P9-CKY-729

WITHDRAWN

JUL 0 3 2024

DAVID O. McKAY LIBRARY
BYU-IDAHO

DAVID O. McKAY LIBRARY
RICKS COLLEGE
REXBURG, IDAHO 83460-0405

LITERATURE AND LEGAL DISCOURSE
Equity and Ethics from Sterne to Conrad

The intersection between law and literature is a developing area in literary studies. Recent work has argued that literature provides an imaginary forum in which legal ideals and practices may be tested. In *Literature and Legal Discourse: Equity and Ethics from Sterne to Conrad* Dieter Paul Polloczek develops this idea by comparing the notion of equity, or ethics, in fiction with its legal equivalent. He shows how the novel, with its increasing social scope and formal sophistication provided a means of transmitting, questioning and refining society's traditions, values and modes of self-questioning. Polloczek analyzes the links between actual legal fictions such as substituted judgments, notions of equity, literary tropes and the construction and representation of social bonds through sentiment, philanthrophy and marginalization. Polloczek's study is both theoretical and historical, covering a period that extends from the eighteenth century to the modernist period and includes texts from Sterne, Bentham, Dickens and Conrad.

LITERATURE AND LEGAL DISCOURSE

Equity and Ethics from Sterne to Conrad

DIETER PAUL POLLOCZEK

CAMBRIDGE
UNIVERSITY PRESS

PUBLISHED BY THE PRESS SYNDICATE OF THE UNIVERSITY OF CAMBRIDGE
The Pitt Building, Trumpington Street, Cambridge CB2 1RP, United Kingdom

CAMBRIDGE UNIVERSITY PRESS
The Edinburgh Building, Cambridge CB2 2RU, UK http://www.cup.cam.ac.uk
40 West 20th Street, New York, NY 10011-4211, USA http://www.cup.org
10 Stamford Road, Oakleigh, Melbourne 3166, Australia

© Dieter Paul Polloczek 1999

This book is in copyright. Subject to statutory exception and to the provisions of relevant
collective licensing agreements, no reproduction of any part may take place without
the written permission of Cambridge University Press.

First published 1999

Printed in the United Kingdom at the University Press, Cambridge

Typeset in Baskerville 11/12.5 pt [VN]

A catalogue record for this book is available from the British Library

ISBN 0 521 65251 0 hardback

Contents

Preface

In this study, I examine literary fictions and legal fictions in selected texts of the modern period. In trying to make an interdisciplinary contribution to the field of literary study, I also draw on such diverse discourses as the history and sociology of law as well as contemporary cultural anthropology. My main goal is to discuss the relationship between the marginal, the equitable, and the unparalleled as one way of tackling the question of ethics in contemporary literary study. Narrowing the scope of this question, I focus on how, during the modern period, the equitable force of conscience informed the languages of sentiment, philanthropy, and solidarity. Essentially, I argue that this branching out generated complex literary responses to a gradual disjunction of equitable justice and critical reason.

For the purpose of this argument, I single out two specific legal fictions, Civil Death and Substituted Judgment. They are both striking metaphors of marginalization and divining rods for the nexus of law and literature in modern England. In the light of Bentham's critique of legal fictions, I reread different cross-overs between literary fictions and legal fictions in the canonical authors Sterne, Dickens, and Conrad. These cross-overs indicate how literature's marginal impact on dominant notions of equitable justice supplemented a significant number of common-law practices.

Sentimentality, utility, philanthropy, and solidarity can be considered nonlegal rhetorical institutions of equitable justice. In my readings of Sterne, Bentham, Dickens, and Conrad, they prove to be implicated in, and acting upon, problematic relations between altruistic and economic personality, a judge's and a subject's conscience, sympathetic and responsible character formation, and racial and national identity. In each case, the two legal fictions and the rhetorical institutions of equitability are alike in performing critiques of institutions within the very institutional setting that allows them to operate. Thus they often end up reproducing the very authority whose exclusionary practices they serve to question.

Literary fiction is certainly implicated in that same process as well. For it cannot simply transcend a cultural mechanism of which it also forms a part. But it is not altogether governed by that which it supplements. In the final analysis, I specify the role of literature's marginality with respect to modernity's more general features of marginality. By reading Sterne's, Dickens's, and Conrad's texts in their relation to the common law, I underscore significant literary attempts at revisiting dominant notions of equitable justice – attempts at both demarcating limits of distributive and compensatory justice and enacting reproductions of its institutional authority.

This book raises the question of how modernity interconnects the marginal, the equitable, and the unparalleled as a question of ethics for literary study today. Such an emphasis also marks its point of departure from those new historicist, neopragmatist, and deconstructionist approaches to "law and literature" on which it occasionally draws. Two goals motivate and define this departure. First, my readings of how selected legal and literary fictions affected modernity's distribution of discourses on marginality are intended to make a contribution to the theory and history of fictions. This is to open up new perspectives on today's tensions between the openendedness of equitable justice and the performative aspects of agency. Secondly, my readings identify postmodern and postcolonial questions of gender, class, and ethnicity in modern canonical European male writers. By establishing such a link, they can serve to reexamine some of the border conditions of canonicity and marginalization that dominate the current political arenas of academic multiculturalism.

I thank the Alexander-von-Humboldt Foundation of Germany for a generous grant that allowed me to write down major portions of this study at the University of California Irvine; Wolfgang Iser for always inspiring and supporting my work; Brook Thomas for hosting my stay at Irvine; Murray Krieger, J. Hillis Miller, Steve Mailloux, and John Paul Riquelme for their endorsement; Jacques Berthoud, Robert Folkenflik, Alex Gelley, Jean-François Lyotard, Robert Newsom, Richard Kroll, and Byron Santangelo for important comments; the journal *Conradiana* for permission to reprint material from an earlier essay on Conrad; and Cambridge University Press for editorial advice.

CHAPTER I

Introduction

Use every man after his desert,
And who should 'scape whipping?
Shakespeare, *Hamlet*

Art about ethnicity or race, about class, about gender and sexuality –
in short, art that reflects, transforms, or engenders the shifting phantom of human identity – has been advanced by many as the crucial
work for our time. The sixties and seventies saw the collapse of an
organic historicism which considered important those works of art that
embodied the contradictions of the cultures in which they were embedded. The eighties saw the decline of the "theory canon" in humanities and art departments, due to its failure to construct a rationale
especially for literary curricula. Contemporary criticism in the nineties
has so far been focusing on the various relations between dominant
components of cultures. Among those components, literature and art
are now considered to play an even more marginal role than they
used to.

At the same time, critics have shifted their attention toward the
phenomenon of marginalization as such. Never have so many assumed
that the "othering" of minorities is an important factor in fashioning
dominant or mainstream modes of culture. "Othering" in advanced
industrial cultures, it is frequently argued, generally takes on more
sophisticated forms than oppression and exclusion. An increased degree
of inclusion, resulting from the accelerated processes of modernization,
has paradoxically made it even harder for minority groups to authenticate the articulation of disadvantages by means of complaint, appeal, or
resistance.[1]

Over almost a decade, the most committed proponents of cultural
criticism in advanced industrial societies have therefore been investigat-
ing such links between inclusion and marginalization. These days, the
networking structures of global communication often serve as ambiguous

I

signs and symptoms of the nature of those links. Interactivity is currently being assessed in contradictory ways, sometimes in terms of a radically participatory democracy that enables postmodern and postcolonial subject constitution through the mechanism of interactivity, sometimes in terms of a covertly neocolonialist buyout of environmental globalism.[2] As a result, criticism in the nineties has been dominated by attempts to illuminate, and articulate possibilities for, the notion of the marginal.

THE MARGINAL

Minority literature, however, represents only one single instance of what the constraints and possibilities of marginality can mean for literature.[3] The marginality of modern literature in general emerges from its relation to socially more relevant ways of organizing and transforming knowledge. This type of marginality can be said to derive from the fast-changing conditions of literature's inclusion in modern cultural processes, rather than its exclusion from them. Barbara Herrnstein Smith identified the reasons for these shifting grounds of inclusion with a crucial feature of modernity as such: the "contingencies of value."[4] In this view, the production of literary texts in the modern period must be seen as competing, if not complicitous with more general parameters of production: the varying dynamics between use value and exchange value.

Multicultural criticism has frequently drawn on this link between, on the one hand, the seemingly total commensurability of value and, on the other, the seemingly total commensurability of signification in modern Western cultures. If virtually every value seems exchangeable with another, does the same hold true for linguistic signs as well? If so, standard separations between durability and transience are no longer as universal as they seemed. The numerous arguments made about this link are generally concerned with two related questions: first, whether the notion of contingencies in terms of value and signification leaves remainders which may resist absorption into total commensurability; and second, whether the very desire for such remainders to be generated in response to a modern experience of total commensurability is a key feature of modernity itself.

Similarly, practitioners of the literary, supported by modernist and poststructuralist theorists, have insisted that making claims for literature's oppositionality need not interfere with the necessity to ditch universalisms. Significantly, this tendency seems to persist, despite the very dehistoricization and nostalgic appropriations of the institution "literature," especially on the part of the New Critics, that along with other factors triggered the multiculturalist turn against literature's de-historicization in the first place. More importantly, it still seems possible today to advocate multiculturalism and at the same time not to restrict literature's marginality to the critical vocabulary associated with the role of minority literature.[5] Postmodern literature is usually said to have inaugurated, or at least enhanced, the very collapse of "high"–"low" distinctions that made multiculturalist approaches to the literary possible. Similarly, modern literature – no matter whether considered established or not – may be equally far from being stripped of the potential to collapse, if only for brief intervals, unexamined distinctions between the "hegemonic" and the "nonhegemonic."[6] The notion of "literariness" has rightfully come to be considered a theoretical fetishism of sorts. Yet the possibility remains that the literary has meaningful existence, within the multicultural frame of reference, as a marginal discourse. As such, it may well exceed those definitions of "literature" which are currently being proposed on the basis of un-equivocally "nonhegemonic" criteria.

Prominent multiculturalist critics such as Judith Butler, John Guillory, and Homi Bhabha tend to use examples from literature to illustrate and privilege various remainders – gender, class, and ethnicity, respectively[7] – to modernity's total commensurability of signification. They formulate these remainders in terms of critical practices, each serving to emphasize and foster a culture's "differences within." Despite their different approaches, all three see literature embedded in cultures, both according to a logic of "supplements" and a deconstructive view on ethics: The opposition between the particularity of literary "textures" and a culture's more general "textuality," of which literature forms part, must be seen as one of mutually dependent (rather than merely contradictory) identities; and these identities are always also defined by the remainders of what each identity is not.[8] Butler, Guillory, and Bhabha would readily acknowledge the difficulty that their goal of maintaining arenas of genuine political contestation may be implicated in the power relations within which norms of modernization, history, law, and civil society are reinforced over time. Notwithstanding this acknowledgment, they continue to insist on a certain distinctness of the "hegemonic." For only then can they declare their critical practices political alternatives, or "supplements," to dominant ideas of distributive and compensatory justice. Only then can they have "counterhege-monic discourse" emerge as an irreducibly supplementary function of modernity.

One unintended effect of such an approach is that the supplementary quality claimed for literature may have to be subjected to whatever "counterhegemonic" criteria current discourses on "supplements" introduce into arenas of political contestation. This effect is particularly dangerous if merely created to convert the increasing social marginality of literary study and literary criticism today – especially when compared to the role of mass media – into an occasion, predominantly inside the professional domain, to declare political expression criticism's cutting edge. To be sure, the rise of political expression in recent criticism – especially in certain versions of neopragmatism, new historicism, gender and postcolonial studies – has exposed many aspects of modern art as both an expression of and an appeal to the language, assumptions and favored mythologies of patriarchy, as well as the ethnocentrism of the high merchant classes. But literature's relation to a more general cultural "textuality," in which it participates, cannot be reduced, as for instance the neopragmatist Walter Benn Michaels believes, to just being part of it.9 The way a culture produces discourses and has them circulate may inform, but need not necessarily govern literary discourse. This ambiguity explains why one cannot easily dismiss canonical modern literature of the West merely because its creation is now (correctly) being seen as tinged with something immoral, disloyal, and exploitative of intimacies and experience.

Clearly, the supplementary quality, not only of modern literature in general, but also of the various corrective devices already built into norms of modernization, law, and civil society, is nowadays itself traded as a complex object of political contestation. One example is the argument between Michael Walzer, who sees distributive justice as largely based upon the political communities which practice it,10 and Seyla Benhabib, who claims that contemporary feminism's need to insist on notions of agency is largely incompatible with such communitarian pluralisms.11 Given this situation, to insist on a distinctness of the "hegemonic" may not be all that difficult if one is dealing, for instance, with modernity's "shift to the postcolonial site."12 If applied to rereading canonical texts, however, those texts will then have to be declared complicitous with "hegemonic discourse" to the extent that canonized texts do not always allow for nonstereotyped identities to emerge from the margins of culture.

This is an undesirable, because potentially reductive, effect. One way to avoid it is to examine literature's supplementary quality more specifically in relation to nonliterary manifestations of "supplements." One such manifestation, which proves especially useful in examining the problem of inclusion and marginalization, is the relation of equity to the letter of the law.

THE EQUITABLE

Equity is known as a maxim applied and instituted in the majority of Western legal systems. Aristotle first formulated it as a correlative, in the context of Greek tragedy, to the consideration of mitigating (or sometimes exacerbating) circumstances that connect criminal action with tragic error. As a mode of justice, Aristotle's notion of equity sometimes contravenes the letter of the law, or its rhetoric, especially where the law does not honor considerations of character, as in the case of Antigone, or special circumstances, as in the case of Oedipus. Both the letter of the law and equity supplement the law's "spirit," or the legislator's general intentions in creating a specific law. The sense of equity as a corrective can thus potentially blur clear-cut distinctions between "intention" and "letter." Equity may supplement the letter of the law in order to ensure that a given interpretation of the "letter" will express the "spirit" of the law. But equity may also supplement the "spirit" of the law, or even the very supplementary relation between "letter" and "spirit," in order to underscore a more fundamental mismatch between "letter" and "spirit."

It seems not entirely wrong, while certainly a gross oversimplification, to say that lawyers and legal theorists tend to deal with the first option – a rule-bound jurisprudence of equity – and literary practioners with the second – a less formal, more allusive supplementary notion of equity. But the question as to whether equity does or does not "belong" to the law is not just an institutional one. The answer also depends on whether equity is associated with something general, such as a universal rational order of justice, or something particular, such as the judicial discretion to interpret the law according to rules and precedents that can change over time. Similarly, it depends on whether the law is associated with something general, such as the predictability and security of rules, or something particular, such as the alterability and flexibility of rules and precedents over time. Thus, what is general about equity is its concern with what is universal; what is particular, its concern with what is flexible. Conversely, what is general about the law is its concern with what is predictable; what is particular, its concern with what is posited. Different conflicts between the general and the particular may emerge, therefore, depending on whether equity is or is not considered part of the law. If it is part of the law, then the security, validity, and accessibility of rules may conflict with the potential unpredictability, arbitrariness, and privacy of judicial discretion. If not, then different aspects of judicial discretion, such as a judge's "genius" or "paternalism," may conflict with non-judicial forms of discretion, such as the readiness of individual conscience to ascribe or accept guilt.

My point here is not to compile a taxonomy of supplementary relations between law and equity in terms of the general and the particular. Rather, I want to connect them with the various supplementary relations between dominant and marginal discourse, official and unofficial stories, or included and excluded voices, that I discussed earlier. The complexities are similar and thus invite careful comparison. Let me suggest just a few cases in point. Literary discourse today may be marginal compared to other forms of organized knowledge. But not all literature is equally marginal. Excluded as well as included texts can represent degrees of marginality. Similarly, literary rhetoric is sometimes described as less instrumental, and perhaps more concerned with universal matters, than nonliterary, for instance legal, rhetoric. But not all literature represents the same values to all human beings. Literary as well as nonliterary rhetoric grows out of a particular place and time. Literature may therefore not provide minorities with an absolute sense of justice, nor represent an openendedness of justice as inequities committed by the law's exclusions. But the fact that it grows out of a particular place and time, and that the truths it might reveal to some are not necessarily self-evident, does also not deny it a significant supplementary relation to the law.

For Aristotle, equity was a means of adjusting universalist human assumptions in legislation and legal practice to a cosmic order of justice.[13] He considered the "poetic fictions" of Athenian tragedy an appropriate means ("mimesis") toward that end. For him, the "particular," incomplete, and nonabsolute quality of justice and injustice[14] that tragedy helped to express also shaped the function of narrative in the Athenian courts. To enhance public debate in the community, it was not enough to use such narratives simply to appeal, by means of persuasion, to the moral quality of certain rules or opinions. For rules and opinions were human-made, and as such fallible. Sometimes, the appeal to a universal, rational order of justice was needed. To the extent that "poetic" fictions (tragedies) performed such an appeal, they could then be considered an "equitable" form of legal fiction: they would be used to create a plot whose truth about human action is self-evident. When such an act of *mimesis* was successful, however, those fictions would also indicate the very limitations of public rhetoric, or persuasion, in creating justice.[15] But in the early modern period, that sense of a universal order of justice suffered a gradual demise. Eventually, the "equitable" Aristotelian unity of "poetic" and legal fictions fell apart as well. The traditional function of Aristotelian *mimesis* shifted towards that of representing, enacting, and supplementing the complex networks of institutions, practices, and beliefs that constituted Renaissance culture as a whole.[16]

This shift also caused a disjunction of equity and legal fictions. It contributed to the widespread modern complaint that legal fictions may be used to feign equitability in order to cover up abuses of judicial discretion. For after the Aristotelian system of rhetoric, ethics, and *poiesis* had fallen apart, neither law nor literature could confidently claim any longer to be able to contain a comprehensively equitable function of fictions. Both discourses, however, adjusted to the widening gulf between equity and legal fictions. In British common law, an institutional separation of common-law and equity courts was intensified which had been in place ever since equitable jurisdiction was associated with the authority of the Crown; it lasted until late into the nineteenth century.

The Lord Chancellors, originally clerics (such as Thomas à Becket and Cardinal Wolsey), dispensed justice according to conscience rather than strict legal forms. Later the rules and remedies of equity jurisprudence [. . .] were institutionalized in the Court of Chancery. [. . .] Equity started out as a truly discretionary jurisdiction. This proved intolerable, and rules of equity emerged; nevertheless equity procedure remained relatively formless, and the result eventually was tremendous delays and uncertainty.[17]

Shakespeare examined some of the "para-legal" consequences generated by the disjunction of equity and legal fictions. Luke Wilson demonstrates how the literary fiction of Ophelia's suicide in *Hamlet* and the contemporary common-law fiction of suicide in terms of "self-felony" *(felo de se)* mutually affected one another. The literary fiction of the gravedigger who declares Ophelia's self-defense a self-offense (V, i, 9) translated "with a twist [. . .] already anticipated in the legal text[s]" the legal fiction's explanation of self-defense as suicide. Wilson argues that in early modern England, rhetorical institutions as different as law and theater began to "implement" metaphors into one another's discourses; and that instead of adjusting human to divine justice, this "alignment between two implementations of metaphor" reveals how the law came to take part in the shaping of modern subjectivities by way of manipulating expectations toward culpability.[18]

Enlightenment thinkers frequently associated equity, somewhat in the spirit of Aristotle, with a rational use of critique that operates above and beyond the logic of precedents. They did so in order to develop reliable means of questioning – questioning the foundations of those long-standing assumptions which had been used to legitimize exclusionary practices. But towards the end of the nineteenth century, science came to replace right reason, and moral philosophy, as a safeguard against improper uses of rhetoric. Equity became absorbed into law, and its authority dissociated from aristocratic privilege, essentially for purposes of egalitarian reform. Law should still serve the public interest, but only by balancing competing interests, not by imposing social unity from above. Along with the demise of Enlightenment attempts to ground the rationality of critique in an authority "that would remedy injustices committed by positive law," equity was eventually stripped of the institutional sense of authority traditionally associated with British equity courts.[19] Equity's function has since shifted, rather than declined, toward that of a temporary remainder to the internal differentiations of norms which prevail in dominant political and legal systems.[20]

THE UNPARALLELED

Unlike equity, literary fiction has continued to be a contested (if increasingly marginal) institution. Nonetheless, its sometimes "wayward and unsatisfactory" encounters with the difference between equitability and commensurability in matters of justice are still most accurately described as "a supplement and a corrective to any legal or philosophical propositions."[21] Nowhere are these "wayward and unsatisfactory" encounters more prominent than in the dubious event of reading literary complaints. Such complaints may be articulated in first-person, third-person, or other voices. But the singularity of suffered injustices that a writer sometimes seeks to convey, perhaps in order to make its articulation exemplary for more universal statements, is most likely to be presented as an intensity vociferous, muffled, or stifled, of first-hand suffering. As a shared practice between the sufferer of injustices and the uninjured reader, the articulation of a complaint has a chance of affecting the sufferer's relation to the reader and the world. Both can feel encouraged that the future may be tied to an unsettled issue in the past, an issue reminiscent of a singular event of emergency, and no precedent in support of memory's abstractions from the singular.

As a challenge to interpretation, the articulation of a complaint presupposes a sufferer's code that needs to be cleared by a reader. Displacing the experience of suffering injustice to the experience of reading complaints, the sufferer implies that some form of redemption may be achieved as soon as readers are substituted for victims and particulars erased in favor of universals. In the final analysis, however, there will be no easy and clear-cut distinctions between complaints as shared practices and challenges to interpretation. Once complaints are articulated, they are also likely to cross established lines between intimate one-to-one exchanges and the redemptive forgetfulness of such exchanges in exemplary spectacles. Which at once raises serious questions about the kind of supplementary role literature may be able to play in relation to the law.

To study legal and literary notions of complaint as related forms of appeal is to address two questions currently raised in cultural criticism: first, whether there are, or can be, adequate languages to articulate unparalleled experiences of marginalization; and second, whether literature's marginal status is or is not overrated as an illustration of how modernity's forms of "othering" work according to a logic of "supplements." On the one hand, civil society's arguably most dominant narrative – that of the many repeated tensions and transitions between law and equity – reflects a sense of iterability with which norms may be reformulated as alternatives. At first sight, this sense of iterability seems not unrelated to the one claimed in multiculturalist attacks on "hegemonic discourse" for freezing a culture's "differences within." On the other hand, legal practice frequently normed, and institutionalized, this kind of iterability in order to engender centered (if not generic) types of subjectivity, instead of encouraging the latter's emergence from the margins of culture.

In short, the potential relations between the general and the particular have neither always nor entirely replicated themselves in the potential relations between the dominant and the marginal. On the one hand, literature's supplementary relation to dominant discourses may help to articulate equity's supplementary function, for instance where the letter of the law is silent on particulars. It may also help to expose failures of that same function, for instance where the entire supplementary relation of equity to the law was found corrupt. On the other hand, while courts of appeal can perform other than equitable functions, and as such draw institutional criticism, they nonetheless continue to be acknowledged as rule-governed forums for political contestation. This somewhat paradoxical fact, however, does not necessarily, as a certain number of multiculturalist critics would argue, make literature irrelevant to pointing out modernity's limits with respect to ideals of distributive and compensatory justice. Instead, it rather strikingly resembles another fact, namely that the supplementary function of literature with respect to dominant discourses continues to be used for purposes of exploring the possibilities contained in rhetorical institutions such as appeal, complaint, and call for retribution.

This particular employment of literature seems still desirable. Today, however, few would deny that once we define its marginality by a logic of "supplements," we will also have to reject the traditional assumption that poetic justice may somehow supplement specific shortcomings of distributive and compensatory justice, such as potentially corrupt institutional relationships between law and equity. Deconstructionist legal scholars tried to shift this problematic to the level of textuality.[22] In doing so, they usually see literary texts in a more privileged position than other kinds of texts to articulate the potential inconsequentiality of an appeal as the openendedness of justice. Conversely, they assume that the law tends to obscure that openendedness as its practitioners "normalize" textuality in universal rules for how to link precedents with principles.

The deconstructionist insistence on an openended notion of justice is certainly effective in challenging the ways the law "normalizes" textuality in the positivist terms of legal textuality. One influential example of how this assumption was successfully applied in cultural criticism is Henry Louis Gates's *The Signifying Monkey*, a study on the trickster in African-American literary experience, whose compelling ability to signify and redescribe can escape the kinds of rhetorical and ideological closure associated with the dominant society. In order to achieve such results, however, critics are forced, as it were, permanently to emphasize the artificiality of those voices which articulate injustices. For they must deconstruct any sense of closure that may adhere to the ways in which singular voices insert their complaints into a logic of competition with official or dominant languages of appeal or retribution.

While such projects are successful in opening up that kind of closure, they can at times also reduce the very openendedness of making complaints to a language of comfort. The problem with languages of comfort is that they themselves end up normalizing the singularity of suffered injustice in the name of a deconstruction of genuine agency. To "do justice" to the diversity of relations between the openendedness of justice and the singularity of agency in the modern period, a greater variety of contexts is needed for the literary analysis of gender, class, and ethnicity. I use sentimentality, utility, philanthropy, and solidarity as historical names for those contexts, but do not consider their "history" one of modernity's "grand narratives." The chief purpose of applying this method to selected literary authors is to sort out, in historical sequence, the possible connections between two different trajectories that marginal, equitable, and unparalleled modes of agency could (and can) follow. In the final analysis, it is to illustrate cross-overs between law and literature in more differentiated terms than "counterhegemonic" opposition.

Sterne challenges sentimentalism's assumption that the natural basis of sentiments is autonomous from the artificiality of legal devices. In *Tristram Shandy* and *A Sentimental Journey*, he indicates that that assumption is as problematic as the common-law assumption that the transmission of customs in communities is autonomous from any consideration *not* based on reason. The masculine gaze that defines relationships between sufferers and spectators of suffering on the scene of sympathy appears to change according to different kinds of national law. In contrast, it is precisely the differences between French and English law, ironically, that Uncle Toby's and Yorick's transnational gestures of sympathy on French territory were supposed to transcend. At Sterne's literary interface of law and compassion, the shaky foundations of natural sentiment "supplement" certain problematic natural-law assumptions, in the eighteenth century, about the moral nature of human beings.

To illustrate this point from a nonliterary perspective, and to provide a transition to the nineteenth century, I include a chapter on Bentham's legal discussion of utility, utilitarian conscience, and the ambiguity of fictions. In the wake of Bentham, then, Dickens cross-examines benevolence and welfare. He challenges philanthropy's emphasis on a religious notion of responsibility, which is supposed to compete with contemporary legal measures of generating and protecting welfare. In *Bleak House*, he indicates that that notion is complicitous with the law's efforts to normalize misery by classifying the liabilities for its persistence. For what defines philanthropy's competitive relation to the law is its basic assumption that in order to efficiently alleviate misery, the sentimental scene of spectators and sufferers has to be institutionalized, just as the law institutionalizes changing rights, duties, and obligations. At Dickens's literary interface of responsibility and liability, the institutional foundations of philanthropic compassion "supplement" the impact of Bentham's legal positivism, in the nineteenth century, on the felt need to control the alterability of the law.

Conrad challenges notions of solidarity that are meant to counteract official modes of identification, especially contemporary aspirations to national or racial identity. In *The Nigger of the "Narcissus,"* he indicates that such a nonofficial notion of solidarity may be an alternative to the way official jurisdiction encourages identification. But solidarity also replicates the very mechanism of authority and subversion that its appeal to commonality sought to debunk in the first place. For what defines the need to anchor alternatives in nostalgia is the assumption that solidarity will *subvert* modern cycles of empowerment and resentment. Conrad establishes a literary interface between solidarity's nostalgic standards for the inclusion of marginalized voices and the judicial authority to determine and control the admissibility of evidence concerning marginalization. He examines certain uses of solidarity that are supposed to set human relationships apart from modern struggles for recognition. It turns out that these uses of solidarity "supplement" legal formalism's assumption, which increasingly informed adjudication toward the end of the nineteenth century, that juridical processes should be autonomous from social and political processes.

THE SOCIAL NATURE OF BONDING

In the light of recent discussions about the kinds of interactivity among virtual communities on the Internet, as well as possible copyright conflicts emerging from that type of communication, critics have also been emphasizing the imaginary components of "pre-virtual" communities of the modern period. For instance, the eighteenth-century foundation of literary authorship in the right to own one's own voice was related to the legal concept of a rights-bearing individual who can own property.[23] In such discussions, there is usually agreement to the extent that while kinship, residence, and legal system were factors in determining such communities in terms of the nation, identification of individuals or groups was never natural. Instead, it was largely dependent on how pre-electronic media, for instance legal and literary texts, disseminated the sign of the nation and contributed to positioning the citizen-subject in relation to it.[24]

One much-debated point, however, is whether the legal narrative of the modern period enhanced or obfuscated the political process in which communities are constructed. Were such dominant narratives efficient in allowing dispersed and fragmented individuals to coexist by virtue of the very existence they have "in common"? Or did they use essentialist notions of the nation to reduce multiplicity to fixity and thus effect a "closure of the political"?[25] Current work in the field of trauma studies raises a related question: How do narratives mediate between incoherent experiences and the difficulty of assimilating past to present?[26] Such considerations reflect an interdisciplinary awareness that examining connections between the national past and the present involves questions of organizing narrative.

The organization of narrative through text and interpretation is clearly something law and literature have in common. However, interdisciplinary projects in legal and literary studies are far from agreeing on the relevance of such commonalities. Much less is there any interdisciplinary consensus, especially not in recent years, on whether it is the approximation or the distance between law and literature that ought to be emphasized. On the one hand, there are academic lawyers who remain confident that both fields can learn from one another.[27] On the other hand, literary critics and legal scholars continue to disagree on questions concerning the law's legitimacy. For instance, neopragmatist critic Stanley Fish doubts that the political attacks on the law's autonomy launched by the Critical Legal Studies movement of the seventies and eighties[28] are an acceptable response to those questions.[29] In contrast, deconstructionist legal scholars frequently associate those kinds of responses with a crisis in the law's very ethical foundations.[30] Conversely, economist legal scholar Richard Posner contrasts the instrumentality of legal rhetoric with the noninstrumentality, indeed the inconsequentiality, of literary rhetoric. He continues to feel justified in seeing the cross-overs of literary studies into legal studies as the former discipline's attempt to conceal and displace the loss of its own foundations.[31]

Neopragmatist critics typically deny such a differentiation, generally maintaining that each of those two rhetorics defines interpretive communities according to their cultural, social, or political preconceptions.[32] But while neopragmatists share the relativist assumptions of deconstructionists, they would not necessarily agree with them that literature remains a viable instrument for legal critique. Most liberal humanists, however, want to reserve and uphold just such an option, while they would agree with neopragmatists that both legal and literary rhetorics can define interpretive communities performatively.[33] Against the skeptical claims of their deconstructionist critics, liberal humanists and feminist critics continue to describe beneficial interactions, both historical and speculative, between judicial authority and literature, seeing both as performances of a communal rhetoric open to many voices, and in this sense capable of moral progress.[34]

There are of course many ways – and the ones listed above are far from exhausting the full spectrum – of looking at this particular debate about problematic closures of the political in legal and literary formations of communities. The one I want to suggest is to introduce the possibility of different types of social bonding, relative to those more strictly defined by power struggles and political contestation. To be sure, no type of social bonding is beyond the demands to be nourished and to protect. Both demands require the human need for comfort to be complemented by the desire for another's desiring gaze. But perhaps types of bonding can exist that reach beyond those conflictual human relationships which typically reduce the desiring gaze, first, to the paradoxical demands for recognition from rivals, and second, the paradoxical frustration of desire by virtue of the very realization of its specific demands. Emmanuel Levinas challenged the idea, commonly dated back to Hobbes, that an individual's rights of liberty precede a citizen-subject's obligations reciprocally to honor trust and act justly.[35] Indirectly reformulating the goals of Rousseau's and Adam Smith's projects for postmodern contexts, he proposed to link the notions of rights and responsibilities in a concept of primary sociality, which defines communities by the nonreciprocal recognition of individual voices.

It certainly remains an open question whether Levinas's project can successfully reach beyond the kind of political contestation which is usually involved in competing for recognition. He does succeed, however, in calling attention to a fundamentally social nature of bonding, and what impact that idea may have particularly on those types of bonding whose parties are related no less by affection than by competition. As one consequence, an individual's actions can be considered as strengthened and credited by a community not merely in being seen, or in being part of its spectacles and "the gaze of the other," but also and more importantly in being valued and revalued through their impact on other persons. The conditions and outcomes of those actions create relationships which also modify the value of all the elements to those relationships.

Not all of those relationships, however, are affect-based or guided by nonreciprocal principles of ethical action. Moreover, some of them are more norm-governed than others, especially so in the domain of modern kinship and collective affiliation, where the law, among other institutions, is in charge of stabilizing the referent of property by regulating its proper usage. The law usually also defines rules as to which type of bonding can embody a community's mutual production of value and benefit as a fixed term. But revaluation of human relationships can happen "in the eyes" of the community or interlocked communities. The institutional balance (or imbalance) between the "letter" and "spirit" of the law then operates as an external evaluator.

Alternatively, revaluation of human relationships can happen "in the eyes" of conscience, an internal censor or jury employed to deal with instabilities in the relation between identity and community. If conscience is invoked or its "call" heard, it operates to resolve the conflicts that arise from insisting on the importance of being able to respect oneself as a person only when one binds oneself to an internal constraint against doing harm to another. The legal concept of equity was designed to supplement the original intentions of legislators and judges. Conscience's private space of jurisdiction is indebted to, while acting upon, the public sphere of law and equity.

Conscience may be "used" to undo the force of the law and its promise to gain a purchase on identity, especially where the law compels the individual to become a subject under the terms of dominant discourse. But sometimes this equitable function of conscience shifts toward a more general function: the permanent readiness to accept guilt. In such cases, conscience may well turn out to be complicitous with those social norms which encourage submission to the law. On the one hand, conscience's internal censorship can effectively complement the activity of external censors. On the other hand, the law may present itself to the individual as desirable insofar as it promises to compensate, by conferring upon him or her an identity as citizen-subject, for conscience's permanent readiness to accept guilt.

VALUING CLAIMS TO RECOGNITION

Any negotiation between those two sides which does not instantly privilege the appeal to precedent, law, and cause at the expense of an unparalleled experience of marginalization requires that its representations, usually supported by languages of comfort, will not reduce that experience to conformity with an established rule. The call of conscience may assemble, when its voice hails the citizen-subject, both unparalleled and precedented forms of injury-as-injustice. Therefore, conscience can be considered an ambiguous negotiator between the compulsion to articulate the singular and the substitution of that compulsion by means of advocating the nonsingular.

Conscience does not exhaust itself simply in using the voice that it helps to articulate to mount a justification of an excessively singular experience, gathered at the limit of where languages of comfort can reach. For in the case of such a type of justification, it would be merely instrumental in restoring the primacy of norms, whether enforced by the law or other institutions of power. This view would in fact correspond to Michel Foucault's position that on the postmonarchic scene of modernity, norms become the condition for discourses that make generalizations about unprecedented and unparalleled events. Foucault's position seems convincing only to the extent that it can explain the transition modern law made from presumed essentialisms like the social contract to the self-referential "sovereignty" of norms, which gradually began to define modern communities' observations of themselves.[36]

But conscience cannot be entirely discredited as a mechanism that submits constitutions, codes, and laws to common standards, which then form the normative basis for judgment. The reason is that conscience may also sustain the excess of singularity to a point where its activity will dislodge comforters from the position of judges and arbiters to that of singular complainants. Such substitutions are primarily neither amiable nor social in their effect unless they freeze into the detached indulgence of socially legitimate feeling, such as sentimental pity, philanthropic compassion, and enthusiastic solidarity. Therefore, conscience can be said to operate, with respect to the articulation of marginal voices, along and across the limit of singular complaints. Its ambiguous or liminal quality enables conscience continuously, though not necessarily consistently, to put a challenge to the ways dominant languages of mutual benefit administer singular experiences of marginalization, that is to say, how those languages operate by virtue of their indifference to everything they do not already include. To be sure, conscience may always become defunct in the absence of specific boundaries that it is permitted to cross. But it may also help to articulate marginal voices to the extent that the resentment which fuels that articulation can give recognition a cultural range that it would otherwise lack.

The distinction between external and internal revaluations of relationships is, however, clearly a heuristic one.[37] To make such distinctions in terms of law versus equity, on the one hand, and justificatory versus singularizing conscience, on the other, means to be already implicated in the respective assumptions that underlie concepts of equity or conscience. In fact, the importance of equity's supplementary relation to the law changed considerably throughout the modern period. British common law can serve as the prime illustration of that change. The institution of equity courts was flourishing when legal theory and practice were still informed by natural-law assumptions about human nature. It declined in what is called the formalist period of the mid-to-late-nineteenth century when legal theory and practice came to be based more strictly on principles and precedents, rather than policy considerations.[38]

Similarly, the importance that Hobbes conceded to conscience after the civil war underwent considerable changes in later centuries, both in support of and in opposition to the law. These can be traced from the emergent need during the eighteenth century to repoliticize morality, for which purpose Enlightenment thinkers employed the authority of conscience, to the disparaging connotations with which Nietzsche, D. H. Lawrence, and Henry Miller dismissed that authority as an self-consumption of the will, resulting as they believed from the failed promises that the internalization of guilt creates. Thus, instead of artificially separating external from internal revaluations of human relationships, it seems more appropriate to open up historical perspectives on the various spaces that politics and law left conscience to operate in.[39]

Therefore, I want to argue that equity and conscience negotiated, under the conditions of modernity, the question of marginality as a question of access to recognition. To open up historical perspectives on that negotiation is to examine how revaluations of social bonding came to be seen as a central issue of modern political life. Appeals to law and equity are certainly part of the law's normative and cognitive strategies for assigning value to persons. At the same time, to value claims to recognition is also to go beyond measuring injustices distributively in terms of physical injury and reputational harm. Appeals that encourage, or are encouraged by, a call of conscience suggest at the least a possibility of withdrawal – at the interface of conflicting normative, cognitive, and affective orientations – from those processes of revaluation which external supervisory institutions hold out as promises.

Three historical perspectives that allow the revaluation of human relationships to be modelled as a particular feature of modernity are sentimentality, philanthropy, and solidarity. In systematic terms, all three reflect to varying degrees the impact of conscience's internal censorship on social bonding. In historical terms, they are contexts in which Sterne, Dickens, and Conrad shaped modern novels to compare and contrast the supplementary relation of literary language to more dominant languages with that of equity to the letter and spirit of the law. Their different objectives may be defined, in the case of sentimentality, as the promise to unfold the moral foundations of human nature; in the case of philanthropy, as the project of linking benevolence with benificence; and in the case of solidarity, as a nostalgic projection of commonality that does not need a common enemy. Sterne, Dickens, and Conrad turn sentimentality, philanthropy, and solidarity into sites, as I demonstrate, on which to examine an interaction between certain legal and literary languages. This observation does not imply, however, that the sites themselves go unexamined in the process. Instead, they are also indebted to the legal assumptions to which they serve to generate alternatives. The chapter on Bentham illustrates this point from a nonliterary perspective.

Neopragmatist and new historicist approaches to such a reciprocal model of modernity generally investigate, despite all their differences and internal varieties, the historical instances of how languages such as those of sentiment, utility, philanthropy, and solidarity can become sites for the production and circulation of other languages (and vice versa). These approaches have so far provided a variety of useful analyses on which interactions between law and literature may be modelled. Their disadvantage is that they often describe such interactions as being simply mimetic of, and on those grounds complicitous with, modernity's general mode of production and circulation of goods.[40] This is a view which may well deny literature the possibilities embedded in Butler's, Guillory's, and Bhabha's claims about political performativity.

In contrast, it is the performative aspect of legal and literary languages that should become the focus of comparison. The differences literature can make certainly exist within the same cultural framework that allows modernity's circulation of discourses to appropriate the very making of differences. The differences themselves, however, do not simply reflect an economy based on turning sexual, class, and ethnic difference into moral or metaphysical difference. Instead, I focus on how Sterne, Dickens, and Conrad connect different revaluations of human relationships with one another. My readings are strategically motivated by the attempt to see the complexities of literary texts in excess of the disparaging connotations of their complicities. In the final analysis, I argue that literature of the modern period could indeed affect, in constructive and occasionally successful ways, certain conditions of marginality.

CHAPTER 2

Trappings of a transnational gaze: legal and sentimental confinement in Sterne's novels

As for sentimentality, that was sometimes the charge against him for his view of the French. If accused he would always plead guilty, claiming in mitigation that this is what other countries are for. Julian Barnes, *Cross Channel*

DEFOE AND STERNE

In the eighteenth century, traveling became an ever more popular way for British subjects to encounter other countries. At the same time, reports, diaries, and treatises frequently reflected the extent to which the travelers' sympathetic fellow-feeling might actually be menaced by cross-cultural challenges. Laurence Sterne's novels form no exception in this regard. What makes the transnational experiences of some of his characters in France quite distinct, however, is the surprising fact that they start making promises when their sympathy seems put to the test. This is indeed surprising, because at the time, sympathy was generally considered a natural impulse, and promises ritual artifices. In such volatile situations, Sterne usually suggests some sort of a breakdown of civility. A sense of crisis calls for equitable justice. Obviously, the sentimental traveler is seeking to supply sympathy with the very transnational legitimation that national (French) law seems to deny it.

To emphasize the impact of legal pressures on sentimental personalities in such situations, Sterne generally focuses on the threat of impending confinement. In doing so, he can more effectively investigate the legal and sentimental aspects of what a "death of civility" may mean to British travelers. In this chapter, I want to show two things. First, some cross-overs, in *Tristram Shandy* and *A Sentimental Journey*, between the spheres of law and sentiment turn out to be more differentiated and complicated than previously attested. Second, Sterne neither exclusively privileges nor dismisses literary fiction as an adequate site for cross-examining those disparate cultural spheres. To unfold this particular intersection between law, sentiment, and literature, I highlight moments when contemporary legal fictions make their entry into Sterne's texts. Somewhat appropriately, one of those legal fictions is Civil Death. A brief detour via Daniel Defoe will underscore its importance for Sterne.

By the time Defoe's Robinson Crusoe returns to England and finds out that his income has been donated to a monastery, to be used "for the Conversion of the Indians,"[1] Robinson's self has undergone multiple conversions. In order to reclaim his fortune, Crusoe must legally recall himself from "Civil Death" and take an oath that he has been alive and the same person during his period of absence from England.[2] David Marshall demonstrated how Crusoe and other fiction-makers in Defoe's texts correspond, with regard to their narrative practices, to Defoe's own impostures, impersonations, "moral justifications," and "almost legalistic denial[s] of responsibility" for many claims about truth and moral purpose made in the prefaces to his fictional texts.[3]

Suggesting religious autobiography as a frame of reference with respect to Defoe's own vacillating identities, Marshall indicates that Defoe simultaneously justified and denied the fictional status of his texts.[4] Defoe apparently needed to uphold a veil of deceptions in order to set the stage for allegories, and thus for apologies, of a salvation associated with impersonations. At the same time, he was eager to dissociate, in his *Serious Reflections*, the "double imposture" of both justifying and denying fiction from generic lying.[5] The "double imposture," bent toward the religiously inspired design of a displaced salvation, should be exempt, he suggested, from being censured even if impersonations as such cannot exempt the impersonators (as well as their observers) from the anxiety that their impostures could be nothing but hypocritical contrivances.

The claim for justice in using fictions, characteristic of many apologies for fiction both before and after Defoe, is a claim for equitable justice – a mode of justice not sufficiently covered by the rigid letter of instituted law. Figuring prominently in the Aristotelian tradition up to Sidney, equity was declared an important function of fiction.[6] Similarly, British common law institutionalized the practice of legal fictions by means of appropriating similar practices in Roman law. Seventeenth- and eighteenth-century common-law theorists such as Hale and Blackstone, who defended that practice, argued that it helped to adapt precedents from the context of feudal law to modern day cases where those precedents in fact no longer applied. Hale and Blackstone assumed that legal rules and historical circumstances ought to be mutually adjusted, thereby assuming that, as Burke later claimed, common law evolved organically.

This practice of legal fictions, based as it was on an organic model of legal evolution, went by and large uncontested until Bentham criticized Blackstone's model of equity. He complained that its practice obfuscated the abuses of juridical power on the part of the legal elites. As a way of solving what he considered a rampant problem, he suggested that the organic model be replaced by one of codification.[7] Bentham thus articulated what had arguably always already been a dangerous element of delusion in the theory and practice of common law.[8] He concluded that equity and legal fictions had probably never been as closely connected as the official claims made about their conjunction suggested.

However, for almost one hundred years after Bentham's invectives against Blackstone, the purpose of bringing about equity, expressed in the separation of common-law courts and equity courts until 1870, was associated with the idea that legal fictions were creatively duplicitous. In epistemological terms, legal fictions were undeniable falsehoods. In pragmatic terms, they needed to be considered useful. The "double imposture," as it were, of considering them useful falsehoods was commonly accepted.[9] Hence, it comes as no surprise, given the nexus of literary and legal fiction in both the Aristotelian and the common-law tradition,[10] that Defoe closely aligned the literary fiction of Crusoe's exile with the legal fiction of "Civil Death."

In Civil Death, incarcerated felons were deprived of their civil rights as well as their right to inherit and bequeath and thus metaphorically died to the community.[11] Civil Death originated in the medieval clerical distinction between worldly natural life and monastic contemplative life. *Civiliter mortuus* was later reinterpreted as an expiatory confinement designed to let an old identity die in order to trigger a new and better one. Basically, anyone convicted of treason or felony would lose civil rights and could no longer inherit. Moreover, his or her fortune was subject to forfeiture on the part of the crown. The legal criteria of forfeiture and "corruption of blood" gradually lost their impact in England and were practically not adopted in the United States. Nonetheless, Civil Death often resulted in a transfer of the felon's fortune to heirs *as if* he or she were already dead.

Civil Death would cause life-long prison terms and end the right to sue, to ask for credit, to marry, and to vote. But the relationship between legal and social death as well as the exclusion from inheritance and bequest marks the core of this fiction. In 1870, a statutory change which abolished general implications of forfeitures, for instance in matters of suicide, also ended the forfeiture and "corruption of blood" resultant from Civil Death.[12] Now the fortune would be handed over to an "administrator" instead of the convict losing it forever. But it remained an open question whether or not the civilly dead person was entitled to inherit and bequeath.

Civil Death suggests a link between legal identity and property. The legal understanding of that loss, in cases of treason or felony, of the rights, obligations, and possessions resultant from civic life is certainly indebted to the social image of *vita contemplativa* in monastic retreat. In the context of *Robinson Crusoe*, however, Defoe relates Civil Death more obviously to Whig ideologies of individualism in terms of propertied control. According to Locke, individuals are invested by law with right and property in things, and ultimately in themselves, although not with a sovereign personality adequate to a participation in self-rule. Defoe creates Crusoe's exile from civility as a locus of self-confirmation. Thus he is able to examine the psycho-imperialist "insight" that to construct isolated fictions in order to contrive moral prototypes in open-ended contexts seemingly void of such prototypes is to construct the fiction of recreating the (Puritan) predicament of "finding" meaning in the world at large.

By exiling his castoff and possession-taking hero from the normative space of national law, Defoe has Crusoe venture into the "para-legal" possibilities of how to manipulate relations of liberal individualism and property. Evoking such "para-civil" excursions across the legal boundaries of individualism, Defoe participates in his culture's attempts at rewriting the legal relations between personality and property. Civil Death on unknown islands suggests the confinement of legal subjects in isolated yet transitional spaces. To employ that confinement metaphorically is thus to explore a certain economic dimension of exile. By means of it, Defoe can call attention to the ways the "confinement" of natural-law assumptions about personality – the independence of virtuous citizens guaranteed by property in the sense of what is proper to each citizen – may be transgressed.

In *A Sentimental Journey*, Sterne translates the mechanism of Civil Death into a French equivalent – the *droits d'aubaine*. Once executed, the *droits d'aubaine* would effect the suspension of certain rights pertaining to Yorick's status as a legal subject as well as the forfeiture of his possessions. But the context of Sterne's mid eighteenth-century commercial society differs from the one in which Defoe uses Crusoe's Civil Death. The seventeenth-century notion that for one's autonomous personality to be politically successful one needs material foundations in property was now challenged, albeit not obliterated, by revised capitalist notions of property. In the early part of the century the number of capital statutes in England grew dramatically: "[T]he constant extension of inland and foreign trade from the late seventeenth century, the exploitation of new mines, the wealth of London and the spas and the growth of population were causing more frequent offences against property."[13] However, the "flood of legislation"[14] which caused that increase in capital statutes does not automatically suggest that such a practice of capital punishment renders the structure and operation of authority and power of an "extraordinarily incompetent" parliament in Hanoverian England conducive to "one of the bloodiest criminal codes in Europe."[15]

In fact, John Beattie complicates and revises such explanations for the "bloody code." According to his account, we should even abandon the eighteenth century as a useful unit for discussing these legal developments. For one, the application of most statutes that extended capital punishment to property offences followed a practice dating back to the sixteenth century when major crimes such as murder, robbery, burglary, horse-theft etc. were made capital. More importantly, the eighteenth-century penal system was transformed not so much by an increased infliction of actual death sentences (and, in fact, it was still the sixteenth-century statutes that were being applied) as by the broadening of secondary punishments such as transportation and confinement.[16]

Moreover, discussions of property began to move beyond the confines of traditional ownership problems. The juridical sense of property as an individual's right was now challenged by an economic sense of property, mobile and imaginary property such as the public debt.[17] The notion of mobile property no longer simply designated propertied independence as defined by civil and common law. As monetary property became more imaginary, literary fiction also depended more directly on its forms of commodication.[18] Similarly, the idea of personal authorship came to be more frequently associated with its subjection to controversial copyright laws.[19]

The emergent desire to discover economic laws that would account for a reformulated individualism as contingent on the commercial exchange of commodities now reflected a modified notion of property. Private ownership was no longer exclusively based on a sense of appropriation vesting a person with rights of title, but also on a sense of transitional personality. The entitlements of that type of personality became both subject to production and exchange and justifiable through political or legal conventions.[20] Traditional civility was rewritten by natural jurisprudence and moral philosophy as a sentimental progression of the passions, paralleled by the progress of commerce, toward refinement and politeness.

Sentimentalism's doctrine of innate and spontaneous benevolence has been described – in the wake of Terry Eagleton's observations on ideologies of pathos as crucial to the construction of the bourgeois subject[21] – as an economic strategy. Robert Markley interprets this economic strategy as one that was transforming paternalistic hierarchies into *laissez-faire* individualism. He argues that that strategy resulted directly from the (bourgeois) political strategy of having to compete with the aristocracy for moral authority: "For many middle-class authors, sentimentality – the generosity of feeling – becomes their claim to a cultural power-sharing based on a liberal interpretation of 'Breeding' that equates hereditary power and moral sensitivity."[22] However, it is rather the momentum of civic humanism than liberalism which marks the eighteenth-century transition to economic personality. Liberalism may provide, as Pocock explains, an understanding of sovereignty as creating the rights it exists to protect. But it cannot always, unlike (republican) virtue, ground sovereignty in personality.[23]

This is not to say that liberalism and republicanism were necessarily incompatible in the seventeenth and eighteenth centuries. "Classical works of the period, such as James Harrington's *Oceana* and Trenchard and Gordon's *Cato's Letters*, can be categorized only as liberal-republican; they effortlessly combine a commitment to popular sovereignty with an acceptance of both constitutional limitations and, within the bounds of justice, the private pursuit of personal interests."[24] In commercial times, virtuous citizens do redefine the passions in terms of transactional manners. But they defend, until late in the eighteenth century, the society of production and exchange by means of humanism, not liberalism:

[T]he new world of the social and the sentimental, the commercial and cultural, was made to proliferate with alternatives to ancient *virtus* and *libertas*, largely in consequence of the jurists' fascination with the universe of *res*. Now, at last, a right to things became a way to the practice of virtue, so long as virtue could be defined as the practice and refinement of manners. A commercial humanism had been not unsuccessfully constructed.[25]

Analyzing "the emergence of parliament as an active law-making institution" in the eighteenth century, David Lieberman details the various jurisprudential ways in which Bentham responded to what Pocock separates in terms of the "law-centered paradigm" and the "paradigm of virtue and corruption." He demonstrates how Bentham perceives those "paradigms" as different stimuli "for [a] more general reflection on the nature of England's legal inheritance [that is, the vacillation between principle and precedent], the challenges to the nation's institutions posed by social and economic growth, and the appropriate avenues in England to legal reform and improvement."[26]

These considerations are important insofar as they help to revise a number of myths sometimes endorsed in post-Foucauldian criticism. Humanist sentimentalism did not exhaust itself in merely forming silent conspiracies with economic determinism[27] and dissimulating simple doctrines of the harmony of egoisms through *laissez-faire* market behavior. It was considered a truism even in Sterne's day that the emergence of commercial society, with its stress on the unintended public benefits derived from blind selfishness, was marked by major defects of a moral and civic character. To be sure, there was some agreement that the revolution associated with commerce and manufacturing might have eliminated gross forms of dependency and domination. But it did of course not go unnoticed that instead of abolishing oppression and social conflict, some effects of that revolution actually widened the scope for contest, envy, and conflict between individuals, between new and different orders of society, and between private and public interests.

This is true even for someone like Adam Smith. Like Hume, Smith was certainly not very sensitive to an egalitarian notion of economic justice when he, in *The Theory of Moral Sentiments*, attempted to aestheticize utility by linking art and commodity through a (class-defined) notion of taste. But he must not too readily be subjected, as Donald Winch correctly points out, to the nineteenth-century "liberal capitalist perspective."[28] Smith did treat the harbingers of commercial society, the merchant and manufacturing classes, with considerable reserve, especially as regards their collective capacity to combine against the public interest. In fact, John Guillory argues that it was only after *The Theory of Moral Sentiments* that proponents of the aesthetic disengaged themselves from political economy and subsequently "betray[ed]," by substituting value for taste, "the continued pressure of economic discourse on the language of aesthetics."[29] Rather, Smith's scene of sympathy is a response to the increased complexity and contingency of experience in the eighteenth century. The "recognition of the other *as another*" challenged, as Niklas Luhmann points out,[30] the probable limits of social behavior at a time when power came to be seen as based on the subject's reflexive position towards its own powers: "*Curiosity* became a legitimate motive for pursuing knowledge, *profit* became something like income without a contractual base (i.e. without social legitimation), *raison d'état* became a political maxim, and *empassioned love* became a sufficient basis for choosing a partner."[31]

In such a context, Sterne's allusion to Civil Death differs from Defoe's metaphor of a civic virtue suspended by possessive individualism. Sterne no longer needs to disconnect property from notions of autonomy. In his day, the law frequently served to recuperate the problem of opaque motives in human transactions. It was certainly intended to protect rights to and the transfer of property. But it could not provide the means to determine character in the sense of what is proper to participants in *any* kind of exchange situation. Given this situation, Sterne's sentimentalist use of the metaphor of legal confinement represents an apology for commerce that is related to, though not simply identical with, similar apologies in moral philosophy. The "death" of civility – an anticipated decline of Pocock's paradigm of republican virtue and corruption – is reformulated, in both discourses, as a renewal of personality based on a movement from confinement to refinement.

Exploring the possible functions of sentimental apologies for commerce, Sterne makes use of Civil Death's performative force. He does so in order to connect what Pocock separates as the paradigm of republican virtue and corruption and the law-centered paradigm. To be sure, both sentimentalism and moral philosophy necessarily differ from the practice of (criminal) law, which for obvious institutional reasons must insist on confinement. But Sterne suggests, as I will show, that their claims for a renewal of personality replicate the mechanism of the legal fiction Civil Death itself. They translate old identities into new ones – by means of "spying" into others' hearts – and thus create modular identities.

A SENTIMENTAL CONFINEMENT OF REFINEMENT

Mockingly alluding to the traveler's Civil Death abroad on the first page of *A Sentimental Journey*, Yorick mentions the potential effects of the French "*droits d'aubaine*." According to that law, all his belongings would be seized by the king of France if he (Yorick) died, of "indigestion" from "a fricasee'd chicken," on French territory: "All the effects of strangers (Swiss and Scotch excepted) dying in France, are seized by virtue of this law, though the heir be upon the spot – the profit of these contingencies being farmed, there is no redress."[32] In *A Sentimental Journey*, Sterne time and again dramatizes and satirizes the legal tensions arising from Yorick's crossing the national border. Only upon entering French territory does Yorick become aware of the fact that France is "at war" (*SJ*, p. 92) with England. In Paris, that neglect causes him passport problems and the danger of incarceration in the Bastille. Employing sensibility as both an argument in defense and a narrative mode before the Count de B**** (and the reader), however, he succeeds in explaining that he came to spy neither the "nakedness of the land" (*SJ*, p. 107), nor that of its women, but the "*nakedness* of their hearts" (*SJ*, p. 108).

With the help of a passport unexpectedly issued by the Duc de C***** that declares him Shakespeare's Yorick, the King of Denmark's jester, Yorick manages to set himself free. When Sterne first visited the Comte in 1762, he was flattered to find a copy of *Tristram Shandy* open on his table. Sterne's Yorick, however, finds a copy of Shakespeare's works on the table. The passport provided by the Count de B**** sets him as free from a prospective incarceration as he wishes the captive bird and the human captive (that he was sentimentally evoking) should be. It seems to please the Count de B**** to identify him, Parson Yorick, the character from *Tristram Shandy* and author of *The Sermons of Mr. Yorick*, with the former owner of that famous skull portrayed in Shakespeare's gravedigger's scene in *Hamlet*. Yorick sets himself free from the impending yoke of incarceration by evoking sympathy for himself as he is evoking sympathy for a fictional character whose legal identity is to provide him, in the form of a passport, a passage to liberty. The liberating interior space of Yorick's sentimental imagination, however, marks yet another type of confinement that Sterne's novel explores narratively. Sterne thus structures the complexities of Yorick's confinement in terms of his legal and sentimentalist perspectives.

When Yorick learns that the king of France would be entirely unrelenting as regards his incarceration – a moment foreshadowed by the king's imagined seizure of Yorick's belongings according to the *droits d'aubaine* – he begins to envision the horrors of the Bastille. His first reaction is to play down those horrors. He imagines merely a limited period of time spent at the king's expenses "with nine livres a day, and pen and ink and paper, and patience, albeit a man can't get out, he may do very well within – at least for a month or six weeks; at the end of which, if he is a harmless fellow his innocence appears, and he comes out a better and wiser man than he went in" (*SJ*, p. 95). Similarly, Tristram Shandy plays down the horrors of an incarceration on French territory that have resulted from his failure to pay the king six livres four sous for the "post-chaise" to St. Fons.³³

Like Tristram, Yorick gradually suspends his brave attitude toward the Bastille. Initially, he rather quickly concludes, "'Tis true [. . .] – the Bastile is not an evil to be despised – but strip it of its towers – fill up the fossé – unbarricade the doors – call it simply a confinement, and suppose 'tis some tyrant of a distemper – and not of a man which holds you in it – the evil vanishes, and you bear the other half without complaint" (*SJ*, pp. 95–6). At this point, a child-like voice interrupts Yorick's soul-pampering. A starling hung up in a cage laments about its lost liberty and whispers a desperate "'I can't get out – I can't get out'" upon Yorick's helplessness to get the cage open without pulling the cage itself to pieces. All of which causes Yorick to overthrow his "systematic reasonings upon the Bastile" and ceremonially to invoke for some abstracted notion of human nature the blessings of liberty against the backdrop of the "bitter draught" of "slavery" for "thousands in all ages" (*SJ*, p. 96). Haunted by his encounter with the captive bird, Yorick confesses, "I begun to figure to myself the miseries of confinement. I was in a right frame for it, and so I gave full scope to my imagination" (*SJ*, p. 97).

Picturing the millions born to slavery "distract[s]" Yorick, however "affecting" the idea of it might be; he needs something that he can bring "near" himself (*SJ*, p. 97). Thus a certain sense of individuality with regard to incarceration serves the purpose of such a projected moral sentiment much better. Suggestive of an artist's creation, Yorick designs a picture which is to make him a spectator of the same: "I took a single captive, and having first shut him up in his dungeon, I then looked through the twilight of his grated door to take his picture. [. . .] – I burst into tears – I could not sustain the picture of confinement which my fancy had drawn [. . .]" (*SJ*, pp. 97–8). This picture of confinement becomes unbearable the moment an iron enters the captive's soul and defies sympathetic visualization. Yorick nervously rushes out to obtain a passport, picturing on his ride from Paris to Versailles the travels of his captive starling from England to France, where the whole nation seems to have turned into an enormous cage for the bird, its desperate song for liberty "being in an *unknown* language at Paris" (*SJ*, p. 99).

Failing to liberate the captive bird, Yorick has now created a story of poetic justice of sorts, perhaps not so much in order to compensate for the bird's captivity as in order to establish a training ground for sentimentally evoking unjustified and miserable incarceration. This story will help him create sympathies for himself on the part of the Count de B**** – whose influence in the Duc de C*****'s office Yorick needs to obtain a passport. For the sake of making his argument before the Count, he tends to supplant intellectual authority with the power not only to display but also elicit the Count's susceptibility to the emotions running predictably high in a spectator of suffering.

The legal backdrop of a gothic French law against which Yorick contrives his argument, highlights, as Stephen Cox argued more generally, sensibility as "a wild card that can be played in virtually any hand, lending itself to virtually any argumentative purpose." In Yorick's and many other cases, "the argument *of* sensibility was constantly turning into an argument *about* sensibility."[34] In fact, Yorick has now incorporated that very evocation of the bird into his own strategies: "I beg leave to inform [my readers], that that bird was my bird – or some vile copy to represent him" (*SJ*, p. 99). He makes the bird his own in placing it on his coat of arms as an emblem, or "vile copy," of liberty. In doing so, he has created but another "picture of confinement" for the bird.

The call of his conscience allows Yorick to employ sensibility in order to escape situations of confinement. However, his conscience is also responsible for the creation of another type of confinement – an objectification of "objects" of suffering in outbursts of sympathy. This type of confinement seems to inhere in Yorick's very own practice of sensibility. In a sense, conscience, traditionally conceived as a corrective to the law, here betrays a certain complicity with the latter's effects. Sterne thus emphasizes the problems that arise from attempts to locate the sentimental basis of social bonding in conscience. But he does not entirely surrender virtue to the sphere of commercial ideologies. Instead, he translates the problem of conscience's complicity with the law into the legal complexities of commerce. By means of such a translation, he can open up alternative ways of correcting the shortcomings of conscience.

One such alternative is, as I will show, the notion of promise. Sterne can make use of promises as correctives to conscience's complicity with the law because they share with the operations of conscience a certain transitional quality. Conscience is private but informed by public expectations. Promises are less private than intimate bonds but also less open to public sanctions than contracts. Moreover, conscience's moral force is not legally actionable. Similarly, the way promises are considered binding is reflected in the moral rather than legal force of available penalties. However, before fully unfolding this liaison of conscience and promises, it will be useful first to explicate the legal and sentimental tensions that Sterne establishes between conscience and confinement. John Bender and Ann Jessie Van Sant proposed different contexts for Sterne's use of confinement. While Bender reads confinement in terms of the penitentiary, Van Sant reads it in terms of sensibility. A cross-examination of those readings will help to explain how the discourses of law and sensibility intersect in Sterne's notion of conscience.

Bender's eighteenth-century study explores the mutual reinforcement of prisons and novels. He holds that confinement forms the common bond between prisons reformed as penitentiaries and what emerges as realist narrative based on authorial control.[35] The realist novel, Lockean and Humean philosophy, and the penitentiary institutionalize for him the fiction of a self conceived as empirically real. This fiction may be constructed, manipulated, and transformed on the basis of punishment in terms of a poetics or narratology of character. According to Bender, new systems of political and moral consciousness inform the pentitentiary, seeking to bring about the maintenance of order in the urban labor force, the salvation of the soul, and the rationalization of personality.

The old prisons are characterized by a certain randomness with regard to authority, control, and restriction. Bender associates the latter with Victor Turner's anthropological notion of liminality in the sense of an initiation rite or symbolic rebirth. In contrast, the new penitentiaries focus on a reformation of criminals which amounts to the formation of institutionalized notions of character. Sentences, both legal and grammatical, are no longer executed but served. They unfold, like a realist plot, within causal ideas of time and controlled principles of shaping personalities (pp. 33–4).

Sterne's Yorick seems to perform a similar move from old to new prisons when he pictures his confinements. At first, he imagines the Bastille as a liminal ritual of rebirth, as he sees himself "come out a wiser and better man than he went in" (*SJ*, p. 95). Later, his sentimental interior space of confinement resembles Bender's picture of the penitentiary when he feels remorse about exaggerating his needs before the Duc de C****: "How many mean plans of dirty address, as I went along, did my servile heart form! – I deserved the Bastile for everyone of them. Then nothing would serve me [. . .] but putting words and sentences together [. . .]" (*SJ*, p. 100).

In his remarks on Sterne, Bender claims for Yorick's evocation of the captive a paradox of "absorptive spectatorship" (Michael Fried), a fascinated attempt at identification based on the isolation of the spectator from its object (pp. 233–4). The absorbed spectator has strong affinities with Adam Smith's "impartial spectator" in *The Theory of Moral Sentiments*. According to Bender, Smith's psychology of reformative punishment conceives of the modular identity implied in the concept of character as the interior personification of juridical presence. This "reciprocal nature of conscience" (p. 218) prefigures the introjection of an image of superior external power commonly known as superego.

Similarly, Yorick appeals to his spectators for sympathy and imagines himself, in that very process, as a spectator of his own sympathetic scenes. Ultimately, however, Sterne undercuts Yorick's emotional remorse. He thus also undercuts the reciprocal nature of conscience suggested by Fried's tableau of absorptive spectatorship and Smith's impartial spectator. Yorick simply has his imagined captive personify his (Yorick's) motives for attaining a passport and a new fictional identity. His liberty results from a "mistake about his identity" (pp. 235–6). This ironic self-consciousness counteracts the sentimental identification with confined objects of suffering. At the same time, it parodies those narrative features which used to mark the realist novel as subservient to the goals of represented confinement.[36]

Van Sant's study explores the psychological and physiological ambivalences in the field of sentiment and sensibility. She contends that sentimental narrative relies on both pathetic and scientific demonstration.[37] Pathetic demonstrations that characterize the age of sensibility rely on a traditional significance of sight in moving the passions. This significance derives from classical rhetoric. Scientific observations of a confined sentimental "object" add to that traditional importance of sight the notion of an experimental approach to character and character formation. This approach derives from empiricist investigations of psychological responses characteristic of the eighteenth century.

In addition to the importance of sight, there is an emphasis on touch in many discussions of sensibility. That additional emphasis accounts for the physiological approach, in what Van Sant calls eighteenth-century "sensationism," to psychological responses. Thus, the entire cultural sphere of sentiment and sensibility somewhat resonates from an ambiguity regarding the question as to whether psychological or physiological factors play a more important role for the delicacy of sight and touch.[38]

Sympathetic visibility uses philanthropic "objects," that is to say, people who suffer. They serve as instruments of both pity, in terms of pathetic demonstration, and curiosity, in terms of scientific demonstration. Correspondingly, these particular types of demonstration evoke a both sympathetic and investigative reading. Thus they align the gazing on suffering with experimental approaches to character formation (pp. 16ff). Van Sant reveals sentimental narrative in both everyday life and literature as frequently based on narrative confinement and trial. Both the Magdalen House for the reformation of repentant prostitutes and the Philanthropic Society in charge of educating the children of the "vagrant and criminal poor" (pp. 45ff) share with novels such as Richardson's *Clarissa* (pp. 60ff) a form of narrative that isolates or confines "objects" of suffering.

The purpose of that confinement is to establish a figurative trial of sympathetic character inspection. In such a figurative trial, sympathetic visibility serves as the corollary of legal evidence for the presence or absence of character. The tension between sympathetic and investigative readings of sentimental narratives also accounts for a potential of violence in traditional narratives of suffering, as the case of *Clarissa* demonstrates. In the wake of eighteenth-century "sensationism," one would have to conclude from Van Sant's observations, sympathetic visibility and legal evidence are used mutually to support each other's functions.

The emphasis on touch superimposes the tactile aspect of feeling over a notion of feeling as seeing and knowing. It shifts attention from the spectatorial event to the body of the spectator. The emphasis on touch shifts the focus from the scene of pitiable distress to the internal "vibrations" of corresponding sympathetic pain or agony in the observer. The language of sight first activates and then translates those vibrations into a language of internal motion (pp. 83ff).

Van Sant claims for Sterne's Yorick in *A Sentimental Journey* a "miniaturization of experience" (p. 101), a sentimental "microsensation" (p. 103) that creates the fictional territory of his adventures as an internal landscape. The external events described by Yorick serve him as a screen for recording his own experiences. His sympathy for Maria's distress, for instance, works as evidence in his self-investigation, when during the encounter with her he exclaims: "'I am positive I have a soul; nor can all the books with which the materialists have pestered the world ever convince me of the contrary'" (pp. 99–100, *SJ*, p. 138).

Sensation therefore replaces adventure as the basic narrative unit. The trifles of minuscule occurrences like the exchange of a snuff-box in

Calais turn into physiological adventures in Yorick's nerves, fibers, and blood vessels (*SJ*, pp. 44, 28) Such miniaturized experience may both aggravate and enhance feeling. But it also represents the subject's withdrawal from more ordinary aspects of experience. In microsensation, the *re* finement of sensory power thus resembles the *con* finement of experience. The ambiguity between a delicacy in the sensory apparatus and an isolation from the world resulting from heightened sensory capabilities has here entirely shifted from the observation of a philanthropic "object" to the body of the man of feeling. This is the concept of a body whose boundaries are defined by the notions of refinement and confinement, a body that Van Sant calls "parodic." She uses the term "parodic body" to suggest that while refinement allows the subject to reinvent itself by escaping confinement, the effects of that reinvention lead the subject into a different sort of confinement, an isolation from ordinary experience. Consequently, since the effects of microsensation can both heighten and trivialize experience, sensibility both enables and parodies Yorick's sentiment (p. 107).

This double-edged parody of sentiment becomes most apparent when pathetic experience contrasts with sexual experience. Yorick's physiological body seems associated, by way of its refinement, with standard views in eighteenth-century England of a feminized body typical of characters in sentimental novels. This feminized standard was "used in general culture and in medicine to characterize the nervous system," Van Sant maintains (p. 106). It suggests a certain imagined immateriality of the idealized feminine body made available through microanalysis (pp. 105–6). However, the sentimental novel often transforms sexual experiences of which the feminized body is capable into pathetic sites of sentiment, which are "countered by the physiological body on which [sexualized experience] depends" (p. 107). Sterne certainly has Yorick waver between physiologically pathetic scenes and physiologically sexual scenes. But he also ridicules sexual suggestiveness. He frequently substitutes the sphere of sexuality by a "parodic juxtaposition of benevolence and impotence," which once more isolates Yorick from "ordinary physicality" (p. 108).

Bender's and Van Sant's readings of Sterne emphasize different notions of confinement. Yet both associate such confinement with trial and punishment of the self understood as an isolated character. Each emphasizes that confinement is of a duplicitous nature. But each defines such duplicity in different terms. For Bender, confinement belongs to what he understands as the (narrative) judicial self-consciousness of

eighteenth-century realist narrative: an identification preserving isolation, modular identity highlighted as the paradox of absorptive spectatorship. Sterne's ironic self-consciousness exposes that paradox by
means of parody. For Van Sant, confinement as a result of microsensation is both enabled and (parodically) exposed by sensibility.

Bender's reading conceives of confinement as something that Sterne's
text exposes because the restrictions and limitations of the self-as-fiction
need to be unveiled. Van Sant's reading allows for a confinement that
triggers the very transgressions of itself. Such an understanding integrates the transgression of confinement within the discourse of sensibility. Bender's concept, however, must exclude that transgression on the
premise that narratives of moral sentiment do confine but do not
transgress what they isolate in confinement.

In fact, Bender presents a melancholic reading of confinement that is
obsessed with the futility of reform. It somewhat reflects a sense of
longing for the old prison system with its carnevalesque features of
theatricality and accounts of reality not based on the yoke of conscience
and on materialistic utilitarianism as behaviorist ordinances. Implicitly,
his account endorses a symbolic exchange of earlier religious, govern-
mental and narrational practices. Insisting on an alternative between
reform and rebirth, Bender thus runs the risk of ending up in melancholic deadlocks.

In contrast, Van Sant implies an idea of revision that can undo the
melancholic deadlocks emerging from the alternative between reform
and rebirth. Revision, as opposed to reform, suggests the possibility to
correct, by means of parody, the reductive aspects of sensibility (refinement as confinement) from within the "parodic" structure of sensibility.
If parody is considered merely one aspect of this self-corrective function,
Van Sant's notion of sensibility resembles the equitable functions of the
law.

However, it is not hard to imagine situations or contexts in which the
effects of sensibility will themselves stand in need of reform. Such need
for change may well be motivated by concerns that lie outside Van
Sant's "parodic" structure of sensibility. Frank, for instance, pointed
out[39] that even a sentimental writer such as Sterne, who in *A Sentimental
Journey* often ironically undercuts the sympathetic feeling that puts the
parodic body "on the rack" (Adam Smith) of its readers' microanalytical
gaze, may be shown to have reduced the sentimental male character to
his class aspirations. This argument, which I will later on treat in more
detail, implies that the parody of sentiment becomes a symbolic space of

jurisdiction that may itself stand in need of reform. Liberation from confinement carried out by means from without or from within the structure of sensibility – such an alternative between reform and revision seems to be Sterne's literary response to the complexities of confinement.

Reform and revision are useful concepts to describe certain legal and sentimentalist appropriations, in late eighteenth-century England, of transitional personality in terms of modular identities (Bender) and parodic bodies (Van Sant). The prison reforms are based on legal subjects created as fictions that can be modulated (and manipulated) by the panoptical means of internalized self-"reform." The refined body of sensibility is based on a concept of sympathy supposed to set forth "good nature" as the self-"revising" sentimental imagination of otherness. Modular identities and parodic bodies can be said to operate as two related modes in which transitional personality shifts private and public subject positions between spaces of production and exchange as well as political and legal conventions.

Both the legal and sentimentalist appropriations of transitional personality combine their own limitations with transgressions of those limitations. Modular identities may be subject to secret manipulation only as long as the status of legal identity as a modular fiction remains the arcane knowledge of judges and lawyers. Modularity as such becomes less scandalous where its practical uses are acknowledged as something that may also be (non-secretly) manipulated according to public opinion. On the one hand, Civil Death to some extent already contains the mechanisms – modularity expressed in notions of reform or revision – with which critics of its practice in common law set out to call for an end of that practice. On the other hand, Civil Death does not contain mechanisms to reconcile the assumption that falsehoods may be employed as practical means to be truthful to law and equity with the historical fact that equity courts for a long time continued to be the legal elite's bastions of secrecy and power.

Similarly, parodic bodies, as in Sterne's parodic juxtaposition – regarding Yorick's self-removal from ordinary physicality – of benevolence and impotence, vacillate between the transgressive element of parody and the very limitations to which that transgressive element remains indebted. Parodic bodies may be derived, on the one hand, from the very notion of sensibility and delicacy whose miniaturization of experience – the "confinement" of refinement – they are designed to transgress. On the other hand, the parodic body is gendered – gendered in the sense that Sterne/Yorick derive mock-heroic sentimentalism from the imagined immateriality of an idealized feminine body made available through microanalysis. In other words, the parodic body is both means and expression of a sentimental imagination defined by masculine standards of transitional personalities.

Ronald Paulson recently argued that Sterne presents the corporeal site of sentimental love as a "revision or refinement" of Hogarth's aesthetics.[40] The latter may be described as a projection of Shaftesburian disinterestedness on the spectacle of the human body. As Paulson points out, Sterne "revises" or "refines" Hogarth's "revision" or "refinement" of Shaftesbury's Platonic abstractions. Sterne does so by way of employing it in *A Sentimental Journey* to unlock the prison of Yorick's body. In performing that function, however, this revised gaze on the body may no longer be merely centered on the female body, nor exclusively defined by curiosity, pursuit, and seduction. Yorick's gaze is likely also to be addressed to an "implied female reader." In Calais, this "is what causes Yorick to give the monk alms in order to make himself look good in the eyes of the woman."[41] Thus Sterne's parodic body is gendered on both the heterosexual and homosocial level. This duplicity reveals his version of sentimentalism as a specifically masculine attempt at rewriting the moral and commercial relations of personality and property. Yorick's sentimentalism is, as Carol Kay maintains, essentially a "remasculinization" of the feminine: "Perhaps Yorick does not need very much sentimental education at the hands of a woman, because he already has all the valuable attributes of a woman. By the process I am calling remasculinization, Sterne has appropriated softness, delicacy, and modesty for his male character."[42] In this sense, Sterne's enactment of the legal and sentimental tensions of confinement may be said to replicate only *certain* tensions, within masculine standards of transitional personalities, of the culture of which it forms a part; it is far from encompassing all of them.

In contrast, one must bear in mind that many sentimentalists, along with proponents of moral philosophy, at the time *did* employ their respective notions of sympathy-as-masculine-imagination as a means of encompassing commercial culture. Those attempts at elevating sympathy to a global cultural framework in terms of transitional personalities testify to a continued need, on the part of (male) philosophers and artists, organically to relate individuals and groups to the body politic of which they are a part. While Yorick's parodic body is gendered, the way Sterne "appropriated softness" (Kay) differs somewhat from the way Adam Smith distinguishes between "mere" (female) "humanity" and (male) "generosity":

The propriety of generosity and public spirit is founded upon the same principle with that of justice. Generosity is different from humanity. Those two qualities, which at first sight seem so nearly allied, do not always belong to the same person. Humanity is the virtue of a woman, generosity of a man. The fair sex, who have commonly much more tenderness than ours, have seldom so much generosity. That women rarely make considerable donations [raro mulieres donare solent] is an observation of the civil law. Humanity consists merely in the exquisite fellow-feeling which the spectator entertains with the sentiments of the persons principally concerned, so as to grieve for their sufferings, to resent their injuries, and to rejoice at their good fortune.[43]

Sterne highlights one particular function that modular identities and parodic bodies perform for "remasculinized" sympathy. This function is a nonlegal variation of equity. We remember, according to the Aristotelian concept of equity that informs common-law practice, the particular circumstances of a case may be used to modify the universality of the law that applies to it. In his interpretation of the law, a judge must translate the legislator's or a previous judge's intention into the adjudicative intention that is to be formed by looking at the particular circumstances of the present case. Sterne suggests, as I will demonstrate, that "remasculinized" sympathy may complement the function of the law in certain situations. He specifically focuses on those situations in which appeals to the notion of equitable justice that is institutionalized in British equity courts do not honor the "good nature" of British subjects in France. In a further step, he also calls attention to the complexities and problems of the promise he is holding out. For this purpose, he translates the mechanism of Civil Death into the *droits d'aubaine*.

In classical common-law theory, legal fictions such as Civil Death were considered vehicles of equity. But they could always also be used to manipulate the intentions of the legislator or a previous judge, which needed to be translated into the context of a particular case. In other words, they could be used to manipulate intentions for purposes other than equity. In order to emphasize the complex effects of sympathy on social bonding, Sterne implements the legal fiction's mechanism into his protagonists' "sentimental commerce" with others. This particular version of sympathy particularly comes to the fore, in *Tristram Shandy* and *A Sentimental Journey*, in the context of liminal and transitional situations. These are situations outside the sphere of national law, where it is often unclear whether, how, and which code of law or code of behavior might apply.

War and traveling represent important aspects of those liminal moments of crisis where death and Civil Death may in fact be imminent. Contractarian assumptions about social bonding are then of course in question. Vowing to help protect the king's subjects against the enemy abroad, the soldier fighting on French soil may end up – as Toby experiences in the case of Le Fever (*TS*, vi vi, pp. 334ff) – suspending certain expectations about how state institutions are supposed to protect him, in times of peace and on domestic soil, against harm or even death. In fact, the king will not be expected to protect against harm those soldiers of his who fight to protect his other subjects against harm. Similarly, Yorick can be said to be aware of having suspended, as it were, his rights, duties, and obligations outside the nation's legal space when he envisions his prospective incarceration in the Bastille. In this situation, he almost feels *as if* he were to be subjected to an equivalent of Crusoe's Civil Death. Both Toby and Yorick engage in forms of "sentimental commerce" in order to counteract the law that requires Toby to return to combat and Yorick to provide a valid passport.

Sympathetic forms of commerce, often figured as concrete objects like swords and snuff-boxes, begin to serve as a means of escaping national, class, and especially legal prohibitions on some universal and unfettered intercourse. Sterne's notion of sympathy emerges in situations of war and traveling as a "para-legal" mode of equity. In such situations, Toby and Yorick must establish social bonds with strangers that are, as I will show, less emotionally binding than intimacy and more morally binding than contracts. Thus, Sterne underscores their sentiment by introducing elements of promise. On the one hand, he adopts a number of Hume's assumptions about promises. On the other hand, he frequently collapses the basic distinction between natural sentiments and artificial promises which underlies theories of moral sentiment. As one consequence, Sterne uses Toby and Yorick to enact a fundamentally paradoxical quality of promising, namely that "[it] invites a reexamination of the commitments that it supplements."[44] In doing so, he brings to his readers' attention a series of conceptual, psychic, and moral tensions and contradictions that the sympathetic urge to escape confinement generates.

To employ sentiment certainly means for Sterne to counteract, often by means of irony, the empiricist epistemologies that dominated normative discourses like that of the law. The way he ridicules the marriage settlement of Tristram's mother (*TS*, I, xv, pp. 33–6) can serve as an example. In Le Fever's case, however, Sterne keeps irony at a minimal level in order to show how legal artifices such as promises can in turn penetrate, rather than remain distinct from, the domain of sentiment.

The notion of promise in British common law – considered between 1600 and 1800 as *per se* morally binding, according to P. S. Atiyah – was "never treated as even prima facie a sufficient fact for the creation of a legal obligation. [. . . A] promise was only legally actionable if the promise was to do something which the promisor ought to have done anyway."[45] Toby gives his promise in return for receipt of some "consideration," which he assumes to be trust and which he, as a promisor, is presumed to want. He receives trust and in return gives his word, thereby giving the promisee a right to future services and, simultaneously, putting his reputation in the promisee's safekeeping. A promise being a convention surviving alongside legal contract, the promisee cannot rely on monetary damages, before there are magistrates to assess them, but can instead rely on the promisor's chances of never being trusted again in case of the latter's failure to perform.

Le Fever is a lieutenant formerly serving with Toby in Flanders and, having tragically lost his wife and then his health, now on his death-bed. Toby's sentimental encounter with him takes place in the context of an imagined common bond of sympathy between soldiers. Upon request by the landlord, Toby sends Trim, as well as food and drink, to comfort someone who, even though a stranger to him, seems a "'compassionate fellow.'" For "'there must be something more than common in him, that in so short a time should win so much upon the affections of his host'" (*TS*, VI, vi, p. 335). This rendition of Toby's humble goodness in the private sphere certainly risks bathos when compared to the competitive virtues expected of a soldier. However, while this is the reason why Sterne often uses irony to distance Toby from pure sentiment, such irony is missing during the encounter with Le Fever.[46]

Sterne suggests the trench fighters' code of honor as a code of familiarity and mutual affection. Toby projects onto the "good-natured soul" of the unknown soldier Le Fever a nostalgia for his own experience in Flanders. More precisely, Toby projects onto Le Fever his own wish that pitiable but good-natured souls should receive equity, even if issued only by the powers of heaven, and be compensated for the justice withheld from them on earth. Toby finds himself "coop'd in betwixt a natural and a positive law" (*TS*, vi, viii, p. 340). He feels caught between the fellow-feeling of bending "his whole thoughts toward the private distresses at the inn," where Le Fever is staying, and the formal obligation toward the allies not to surrender Dendermond, "to be relieved or not by the French king, as the French king thought good." Eventually, Toby gives up the siege of Dendermond and considers only "how he himself should relieve the poor lieutenant and his son."

– He shall not die, by G–, cried my uncle *Toby*.
– The ACCUSING SPIRIT which flew up to heaven's chancery with the oath, blush'd as he gave it in; – and the RECORDING ANGEL as he wrote it down, dropp'd a tear upon the word, and blotted it out forever. [. . .] The blood and spirits of *Le Fever*, which were waxing cold and slow within him, and were retreating to their last citadel, the heart, – rallied back, – the film forsook his eyes for a moment, – he looked up wishfully in my uncle *Toby*'s face, – then cast a look upon his boy, – and that *ligament*, fine as it was, – was never broken. – (*TS*, vi, viii–x, pp. 341–3)

The "ligament" of sympathy is a bridge of microsensation across the abyss between self and other. As the reader learns later, Toby turns it into the moral bond of a commitment that he can direct toward the well-being of young Le Fever.

Toby's commitment is necessitated, as it were, by his failure to fend off old Le Fever's death by means of sympathy. For Toby seems to fail, in merely exercising sympathy, to enact the vision proposed by Adam Smith to reestablish the merits of a sufferer wronged and slain in a quarrel:

When we see one man oppressed or injured by another, the sympathy which we feel with the distress of the sufferer seems to serve only to animate our fellow-feeling with his resentment against the offender. [...] If the injured should perish in the quarrel, we not only sympathize with the real resentment of his friends and relations, but with the imaginary resentment which in fancy we lend to the dead, who is no longer capable of feeling or any other human sentiment. But as we put ourselves in his situation, as we enter, as it were, into his body, and in our imaginations, in some measure, animate anew the deformed and mangled carcase of the slain, when we bring home in this manner his case to our own bosoms, we feel, upon this, as upon many other occasions, an emotion which the person principally concerned is incapable of feeling, and which yet we feel by an illusive sympathy with him. (*TMS*, pp. 98-9)

Sterne presents a commitment of that sort as generated prior to reflection but simultaneous to other passionate impulses. It serves Toby to sandbag the tides of passion aroused not only by loss (death) but also by longing (love). Widow Wadman's "fever" of love for Toby, for instance, is, according to Walter Shandy's learned opinion, "not so much a SENTIMENT as a SITUATION, into which a man enters, as my brother Toby would do, into a *corps*, – no matter whether he loves the service or no – being once in it – he acts as if he did; and takes every step to shew himself a man of prowesse" (*TS*, VIII, xxxiv, p. 475). Walter's view of love does not merely differ from a relief, without preference, of those who are in distress. He elaborates on it in order to contrast a relief due to a natural compassion, an intimate ritual of exchanged sympathy between self and other, with what in a postlapsarian state of abstract virtues, morals, and laws will have to be supplied by promises, commitments, and obligations.

However, Walter probably would not have to insist on that distinction to the extent that he does if it were an obvious one. To be sure, sympathy may be used in the sense of a projected natural residue, "independently of all modes and customs," to take the place of customs and rules – that is to say, of instituted law. But whenever that happens, sympathy takes the place of instituted law just as much as instituted law, in the sense of seventeenth- and eighteenth-century common law, used to take the place of natural law when the latter was found to fail in coordinating rules and historical circumstances. Natural sympathy, supplanted by law and society, may also play the role of that which supplants the laws, rules, and customs administered by the common law.

EN-GENDERING TOBY'S TRANSFERS OF AFFECTION

Toby uses his sympathy for Le Fever to evoke exactly the contrast Walter suggests by comparing love and war. Joining the military "corps" seems to Walter like becoming in*corp*orated by the physical desires of widow Wadman. He sees it as a threat to be bound by amorous passion, to be in the "service" of femininity such as one would be bound by moral and legal obligations like the military code of honor and the duty of the king's subjects to conquer Dendermond. To be sure, desire is as prereflexive as pity. But in Walter's opinion, it also denatures natural sympathy. He is suspicious about desire's power to capture the nonpreferential energy of fellow-feeling. Therefore, he cautions Toby against any betrayal of natural morality by the physical desire for a single person.

Hence Toby's attitude of modesty, with respect both to widow Wadman and to Le Fever. Of course, the modesty of moral love is as little natural as the alleged immorality of physical desire. Instead, modesty is a product of social refinement designed, as a moral imperative, to limit the immorality of physical desire. As such, modesty is based less on sympathy than on the contradiction that it serves as an instrument to limit a preference-based notion of immorality, namely physical desire. For physical desire already poses a limit to the alleged nonpreferential and, ideally, unlimited scope of natural sympathy.

Sterne emphasizes this contradictory nature of Toby's modesty in two different but related ways. In the case of widow Wadman, Toby's modesty emerges as comical. It parodies its own assumptions. The moral imperative of modesty limits less the immorality of physical desire – an experience that appears to remain largely unknown to Toby – than in fact morality itself. Both Walter and Toby never make a claim for moral love to have turned immoral except as it menaced man's life. In the case of Le Fever, Toby's modesty emerges as grotesque. His act of benevolence – offering to take Le Fever home and to be his servant – grossly misstates Le Fever's actual need for some comfort adequate to his prospective death. Indeed, Toby enters, in Walter's words, into a "sentiment" as much as he enters into a "situation" where his sympathy may break with the behavioral code of an honorable commander laying a siege on Dendermond. Toby's sentiment may break with the brute force of war. But he cannot, by way of employing sympathy, dismiss the brute event of death as unnatural.

In response to that "situation," Toby ensures himself that the intimacy of mutual affection between himself and old Le Fever carries over to young Le Fever. A transfer of affection, however, seems to belong for Toby to the same set of categories that established "natural" modesty as a product of social refinement. Toby is treating the transfer of affections, in order to make it morally binding, in terms of promising a property transfer based on the exchange of his commitment for young Le Fever's trust. His decision to perform the duty of protecting young Le Fever as his ward and to provide for him rests on a noncontractual notion of promise.

When my uncle *Toby* had turned every thing into money, and settled all accounts betwixt the agent of the regiment and *Le Fever*, and betwixt *Le Fever* and all mankind, – there remained nothing more in my uncle *Toby*'s hands, than an old regimental coat and a sword; so that my uncle *Toby* found little or no opposition from the world in taking administration. [. . .] And this, – said my uncle *Toby*, taking up the sword in his hand, and drawing it out of the scabbard as he spoke – and this, *Le Fever*, I'll save for thee, – 'tis all the fortune, continued my uncle *Toby*, hanging it up upon a crook, and pointing to it, – 'tis all the fortune, my dear *Le Fever*, which God has left thee [. . .]. The greatest injury could not have oppressed the heart of *Le Fever* more than my uncle *Toby*'s paternal kindness; – he parted from my uncle *Toby*, as the best of sons from the best of fathers – both dropped tears – and as my uncle *Toby* gave him his last kiss, he slipped sixty guineas, tied up in an old purse of his father's, in which was his mother's ring, into his hand, – and bid God bless him. (*TS*, VI, xii, pp. 346–7)

Toby receives young Le Fever's affection in return for a commitment properly to "tak[e] administration" of property to be inherited by a minor. Since both Toby and young Le Fever only imagine rather than express intimacy, Toby feels "naturally" compelled, if not obliged, to resort to a pawn of trust – Le Fever's sword – for his delivery of paternal affection and commitment. The sword serves as a symbol which creates an obligation to perform his promise of committing himself to Le Fever's well-being.

This choice of representing the promise to perform may seem arbitrary. But Toby thinks of the impulse to commit himself by means of a promise as something naturally arising from his paternal instincts. He thus anticipates Sterne's story of the impoverished aristocrat Marquis de E**** of Brittany in *A Sentimental Journey*. Out of a paternal sense of commitment to his two young sons, that nobleman deposits his status and reputation, symbolized by his sword, at the court. He finally returns, after twenty years of accumulating riches in Martinique, to "reclaim" his nobility (*SJ*, p. 105). Both the Marquis and Toby express a particular commitment with respect to nonintimates, but do so in the absence of contracts. Their cases may be different in that Toby promises to administer Le Fever's well-being, while the Marquis promises not to disappoint the judge's expectation toward the full recovery of his (the Marquis's) deposit. Both, however, pledge their name. Both try to compensate for the fact that a failure to meet the expectations generated by their expressed commitments will have no legal consequences.

The cases of Toby and the Marquis reflect, and complicate, David Hume's account of promises as a convention distinct from natural sympathy. Published in 1740 as part of *A Treatise of Human Nature*, that account describes how promises became the artificial means of creating obligations, which societies use in contradistinction to both oath and contract. To perform that function, Hume argues, promises must meet three requirements. They must involve, unlike the transfer of property by consent such as in barter or gift, a representation of the particular commitment to be performed in the future. Such a representation must be introduced by ritually exchanging with another party linguistic signs of one's reputation. Promises must further include particular remote and general goods within the scope of a voluntary transfer. Only the voluntary nature of transactions will create those obligations which specifically arise from a delay in delivery. Finally, promises must imply a penalty clause that entitles the promisee to a forfeiture of the trust deposited by the promisor. The penalty clause also entitles the promisee to a declaration of social death – a nonlegal equivalent of Civil Death – on the promise-breaker, inviting a communal agreement not to accept further promises from persons standing in ill repute.[47]

Toby only superficially invokes contractarian notions of paternal administration, such as Locke's, when he feels "naturally" compelled to commit himself to young Le Fever's future: "[The natural father's] command over his children is but temporary, and reaches not their life or property; it is but a help to the weakness and imperfection of their nonage, a discipline necessary to their education; [. . .] yet this freedom exempts not a son from that honour which he ought, by the law of God and nature, to pay his parents."[48] There are, however, indications that their sympathy is not exactly reciprocal. At least, they are not as reciprocal as Hume's carefully crafted notion of sympathy as a general principle of moral mutuality would require them to be. Toby creates, by committing himself to his elected minion's concerns, young Le Fever as an other that resembles, structurally, characters in novels of Defoe, Fielding, or Goldsmith. There, the good man sets out, or is sent out, to discover his own moral powers. He is then somewhat expected, after a series of trials, to come into his true inheritance and supplant the dominion of an earthly father. He is, however, expected to do that by acknowledging that father's divine counterpart as someone or something that according to a set of just principles has controlled or plotted his life. Such a theological pattern usually provides an orderly system of rewards and punishments in this life or the next. It is also the same pattern whose political implications Bender extends, as explained earlier, to the concept of omniscient narration.

In Sterne's text, the traditional focus on an accomplished plot disappears, of course, and so does the theological pattern of paternal influence. This is not to say, though, that Sterne transcends the Lockean link between "class differentials" and "gender differentials" in terms of the capability to own property.[49] Rather, the process of sentimental commerce abroad, which temporarily suspends the expatriate male soldier or traveler from "repatriation," reconfigures, as Melinda Alliker Rabb pointed out for Yorick, his gendered identity: "As one meaning engenders another, so any object, action, or expression may acquire gender."[50] For instance, if Toby retains paternal power over young Le Fever, he also begins to mother him with a peculiar sense of tenderness and affection.

Is Toby aware of the moral insensitivity that his involvement in bonds of sympathy between the roles of father and son may do more than simply turn the spectacle of young Le Fever's suffering into an *exemplum* for the sake of his own enlightenment? Does he see a problem in that it also dramatizes the separation between victims and agents of providence as an undesirable emotional gap between the powers of the self and the bare existence of the other beyond any participation in moral spectacles? We cannot be sure. However, we do see that Toby does not confine himself to a notion of sympathy whose moral claims would only amount to emotional luxury at the expense of others in the utter safety of separation between observer and observed. In fact, we do see him take measures against the disquieting prospects of such self-protective identification.

HOW TOBY'S PATERNAL KINDNESS INCURS PROMISSORY LIABILITY

Toby and young Le Fever are virtually strangers. They effectively invoke promises as artificial means to create obligations as they agree to turn an imagined rather than expressed sense of sympathy between nonintimates into commitments. To back up imagined or desired sympathy with, in Hume's words, the nonnatural obligation of a promise – in Toby's words, "'and this [sword] I'll save for thee'" – is to turn noncontractarian. The obligation which Toby linguistically creates seems opposed to the presumably natural sympathy which compels him to do so. It will be perceived as artificial, according to Hume, once that community of readers sympathetic to fellow-feeling in whose context Toby makes his promise recognizes the customary basis of the obligation as such: property, transfer of property by consent, government, marriage etc. Hume goes so far as to say that the fictions of "*symbolical* delivery" society has created in promises may in fact be considered useful, if artificial, rituals invented by the lawyers "to satisfy the fancy" "concerning the transference of property by consent":

The property of an object, when taken for something real, without any preference to morality, or the sentiments of the mind, is a quality perfectly insensible, and even inconceivable; nor can we form any distinct notion, either of its stability or translation. [. . .] In order to aid the imagination in conceiving the transference of property, we take the sensible object, and actually transfer its possession to the person, on whom we wou'd bestow the property. The suppos'd resemblance of the actions, and the presence of this sensible delivery, deceive the mind, and make it fancy, that it conceives the mysterious transition of the property. And that this explication of the matter is just, appears hence, that men have invented a *symbolical* delivery, to satisfy the fancy, where the real one is impracticable. Thus giving the keys of a granary is understood to be the delivery of the corn contain'd in it: The giving of stone and earth represents the delivery of a mannor. This is a kind of superstitious practice in civil laws, and in the laws of nature, resembling the *Roman catholic* superstitions in religion. As the *Roman catholics* represent the inconceivable mysteries of the *Christian* religion, and render them more present to the mind, by a taper, or habit, or grimace, which is suppos'd to resemble them; so lawyers and moralists have run into like inventions for the same reason, and have endeavour'd by those means to satisfy themselves concerning the transference of property. (*T*, pp. 515–16)

Sterne supports the sentimental fiction of Toby's intimacy with young Le Fever by means of what Hume calls the artificial device or ritual of a mysterious transition of property. This ritual of transition is none other than the legally and morally accepted fiction of a symbolic delivery of affection granted by a promise. Toby thus translates the Humean obligation-creating fiction of making promises into his own sentimental act of sympathy. He does so in order "artificially" to perform as binding what may "naturally" defy its transfer into instituted forms of performing obligations. Upon this premise, he can implement the "artificial" mechanism of transfer ("symbolic delivery") exhibited in promises into his own sentimental delivery of "natural" affection. Nonetheless, the very precondition of that implementation – Toby's apparent need to renegotiate the Humean difference between natural sympathy and artificial rituals of obligation-creation – relies on the same ritual mechanism of transfer that is already contained, or implemented, in promises.

Both sympathy and promise, it appears, transfer something. To be sure, they also differ, at least for an "enlightened egois[t]" such as Hume,[51] and they do so in two respects. On the one hand, promises involve an expressed resolution to perform dutifully, which reaches beyond the avowals of intention typical of mere transfers by consent. On the other hand, sympathy is a very powerful principle in human nature, [. . .] has a great influence on our taste of beauty, and [. . .] produces our sentiment of morals in all the artificial virtues [as, for instance, in "fidelity to promises"]. From thence we may presume, that it also gives rise to many of the other virtues; and that qualities acquire our approbation, because of their tendency to the good of mankind. [. . . M]oral distinctions arise, in a great measure, from the tendency of qualities and characters to the interest of society, and that 'tis our concern for that interest, which makes us approve or disapprove of them. Now we have no such extensive concern for society but from sympathy; and consequently 'tis that principle, which takes us so far out of ourselves, as to give us the same pleasure or uneasiness in the characters of others, as if they had a tendency to our own advantage or loss. The only difference betwixt the natural virtues and justice lies in this, that the good, which results from the former, arises from every single act, and is the object of some natural passion: Whereas a single act of justice, consider'd in itself, may often be contrary to the public good; and 'tis only the concurrence of mankind, in a general scheme or system of action, which is advantageous. (*T*, pp. 577–9)

Sympathy and promise also differ in that promises involve – and this seems true for both Hume and Toby – a submission of one's potential non-performance to penalty. Losses of intimacy rather refer to such future services as responses to love and kindness. This is in fact how Hume distinguishes promisors from friends as engaged in "two different sorts of commerce, the interested and the disinterested" (*T*, pp. 521–2): "Men being naturally selfish, or endow'd only with a confin'd generosity, they are not easily induc'd to perform any action for the interest of strangers, except with a view to some reciprocal advantage, which they had no hope of obtaining but by such a performance" (*T*, p. 519).

Ironically, Toby without hesitation extends sympathy to "strangers" such as Le Fever. For he assumes that they stand in need of a pawn of trust with respect to the affection "transferred." He would certainly agree with Hume that the sentiments of others naturally affect him, that is to say, "*as if* they had been originally deriv'd from [his] own temper and disposition" (*T*, p. 593, my emphasis). He may even go along with Hume in admitting that since no "natural passion," but only a sense of duty, leads him to observe the obligation to perform his promise, promises are no "natural obligations" (*T*, p. 518). There is no purely internal or subjective way in which he can surrender his freedom to break the promise. The will cannot strictly speaking obligate itself, Hume claims, so that by invoking promises, we therefore "*feign* a new act of the mind, which we call the *willing* an obligation; and on this we suppose the morality to depend" (*T*, p. 523).

Toby differs from Hume with respect to the purpose of feigning the will. For Toby, it is not as important as it is for Hume to distinguish types of trust – and the vulnerability of those who express it – according to friendship, promises, and consent or authority. To feign intimacy with strangers is to supplant both natural ties with contrived ones and "artificial virtues" such as the fidelity to promises with "natural virtues" such as sympathy. The sentimental soldier abroad meets strangers on the basis of a common military code of honor. Appeals to that code are meant to trigger a sense of heroic human feeling wherever the stranger has been deprived of equitable justice. By resorting to promises, however, Toby employs "non-natural" forms of creating obligation not as opposites, but as supplements, to sentiment. Conversely, since Toby uses a form of sympathy supplemented by the structure of promissory transfer, he is seeking to provide the stranger with a sympathetic sense of equity that has the same structure as that of a promissory transfer. He is anxious to perform a symbolic transfer, or "delivery," of the equitable "justice" so far not rendered to the stranger.

It is historically significant that Sterne uses the notion of trust implied in promises in order to negotiate between two culturally opposed forms of social bonding – the spheres of intimacy and contract. To implement trust into a cultural situation characterized by increasingly complex social relations is to turn risks into possibilities for the future. In a situation where psychological and economic desires begin to overlap, risks with regard to social bonding will become individualized and the norms supposed to regulate them more differentiated, as Niklas Luhmann points out for eighteenth-century societies. People do not yet assume that interdependencies exist in non-contractual relationships. In such cases, trust stands apart from the law. It requires a personal and unverbalized motivation to match one's own actions with the experience of others' actions.[52]

Hume shows what promises can do in the absence of magistrates who enforce penalties against breaches of contract. They can "enforce" a sort of pre-legal Civil Death as a person's social death in terms of communal reputation. Sterne connects Toby's sympathy for young Le Fever with a sense of promissory liability. Sterne thus still reflects Hume's assumption that some ties are natural, independent of general rules or any contrived penalties. Toby would concede that neither all the natural ties nor all the contrived ones are voluntarily assumed by those involved in such relationships, and that not all the voluntarily assumed ones are penalty-backed. He would admit that the penalties involved in promises and in contracts differ according to the way they are enforced. He thus seeks to keep his promise in the same way that he would obey the rules concerning property and its transfer by consent. In addition to changing the moral situation, as in other rituals with instituted roles and offices to structure a transfer, he represents the very conditions under which the ritually invoked penalty – his loss of reputation in a metaphorical Civil Death – will be avoided.

Sterne expresses Toby's "paternal kindness" (*TS*, vi, xii, p. 347) toward young Le Fever as a form of sympathy, backed by promissory liability for the latter's well-being, that resembles Van Sant's analysis of Yorick's paternal sympathy for strangers in distress. It is a paternalism that creates its "objects of suffering" according to certain male standards of the feminine. But what characterizes the difference between Le Fever, as an object of suffering for Toby, and Toby himself, the pity-sensitive spectator-benefactor, is not exactly an equivalent of sexual difference, usually represented as polar oppositions (e.g. passive–active) designed to taper off the anxiety that specific differences provoke. The structure of promissory transfer which regulates the reciprocal flow of affection between them institutes an obligation to renounce the choice of exercising powers of paternal desire.

This is certainly not to say that Toby's paternal desire may not reemerge in a transference of Le Fever's submissive need for sympathetic approval onto his own sympathetic "submission" to young Le Fever's pre-arranged well-being. Toby's promise to take measures against Le Fever's suffering and to work toward his perfectibility may in fact adumbrate a defensive mechanism established against a secret pleasure of domination – disguised in a submissive identification with the role of the victim. However, as Tzvetan Todorov points out, the recognition of otherness within relationships characterized by sympathy and sociality is usually more richly textured than suggested by critiques of struggles for power and prestige and of cultures of resentment and mimetic desire. Disputing Kojève's interpretation of Hegel's master/slave dialectic, he maintains that such recognition must not be reduced to notions of

desire frustrated by its very realization, [or] rivalry accompanied by the paradoxical demand for recognition from the rival. The description is not false, but its claim to universality is exorbitant. The reality of human relationships is infinitely richer. Not everything that is immaterial is desire. Not every recognition is a struggle for power or a demand for a confirmation of a value. Nor is every struggle accompanied by a demand for recognition either.[53]

By renouncing his obligations toward the military community before Dendermond, of which he forms a part, Toby creates an alternative obligation toward a miniaturized community of donors and recipients of sympathy that he has established by deciding to "administer" young Le Fever's life. His promise is meant to suspend the network of fictions involved in the political desires of war. As such, the promise expresses a renunciation that simultaneously affirms itself as a different network of fictions. This mode of renunciation connects the roles and offices involved in the Humean "ritual" of promises. Thus Toby temporarily becomes a stranger to the previous network of fictions (war). His "gaze" on military "objects of suffering" may, in this sense, now be external. But it operates only relative to the network of sentimental fictions of promising that he now inhabits. Therefore, he is only ideally capable of perceiving the fissure between himself and the object of his varying commitments (war, sympathy).

What practically holds his new miniaturized community together is a ritual of renounced desire to distance the "administrator" of another's suffering from a detached experience of it *as* another's suffering. By exchanging the military code of honor for the sentimental code of promise-backed sympathy, Toby exchanges but two modes of renunciation. He may certainly be said to seek the perfectibility of those in need of sympathy. But he also exchanges those two modes of renunciation for the perfectibility of his own "good nature." In other words, Toby exchanges rituals of renunciation, paradoxically, for the sake of his own benefit. It is in this sense that he institutes the ritual of promise-backed sympathy for Le Fever and himself as a responsible choice. Apparently, this choice is without "natural" alternatives, obliging him to renounce any detachment of the "administration" of well-being from the sympathetic experience of suffering.

Truthful to his benefit of perfectibility, Toby turns himself into a promisor who, in a way, promises to "pay" for the benefit received. In the legal terms of the above-mentioned "doctrine of consideration," this admission might have been taken as the very ground of his liability to perform the promise. By promising to "pay" for the benefit, he could have been said conclusively to admit that it is a benefit and what it is worth to him. Since he appears to be the sole and best judge of his own interests, he may consider himself liable *because* he has promised. But his promise is not the reason for the obligation any more than his decision as the judge of his own interests is to a judge a reason for the law that he or she declares makes the promisor liable. In Toby's case, the promisor is himself the judge, but also remains the promisor before a (potential) judge.

In his capacity as judge, Toby conclusively determines what is beneficial (not necessarily only to himself) and what it is worth. In his capacity as promisor, he then becomes bound by his own decision as judge. The admission that the promise entails a benefit may even become appropriate for him as promisor, once he has made his promise. Which explains why, once the promise is made, even he as promisor may come to see himself as bound just because he has promised, and for no other reason. He puts himself in a position in which a judge might find himself if he became personally involved in a dispute on a point of law which he had formerly resolved in his capacity as judge. As a judge, various reasons would have informed his decision on what the law should be. As a legal subject making a promise, the judge would become bound by the law, irrespective of any good or bad reasons that informed his decision on what the law should be.

What makes this "position" so odd is its obvious break with the strongly held ideal that no person, as Burke later formulated it, should be a judge in his or her cause.[54] The reason that this maxim does not bar Toby's perspective is that Toby the promisor is treating himself as a judge only against himself. He is likely to hold himself liable on the promise because, by his own admission, what he has received is a benefit worth what he has promised for it. Even if he were to treat himself as the judge to decide what is beneficial, and what value benefits have, the decision he has made is one he has made against himself. Although he should not, according to the maxim, be a judge in his own cause, he constructs himself, without any limitations or qualifications, as both a moral and a legal subject who, having decided against himself, appears to be the best of all judges. For the judge in him, the source of the obligation is the promise. For the promisor in him, the source of the obligation consists of the reasons which have led him to make the promise or to make a judge's decision.

WHAT DOES SYMPATHY WANT OF ME? OR: YORICK GOES FISHING FOR COMPLIMENTS

Yorick's afterthoughts on the exchange of snuff-boxes with Father Lorenzo, a Franciscan monk in Calais to whom he first refused to give money, illustrate another aspect of this duplicity. Yorick trades rituals of renunciation imposed on the tourist traveler (voluntary suspension of certain rights, privileges etc.) for ritual renunciations of desire implied in responsible exchanges of sympathy. He differs from Toby in that he does not linguistically express his commitment as an explicit promise. Instead, he implies it in the corporeal gestures of reaching out for an intended reciprocal exchange of snuff-boxes. Eventually, he links the monk's later (real) death to his own obligation not to break the sympathetic bond between the two of them.

I guard this box, as I would the instrumental parts of my religion, to help my mind on to something better: in truth, I seldom go abroad without it; and oft and many a time have I called up by it the courteous spirit of its owner to regulate my own, in the justlings of the world; they had found full employment for his, as I learnt from his story, till about the forty-fifth year of his age, when upon some military services ill requited, and meeting at the same time with a disappointment in the tenderest of passions, he abandoned the sword and the sex together, and took sanctuary, not so much in his convent as in himself. (*SJ*, p. 44)

Not only does Yorick commit himself to aspiring to his own perfectibility. He commits himself to place perfectibility in relation to different forms of an opaque interiority that the metaphor of Civil Death suggests. Lorenzo's withdrawal into a monastic form of social death marks his position in their relation as one which appears secluded from Yorick's demand for sympathetic affection. It marks his position as one in which he cannot comply with that demand without rendering his interiority transparent. For what Yorick lacks is not likely simply to lie dormant within Lorenzo. Instead, Lorenzo answers Yorick's demand with what he appears to lack himself, expressed in his longing for sympathy. Sterne renders this encounter of two lacks as a successful instance of exchanged affection.

Yorick and Lorenzo employ the unspeakability of mutual sympathy to appease the abyss of otherness between two strangers. They seek to appease that abyss by resorting to a *sympathetic* renunciation of the desire *sympathetically* to objectify the other. A sympathetic objectification of the other, however, is exactly what happens. Both of them understand the other's inaccessible interiority as such as an objectifiable target of their need to imagine the other's (assumed) need to share their sympathy. Implicitly asking themselves questions such as "What does Sympathy want of me?," they submit to an Otherness that makes their relationship of exchange possible in the first place. As a result, they renounce themselves as "pathological" subjects full of particular desires and interests. They do so in order to participate, in an abstract ethical fashion, in a projected "original" situation prior to all such desires and interests, one which almost projects a sentimental fiction of the social contract.

Yorick later learns from Maria that "pale, thin" Tristram Shandy pitied her and "half *promised*" to see her again (*SJ*, pp. 138–9, my emphasis). At Calais, he did *not* make an explicit promise to Father Lorenzo that he could subsequently break. He has, however, clearly internalized the threat of a penalty hanging ominously over his own respectability. Lorenzo's choice to live a life of monastic isolation reemerges in Yorick's endeavor not to subject himself, by "breaking" the *implicit* promise of sympathy after Lorenzo's real death, to a confinement issued by his own internalized psycho-judicial system. The confinement Lorenzo has chosen is a negative signal for Yorick to objectify Lorenzo as someone with whom he ought to sympathize but not identify. Their mutual acts of sympathy are thus centered, despite their different motivations, around a metaphorical Civil Death, which one lives and the other tries to avoid. Sterne therefore still subjects Yorick's desire to transference, having him posit sympathy so as to be able to appease it through the renunciation of "pathological" desires imaginatively to invade the other's interiority.

In an ironic twist, Yorick eventually reveals, when he visits Lorenzo's grave, that his sympathy for the monk has had a "pathological" taint all along. His sympathy is tainted in the sense that he appropriated Lorenzo's monastic lifestyle – a "sanctuary, not so much in his convent as in himself" (*SJ*, p. 44). In Paris, as I mentioned earlier, Yorick uses the appeal to fellow-feeling for his own escape from a metaphorical Civil Death, as the projected penalty for a withheld-but-implicitly-promised sympathy, into the traveler's sentimental confinement of refined "microsensation." To be sure, in Calais he first revises his opinion of the monk and decides not to enter into an exchange situation with him. But later he makes himself a judge of his own judgmental faculties, which seem to stand in need of improvement by means of sentimental imagination. In fact, now it seems as if he cannot but commit himself to the commemoration of Lorenzo. He begins to identify the sympathy ruling his compassion with an enactment of distributive and compensatory justice that reaches beyond the utilitarian aspects of individual renunciations.

Only a free choice is morally binding. And Yorick certainly assumes that he freely chooses a sympathetic "community" with Lorenzo. At the same time, he does really not exist as a sentimental sharer of sympathetic imagination prior to his choice to "administer" the other's metaphorical Civil Death, and to "administer" it as a judge entitled symbolically to render distributive and compensatory justice. This choice is a paternalistic choice. For Sterne has Yorick assume that the monk is incapable of rendering justice to himself: "[H]e *begged* we might exchange boxes" (*SJ*, p. 44, my emphasis). Lorenzo's withdrawal from social life suggests to Yorick a retreat from any intention to become the judge of his (Lorenzo's) own needs. Yorick's imagination objectifies Lorenzo as someone who cannot help himself.

Furthermore, this assumption of helplessness is gendered. Which becomes obvious the moment Sterne repeats Yorick's ritual of renunciation at the site of Lorenzo's grave:

[. . .] I heard he had been dead near three months, and was buried, not in his convent, but according to his desire, in a little cimetiery belonging to it, about two leagues off: I had a strong desire to see where they had laid him, – when, upon pulling out his little horn-box, as I sat by his grave, and plucking up a nettle or two at the head of it, which had no business to grow there, they all struck together so forcibly upon my affections, that I burst into a flood of tears – but I am as weak as a woman; and beg the world not to smile, but pity me. (*SJ*, pp. 44–5)

We have already seen that Yorick feminizes Lorenzo from a perspective of paternalistic "administration" of distributive and compensatory justice. Here he exposes himself as the idealized feminine body made available, as a "parodic body" (Van Sant), to his sentimental readers by insinuating the option of a "microanalytic" sentimentalist reading. He is asking readers to substitute their imagination for the judgment he himself appears to have lost – as "evidenced" by feeling "as weak as a woman" – just as he substituted his own imagination for the "right" to justice on which he assumes Lorenzo had given up.

Yorick switches positions, as it were, and turns himself into the Lorenzo of his sentimental readers, whom he (Yorick), at this point, is implicitly "begging to exchange" affection. The contemporary reader will have *consciously* felt courted by this sense of sympathetic "commerce." Yorick here glosses his gestures of sympathy as the polite gesture of a refined understanding of "sociality" that creates "the pact between a knowing narrator and a knowing consumer of novels."[55] What makes this politeness rather complex is the possibility that it may not only be gendered in terms of Kay's notion of "remasculinization," but also be connected with the very context of French culture which the sentimental traveler is at this point exploring.

Hume, for instance, considered the smooth and polished manners that enable people to get along and to alter political, moral, and emotional situations by means of unverbalized strategies, as well as the arts of elegant conversation and compliment, a set of values typically found in modern monarchies such as France, where to be prosperous and successful a person had to "render himself *agreeable*, by his wit, complaisance, or civility."[56] To be sure, as every social habit contains its own weaknesses, "modern politeness, which is naturally so ornamental, runs often into affectation and foppery, disguise and insincerity."[57] In a way, Hume explains what self-feminizing – or, rather, "self-remasculinizing" – Yorick asks the sentimental reader to do in terms of a civilized gendered form of authority over a female, "a studied deference and complaisance for all her inclinations and opinions."[58]

Significantly, Yorick does not seem to need to learn much from women themselves, for instance from the grisette in the glove shop or from Maria. As I said earlier, Sterne often replaces conversational intercourse, typically expected as formal politeness, with expressive silences and with Yorick's inclination to translate faces and gestures into refined fictional worlds of sentimental confinement ("microsensation"). This confinement, one would now have to add, is one that also serves to portray Yorick as a man of agreeable manners in the eyes of the reader. In fact, Yorick does not earn a living by commerce. Instead, it helps him, in an indirect way, to acquire, maintain, or support his social dignity. This acquired sense of dignity seems to extend sympathy to French-style authority. It appears to make sympathy uphold the social and political segregation of classes just as much as one would assume that it is meant to overcome them. A case in point is the psychic economy, as it were, displayed by the sense of dignity according to which Yorick conducts "commerce" with the Chevalier de St. Louis, the "patisser" in Versailles. He subsequently justifies his behavior by telling the story of the Marquis de E****, which discloses and underscores the legal abyss between the aristocratic and commercial classes.

More obvious, perhaps, in this regard are situations where Yorick ironically subjects himself to a certain degree of legal and sentimental control on the part of others. We remember that before the Count de B****, he enacts the social powerlessless of Yorick-the-jester as the aesthetic power of a literary character, turning the anticipatory fantasy of his imprisonment in the Bastille into both liberation and financial advantage. Eve Kosofsky Sedgwick goes so far as to argue that Yorick *strategically* enacts such manipulations as a form of vulnerability in order to avoid actually being helpless.[59] Building on this argument as well as on Foucault's observations on eighteenth-century discipline and punishment, Frank explains Yorick's reversal of such subject positions as the "ideological tactic" of a "virtual imperialist of sensibility." She claims that he struggles to counteract his own social marginalization by parodically producing the sentimental: "[Yorick's] fantasizing of himself as a pathetic victim – an object rather than the subject of sentimentalism – functions as an apotropaic gesture by which he both rehearses poverty and powerlessness and wards it off, constituting himself as a multivalent and self-ironic gentleman."[60]

Obviously, the parody of subjecting one's body, or the "body" of one's own text, to the microanalytic gaze of others enacts something. But it does not seem all that obvious that what is enacted here ought to be specified as an "apotropaic gesture." Frank's argument implies that the sentimentalist writes about surveillance and anticipated torture from, as it were, an inside perspective. It also suggests that the benevolist does not help his or her audience to see how the private pursuit of social advancement through aesthetic means can generate cruelty. In Frank's view, sentimentalism is necessarily complicitous with those eighteenth-century systems of surveillance which, according to Foucault, discipline and police the body in order to produce the bourgeois subject – to produce the bourgeois subject as one who can spy the nakedness of others' hearts.

According to this rationale, sentimental taste and conscience are, for Sterne, not just yet pragmatic bundles of idiosyncratic beliefs and desires. Instead, they are actually faculties that have determinate objects, namely a sense of character to be established in terms of class. Moreover, they are employed to replace traditional attempts at combining a moral quest for right action with an adequate aesthetic expression of feeling. In fact, Frank seems to imply that sentiment-producing parody always contributes to generating a body politic of bourgeois subjects who are complicitous with the discipline inscribed on their bodies; yet that such parody can never serve to expose the complicity at work in that production of bourgeois subjects. To be sure, parody may produce sentimentality. But the forms of parody that may be discerned in sentimental discourse cannot necessarily be reduced to a production of the ironic gentleman who exculpates sentimentality's complicity with cruelty.

Sentimental parody, even as it is made to cover up its own ulterior motives, cannot strictly speaking be dissociated from the idea of working for a future in which such cruelty will no longer be institutionalized. On the one hand, Yorick's parodic body is certainly a throwback to a time when such social hope was so obviously unrealistic as to be of little interest to intellectuals or artists. On the other hand, the fact that the parodic body does not seem to articulate any need for a world of "sentimental commerce" in which Yorick could not feel shame does not necessarily imply that he does *not* need, like for instance Harold Skimpole in *Bleak House*, a world of "sentimental commerce" in which he would not have to feel pity. On the contrary, Sterne may just as well have tried to situate morality, as Wolfgang Iser argues with respect to "Momus's glass in the human breast" in *Tristram Shandy* (which was thought to render the soul visible), within a parodic body that causes abstract frames of reference for morality typical of the Enlightenment period to implode. One such frame of reference was a notion of reason that is to be validated and secured by linguistic rationality. Instead of employing sympathy as a cover-up for his hero's class aspirations, Sterne suggests morality as a pre-reflexive cipher for the foundations of subjectivity. Those foundations, however, must remain inaccessible to cognition.[61] "Class" thus emerges as just another form of definition whose "mechanical help" in delineating character Tristram rejects as he insists on "draw[ing] my uncle Toby's character from his HOBBY HORSE" (*TS*, I, xxiii, p. 61).

The assumption, on the part of British moral philosophers and proponents of sentiment, that commerce itself involves agreeable manners was, as is well known, a beacon of hope for the new economies of the mid eighteenth century. In this regard, Hume appears more hopeful than Rousseau, who, in his *Discourse on the Origin of Inequality*, claims that the sociability which inspires taste and commerce deteriorates the morals and that inequality originates in politeness even before the invention of private property. In contrast, Hume believes that the development of industry, commerce, and consumption has triggered, especially as far as the sociable manners in conversations between the sexes are concerned, both a sense of cultural superiority and an "encrease of humanity" in modern Europe.[62] In making this claim, he is clearly indebted to Montesquieu's connection between polite intercourse, taste, fashion, and consumption as based on competitive desire and esteem. The social value of "doux commerce," previously considered luxury, is for Montesquieu, in his *De l'esprit des lois*, based on a sense of competitive honor that makes possible ever finer discriminations between subjects of the monarchy.

Competitive honor is of course an egoistic concern for other people's opinions, rather than the altruistic love of public good which was the virtue of the republics. And Adam Smith was certainly not the first to hint at the danger of letting honor form part of an undifferentiated series of desires such as for wealth and power when he spoke of justice having a special role to play in societies no longer regulated by beneficence:

All the members of human society stand in need of each other's assistance, and are likewise exposed to mutual injuries. [. . .] Society may subsist among different men, as among different merchants, from a sense of its utility, without any mutual love or affection; and though no man in it should owe any obligation, or be bound in gratitude to any other, it may still be upheld by a mercenary exchange of good offices according to an agreed valuation. Society, however, cannot subsist among those who are at all times ready to hurt and injure one another. (*TMS*, p. 124)

The case of Yorick, however, is more complicated. He certainly spreads politeness wherever he goes, for instance by overpaying servants or buying unneeded things from people he cares for. But he also differs from Frenchmen like Monsieur Dessein, the hotel-owner in Calais – who supplies deferential Yorick with the epithet "*homme d'esprit*" (*SJ*, p. 38), thus also alluding to the title of Montesquieu's text – from whom he hires a carriage larger than he needs. Yorick proposes to rent an inexpensive old *chaise* to relieve Dessein from "suffer[ing]" over its business-damaging presence in the coachyard. Dessein, however, insists on his obligation not to hire out a *désobligeant* unworthy of a "man of honour." What starts out as a polite mutual assurance not to exchange "one disquietude for another" ends for Yorick in the image of a reprehensible "duel" of "casuistry" between the forces of deference and authority, where "the buyer [. . .] falls into the same frame of mind [as the seller]" (*SJ*, pp. 38–9). What turns Yorick's deference into anger is the anxiety that in such an exchange situation, he can hardly discriminate anymore between the sentimental commerce he envisions in terms of competitive esteem, on the one hand, and the calculation of advantages within the client economy of host and tourist, on the other. Politeness certainly implies a sense of long-term credit to be "purchased" at the "expense" of extending to the other party an indication of willingness to respect honor. But at the same time, it implies a sense of short-term credit to be "purchased" by restlessly consuming, and incorporating into the commercial situation, other values than the courtly rationality of honor.

Only at first does Yorick seem favorable to those features of French politeness which for many people in England epitomized the inquisitionist tyranny of French monarchy. Upon reexamination, Yorick's internalized psycho-judicial system triggers, in his imagination, the psychological equivalent of a public petition, more typical of England's legal system. Conscience recalls him from the anti-Semitism and racism he expressed against hosts such as Dessein: "Base passion! said I, turning myself about, as a man naturally does upon a sudden reverse of sentiment – base, ungentle passion! thy hand is against every man, and every man's hand against thee" (*SJ*, p. 39). Yorick displaces the asymmetry of aristocratic and commercial classes, which threatens the integrity of his notion of sentimental commerce, onto the asymmetry of base and noble passions. Subsequently he can rationalize that displacement in his sympathetic encounters with the lady whose hand he holds in the *désobligeant*. The same applies to his commemoration of Father Lorenzo, whose snuff-box he holds dearly, "as I would the instrumental parts of my religion, to help my mind on to something better" (*SJ*, p. 44), even after the old monk's death.

This is not to say that Yorick turns honor against commerce. Rather, he learns how to play the one off against the other. He demonstrates this skill for instance in the episode with the Count de B****. There he enacts, as I discussed earlier, *"politesse de cœur"* (*SJ*, p. 114) in exchange for a passport opening up a passage to liberty. The moment Yorick sets foot on French soil, his anxiety over the possibility that the *droits d'aubaine* may effect the confiscation of his property seriously affects his journey through the nation of manners. He concludes that the traveler must enact the sentimental manners of a caring and faithful friend, a *mensch* for all seasons. He feels that he must use the "argument of sensibility" (Cox, see above, p. 30) in order to counteract the French law's lack of equity concerning the protection of property, resorting to a sense of sympathy that he feels ought to be "proper" to agents of "sentimental commerce" from both nations. Yorick plays honor and commerce off against one another in order to attain results desirable both for the "pathological self-interest" he exhibits in his anger against Monsieur Dessein and for the perfectibility of the soul that he aspires to as he commemorates Father Lorenzo.

Nor is it to say that he dismisses the "Catholic ritual" of exchanging a snuff-box like a "holy relic" as merely a nostalgia for philanthropic soldiers like Toby – a nostalgia which would find its *raison-d'être* only in the sentimental commerce of tourists abroad. "[Yorick] does not join in

Catholic ritual; Catholics join him in sentimental ritual, potentially a subtle vindication of the authority of individual conscience."[63] Again, Sterne complicates Hume's account of promises as rituals invoked to establish trust. Hume connects the "superstitions" of a "Catholic ritual" *devoid* of "public interest," such as *"transubstantiation,* or *holy orders,* where a certain form of words, along with a certain intention, changes entirely the nature of an external object, and even of a human creature" (*T,* p. 524), with the practicality of fictional artifices instituted *for the sake of* "public interest," such as the "symbolic delivery" performed in promises (*T,* p. 515). Yorick connects what he would like to see as his "natural" obligation, substituted by the "Catholic ritual" of exchanging objects as relics, symbolically to honor a monk's metaphorical Civil Death in life (and thereafter) with the practicality of an implied promise to do so. He thus submits his "reputation," which is at stake in carrying out such an obligation, to the authority of his internalized psycho-judicial system.

HOW TO TRUST CONSCIENCE BY SUBSTITUTING JUDGMENT

Sterne differs from Adam Smith in terms of his "remasculinized" benevolence. Yet he seems closer to him insofar as the authority of conscience for submitting one's reputation may cause, according to Smith, (male) "generosity":

[W]hat is it which prompts the generous upon all occasions, and the mean upon many, to sacrifice their own interests to the greater interests of others? It is not the soft power of humanity, it is not that feeble spark of benevolence which Nature has lighted up in the human heart, that is thus capable of counteracting the strongest impulses of self-love. It is a stronger power, a more forcible motive, which exerts itself upon such occasions. It is reason, principle, conscience [. . .]. (*TMS,* pp. 193–4)

In volume II of *Tristram Shandy,* Sterne discusses the authority of conscience in his sermon on the text from Hebrews 13:18 that Trim finds in the Stevinus and reads to Walter, Toby, and Dr. Slop. Contrasting with both Dr. Slop's approval of the Inquisition and the trust in good conscience that the text from Hebrews advocates, Parson Yorick dispels the notion of conscience as a trustworthy "'just and equitable'" "'judge within us'" (*TS,* II, xvii, p. 105). Whereas someone is guilty whenever conscience accuses him or her, conscience does not always accuse when there is guilt (*TS,* II, xvii, p. 101). Conscience needs to "'anticipate'," according to Parson Yorick, "'the judgment of God'" and be enforced "'by the terrors of gaols and halters'" (*TS* II, xvii, p. 106). But the law of "'religion and morality'" (*TS*, II, xvii, p. 105) is itself supposed to mediate between conscience, no longer performing its disinterested task of monitoring actions, and the laws of Britain, operating "'not like an *Asiatick* Cadi, according to the ebbs and flows of his own passions, – but like a *British* judge [. . .] who makes no new law, but faithfully declares that law which is already written'" (*TS*, II, xvii, p. 112).

Parson Yorick believes that conscience is unreliable wherever it "'looks into the STATUTES at LARGE'" and "'has got safely entrenched behind the Letter of the Law; sits there invulnerable, fortified with Cases and Reports'" (*TS*, II, xvii, p. 103), and fails to protect what otherwise "'I must lay at the mercy of HONOUR, or some such capricious principle. – Strait security for two of my most valuable blessings! – my property and my life'" (*TS*, II, xvii, p. 108). Once it becomes clear that one cannot properly know one's conscience, as it may be the product of self-delusion, the Humean question arises for Parson Yorick as to whether one can *trust* another person's conscience.

On the first page of *The Theory of Moral Sentiments*, Adam Smith explains that since we cannot know the experience or sentiments of another person, we must copy in our imagination our own sentiments as we imagine ourselves in someone else's place or person. Similarly, Sterne seems to suggest a scene in which people who examine the validity of their own conscience try to represent their external examiners' point of view. They enact in their imagination what they feel as they enact in their imaginations what kind of conscience it is that they enact. Like Smith, Sterne does not give up conscience simply because we cannot know it. In fact, he has Parson Yorick end the sermon with the admonition to the congregation: "'[. . . T]rust that man in nothing, who has not a CONSCIENCE in everything'" (*TS*, II, xvii, p. 112). However, he seems to issue a *caveat* against the inclination, encouraged by the importance of the "gaze" in Smith's "theater of sympathy," to sympathize with the figure of an internalized spectator-judge.[64] Apparently, Sterne does not want his readers to depict that figure merely as an uninvolved witness when they internalize the fiction of successful sympathetic identification with a character who is to play the double roles of actor and spectator.

If conscience cannot always be trusted, this is due, according to the sermon, to the experience that religion sometimes hides behind the letter of some specific law when morality would demand invoking the rule of equity against undeserved punishment. Parson Yorick's case in point is the Inquisition's cold legalism, which is related to the more general British anti-Catholic argument at the time[65] – and variously interrupted by Trim's tears over the story of his brother Tom's imprisonment by the Inquisition in Lisbon which he has been struggling to tell throughout the novel. Bearing in mind that a conscience which works properly (because equitably) works "like a British judge," the reader here might want to contrast France with England. However, it only seems that the Inquisition, "is the figure for anti-justice. Yet the figure is vexed; for one might call the long description of inquisitorial punishment [in Parson Yorick's sermon] a mere amplification of what is, more briefly and tactfully, suggested to be the efficacy of British law: "the terrors of gaols and halters" and 'the scourge waving over his head.'"[66] Indeed, French and British law seem rather similar in their neglect of the law's equitable spirit. True, the spectator's sentimental journey into the sufferer's heart promises a form of equitable justice not rendered by either law. But the sentimental British narrator/traveler to France may nonetheless end up as a promise-breaker. For his conscience of sympathy is no longer an uninvolved witness to the scene of suffering.

Sterne's sentimental spectator of suffering refuses to give up conscience altogether. Consequently, he will have to submit his conscience of sympathy – an equivalent to the aestheticized disinterestedness of reliable sympathy in Smith's Impartial Spectator – to an inspection in terms of its responsibility. This would have to be a form of inspection that simultaneously trangresses the mechanism of inspection responsible for the complicitous gaze. Yet his attempt at grounding sympathy in the "parodic body" – Van Sant's designation of an ambiguity between refinement and confinement – cannot itself exert control over the transgressions of mechanisms of inspection. This is the reason why Sterne needs to back up the transgressive quality of transitional personality in sentimental soldiers, travelers, and narrators with something that will channel the momentum of transgression toward a commitment. Like Toby in the case of Le Fever, Parson Yorick implies that this problem of how to trust conscience may be resolved in the Humean structure of promises, in order to link the interplay of human "passions" and "interests" to the "judgment of God": "'Religion, the strongest of all motives, is out of the question: – Interest, the next most powerful motive in the world, is strongly against me: – What have I left to cast into the opposite scale to balance this temptation? – Alas! I have nothing, –

nothing but what is lighter than a bubble. I must lay at the mercy of HONOUR, or some such capricious principle'" (*TS*, II, xvii, p. 108).

Parson Yorick would certainly not want to dissociate religion from morality. But he must account for those situations in which religion cannot be used to form commitments. Trust in conscience then amounts to nothing '"lighter than a bubble'" – a term that the *OED* lists, as Frank points out[67], as "from the seventeenth century onwards often applied to delusive commercial or financial schemes." Sterne must contrast his efforts to anchor morality in the parodic body's actions with the unintended consequences of what people perceive to be their interests and their capacity for self-deceit, both as to the ends of their actions and the appropriateness of the means of achieving those ends. Thus he places considerable emphasis on the social setting within which these perceptions are formed (the banker, the physician). He implies that in the absence of religious motives, we are somewhat forced to have an *interest* in subtracting, when faced with untrustworthy self-interest, honor from honesty.

Toward the end of the eighteenth century, the concept of interest increasingly connoted economic interest. In Smith's *The Wealth of Nations*, for instance, "the two terms 'passions' and 'interests' [. . .] appear [. . .] as synonyms."[68] This may have been compatible with Sterne's employment of the term "interest" to cover aspirations or ambitions in general: the "most powerful motive in the world [next to religion]" (*TS*, II, xvii, p. 108). Like Hume and Smith, Sterne here expresses the belief that the significant connections between property and power in commercial situations, sentimental or unsentimental, rest on opinions and reputations exchanged in specific communities to form, manipulate, and check conscience. For him, conscience holds out a promise to monitor and judge actions – a promise which itself needs to be monitored and judged.

Like Smith's Impartial Spectator, Parson Yorick's notion of conscience depends on the coexistence of represented and imagined motives in the exchange between the interests of the judge's sympathy with the promisor and the conduct of the promisor judged. By specifically juxtaposing French and English law, Sterne can first invoke a notion of conscience that judges the inequitable punishments inflicted by the Inquisition. Once this particular cross-cultural discourse is established, he can then proceed to modify it as he likens the cruelty exhibited in French law to the efficacy of "gaols and halters" typical of a (now suspiciously) "equitable" enforcement of British law. Similarly, "poor sword's-man" Yorick first renders himself agreeable to Monsieur Dessein, for whom he assumes he is "no way a match." He then feels "the rotation of all the movements within [him], to which the situation is incident" (*SJ*, p. 39). Eventually, he has his conscience recall himself from niggling with him, for "[i]t must needs be a hostile kind of a world, when the buyer [. . .] falls into the same frame of mind [as the seller]" (*SJ*, p. 38).

Yorick seeks to redeem himself from getting caught in the circularity of such power struggles. One the one hand, this effort also reflects Sterne's remark that *A Sentimental Journey* was in fact "his work of Redemption," not only for being less lascivious than *Tristram Shandy* but also for being religious in purpose.[69] On the other hand, Yorick translates his sentimental and charitable exchanges with men and women, which are meant to counteract those struggles, into yet another transactional currency from which he must recall himself. At stake is the idea of paternal redemption itself, which he has translated into the French context.

To be sure, the redemptive authority of the heavenly father seems far more benign than that of the earthly king of France, who by means of the *droits d'aubaine* may disinherit Yorick from his legacy and revoke his right to bequeath. Nonetheless, Yorick uses the redemptive "currency" of identificatory exchange for his own "profit" when he arrives in Calais and "finishe[s] the treaty with [him]self: – Now, was I a king of France, cried I – what a moment for an orphan to have begged his father's portmanteau of me!" (*SJ*, p. 28). He imaginatively substitutes his own charitable authority for the king's legal authority. In doing so, he of course replicates the very hierarchies of power distribution from which heavenly power should have redeemed him. His statement, "– They order [. . .] this matter better in France –" (*SJ*, p. 27), which opens the novel with the gesture of a promise, ominously replicates on earth Parson Yorick's point in the sermon that the "judgment of God" orders these things better in heaven.

Yorick time and again projects himself into substitutes of those exchanges from which he wants to recall himself. In Julian Barnes's words, quoted in the epigraph to this chapter, Yorick is implicitly "claiming in mitigation that this [kind of sentimentality] is what other countries are for."[70] His hand first refuses to distribute *sous*. But then it reaches out to exchange snuff-boxes. It sometimes tries on a glove, sometimes feels a pulse, sometimes commands, sometimes yields – it performs gestures of reaching out and of hesitation whenever sentimental commerce borders on possible commitments. On the one hand, the way Yorick's hand reaches out with sentimental intentions suggests a heart at the service of others. But that does not stop the king of France from threatening him with incarceration. On the other hand, Yorick seeks to redeem himself by pointing (that same hand) to a copy of *Hamlet*. But his subservient relationship with French authorities has also made his heart (ser)vile.

The hand connects with hands in relationships in which what is given must be met by what is taken. It reaches out to express the gesture of a promise not to let a judgment coming from a potentially untrustworthy conscience go unmonitored. The promise of monitoring conscience's judgments forms part of the same order of transaction which the promise of sentimental commerce is supposed to transgress. Therefore, it must itself be monitored in order to maintain a sense of responsibility that still deserves to be called "equitable."

Perhaps it is not too surprising that we find the same double bind between promisor and judge some fifty years later when Lord Eldon crafted a legal fiction by means of which a judge could promise equitably to substitute someone's judgment by means of benevolent imagination. In Substituted Judgment, a judge's decision substitutes for the missing will of an incompetent as soon as the label "incompetent" has marked the incompetent as isolated from the faculty to articulate herself or himself according to the requirements established by the court.[71] Since 1816, the Lord Chancellor in Chancery could extend his authority to administer the fortunes of lunatics and idiots – later generalized in the category "incompetent" – into the judicial realm of equity. Restricted by certain "evidentiary constraints," he was allowed to impersonate the "donative intent" of an incompetent *as if* that incompetent possessed right reason.

This procedure recalls Adam Smith's description of sympathy directed toward an incapacitated sufferer:

The sympathetic tears which we shed for that immense and irretrievable loss, which in our fancy he seems to have sustained, seem to be but a small part of the duty which we owe him. The injury which he has suffered demands, we think, a principal part of our attention. We feel that resentment which we imagine he ought to feel, and which we would feel if in his cold and lifeless body there remained any consciousness of what passes upon earth. (*TMS*, p. 99)

Obviously, the authority with which a judge may move from administered to substituted rights is at stake. Substituted Judgment enables the judge to control the fortune of a lunatic, idiot, or incompetent, including their bodies in the case of organ transplants, where the law of informed consent applies. Equity courts were in a position to grant money by circumventing principles of property transfer. They often did not have to account for the reasons why an incompetent was to be considered less alive and his or her fortune more or less in need of protection.

Substituted Judgment suggests that the judge has access to the un-articulated intention of an incompetent. It further suggests that the incompetent has had a genuine intention capable of being substituted by the judge – an intention which the incompetent would have, if he or she were now capable of having intentions. It inverts the principle of action by proxy, which translates a given will into a set of actions as long as its constituent is still alive. Like Civil Death, Substituted Judgment brackets certain rights, particularly the right to transfer property, by way of substituting intentions. The metaphorical death in literal con-finement (Civil Death) corresponds to the substituted right to control fortunes to be inherited or bequeathed (Substituted Judgment). The substitution is the effect of a metaphor that translates action by proxy into displaced intention and thus "literally" affects premises of property transfer. Like Civil Death, Substituted Judgment focuses on withheld rights and displaced intentions that connect metaphorical death with literal inheritance and bequest.

The mechanism with which Substituted Judgment helps a judge to displace intentions resembles the instances of sentimental "commerce" that we have observed in Toby. The core of this connection is a resemblance between the institutionalized incorporation, in the case of the judge of an equity court, and the sentimental administration, in the case of Toby and young Le Fever, of an "incompetent" subject's will. The analogy suggests a metaphor of the formation of citizen-subjects. This subject formation appears to take place to the extent that it simultaneously requires the subject's acceptance of guilt insofar as that subject's "competence" in facing the eye of the law is "on trial."

But the visual metaphor is challenged once Sterne juxtaposes the mechanism of this nation-specific gaze, which is at the same time a sentimental gaze, with the impersonal glance of a prospective Civil Death (the *droits d'aubaine* transposed into British sanctions regarding the formation of citizen-subjects) that the king of France invisibly but palpably casts on Yorick. Yorick's feelings of guilt, as well as the ways he deals with them, do not result in his submission to French law through an acceptance of its demand for conformity. In the terms of an auditory metaphor, Yorick responds to the voice of the law but does not exactly respond to its demand to respond to it.

In this seemingly trifling difference, Sterne represents the citizen-subject's act of following the voice of conscience as conditioned by two components, which both determine, but do not exhaust, the "transnational" call of Yorick's conscience: first, the voice of whichever law is hailing the subject, and second, the responsiveness of the subject hailed by the law. The call of his conscience does not simply confer upon Yorick an identity as British citizen-subject through the self-ascription of guilt. Yorick responds to the voice of French law to the extent that he anticipates what is to be gained from such a response.

This is different from conscience's typically pre-reflexive complicity with the law, without which turn against oneself no citizen-subject emerges.[72] Yorick is perfectly capable of reflecting whether and why he should accept the terms by which he is hailed. Contemplating his own vulnerability to the law, he manages to fabricate an identity by performing for the Count de B**** (and the reader) a sentimental identification with that "part of himself" which has, "in the eyes" of the king of France, broken the law.

By exhibiting the critical role the parodic body of sentiments plays in evoking sympathetic responses to such fabricated identities, Sterne prevents Yorick's conscience from merely remaining paralyzed in an uncritical relation to the law as a condition of subject formation. He thus allows the reader to contemplate the conditions under which the conscience of British citizen-subjects operates most efficiently. They will feel guilty of having broken the law even prior to the possibility of having access to knowledge of it. However, Sterne also implies that since we cannot know conscience, a contemplation of its efficient operations will not undo its force. There is no discourse on the question as to how conscience is or has been constructed that cannot presuppose a notion of its construction for the raising of that question in the first place.

Hence the Humean question, which Parson Yorick raises in *Tristram Shandy*, as to whether one can *trust* another person's conscience. The "higher authority" that is called upon to decide such "cases" – that is, one's own conscience – must submit itself to a system of checks and balances in terms of trust. Sterne represents these by the legal and moral implications that Hume ascribes to promises. As we have seen, however, that does not mean that Sterne invokes the authority of the law whenever subject formation is complicated by questions of trust. Both legal and sentimental identity are not so much necessitated by the hailing on the part of the law as by the call of conscience. For the latter promises a significant sense of identity by compelling the self to internalize a debt as guilt and subsequently to turn toward one law or to turn away from another.

Sterne is concerned less with a critique of conscience as an ideology than with the inscrutability of human nature as a basis for morality. Thus he does not suggest any undoing of the subject by means of making interventions into the institutional workings of the law. Similarly, he is not willing to dissociate morality from the call of a suprapositive law that promises to relieve the religious subject from his or her original guilt. He would not, therefore, go as far as Nietzsche, who debunks conscience's capacity to generate a promise through the internalization of guilt. Sterne's notion of promise in relation to conscience does not yet represent as disparaging a view of morality as Nietzsche's, who dismisses "bad conscience" as a promise trapped in self-consumption: "[the] instinct of freedom pushed back and repressed, incarcerated within and finally able to discharge and vent itself only on itself."[73] For Sterne's purposes, it is sufficient to show that one's readiness to be compelled by the authority of the law precedes the actual response by which one subsequently yields to the law. Thus he cautiously, though perhaps not very successfully, exempts the status of religious authority from Yorick's insights about the workings of his conscience.

Instead, Sterne is concerned to show that the traveler's passionate pursuit of recognition in France makes even his formation as a transnational subject of sentiments inseparable from home-made inflictions of guilt and condemnation. One might describe this particular formation in a four-step cycle, although its elements certainly form far more complicated relations than the ones delineated here. First, the more Yorick subjects his British habits of moral sentiment to the practice of French *politesse de cœur*, the more he masters its rules, to the extent that his mastery protects him even against the law – the king's master discourse. Secondly, the more Yorick masters those rules, however, the more he is in danger of submitting the workings of his conscience to the rules of French sociality. Thirdly, the more he submits the workings of his conscience to these rules, the more he becomes socialized into *politesse de cœur* by virtue of this very submission. Fourthly, the more he acquires and refines French socializing skills, the more he also reproduces the influence of those skills on the formation of conscience – that is, the formation of a defense mechanism against accusations by means of carrying out a socially and morally recognized task.

Acquitting himself of the French king's accusations, Yorick submits to conscience's demand for a display of guiltlessness. Significantly, he does so in the face of the law's insistent demand for confessions to existing or anticipated charges. In this sense, Sterne both underscores and critically examines the role of legal confinement (incarceration) for the formation of a transnational personality subjected to the demand of sympathy. In the case of Yorick, the fantasy of legal confinement reemerges as a confinement in the accusation of guilt. The sentimental traveler must continuously acquit himself of that accusation by refining his "microsensation."

In his novels, Sterne not only uses material from the discourses of law and moral sentiment, but also reflects it structurally without simply yielding to complicity. At an historical moment when reason cannot guarantee human nature as the basis for morality, Sterne backs up the nature of sentiment with the symbolic fiction of a Humean notion of ritual promise. This sentimental form of promising is "para-equity": it is meant to complement the law where the latter fails to live up to the promise of equity that lies at the core of British common law. However, sentimental promises sometimes turn out to be complicitous with the nonsentimental commerce that they seem to counteract. Similarly, legal fictions such as Civil Death sometimes betray the legal equity for the achievement of which they have been institutionalized in common law. Just as sentimental promises depend on certain insufficiencies or *shortcomings* of the law that they are meant to complement, the legal fiction Substituted Judgment is related to the way Sterne employs the Humean structure of sentimental promises in his novels. The performance of ritual promises remains ambiguous, for Sterne, as it causes the sentimental subject both to reproduce and to transgress the conditions of its own formation.

Sterne invests sentiment with two alternating types of fictions – those operating in the law to match principle and precedent as well as those operating in ritual promises to manage delayed delivery in commitments. He may not be able to establish a literary discourse capable of grounding morality in human nature. But he can liberate human nature from its identification with either one of the two alternating types of renunciations entailed in law and sentimental promise: the renunciation of the ethical subject's "pathological interests" and the renunciation of the "remasculinized" subject's sexual passions. He can thus, without touching upon the common law's own shortcomings in generating distributive and compensatory justice, use his narrative to revisit the fictions by means of which his culture negotiates the renunciations deemed necessary at the time to shape an ethical community.

By juxtaposing England with France, Sterne demonstrates how notions of the supreme good, which are at the bottom of a morality to be grounded in human nature, may be experienced in the context of a transnational gaze – that is, the internalized gaze of representatives of another culture, on whose judgment the soldier's and the traveler's conduct depend. The lack of a genuine transnational perspective certainly forecloses any translation of the supreme good into a common good. But Sterne refuses to solve that problem simply by making the good contingent on an affirmation of the primacy of justice over the good. The reason for this refusal lies in one crucial problem that presents itself to the subject of justice: for the subject to pass coherent ethical judgments on the actual state of both England and France, he or she will not only have to renounce pathological interests and sexual passions. He or she will also have to eliminate any consciousness of the fact that this position is a product, not of human nature, but of artificial forms of commitment such as oath, promise, or contract.

Sterne is far from denaturalizing morality when he indicates the ethical subject's positions by means of associating them with legal fictions such as Civil Death and with Humean "artifices" such as promises. Rather, he allows the subject's identity to become modular, and its body parodic, in order to suggest that the specific renunciations necessary to uphold a cultural system of distributive and compensatory justice are not sufficient to justify "good nature" as the basis for ethical conduct. In doing so, he refuses to submit sentiment to the "panoptical" danger that a total transparency of justice may entail the total impenetrability of the position from which the ethical subject passes judgments. Thus Sterne achieves nothing less than to open up the conflicts over power that are at work in the internalized sentimental gaze of others to a greater diversity of the demands and grants of recognition.

CHAPTER 3

Reinstitutionalizing the common law: Bentham on the security and flexibility of legal rules

The malleability of human reactions allows utilitarians to ask whether the attitudes whose gratification or frustration determines how much happiness an institution produces are more or less the effects of the institution in question
Alan Ryan, *Property*

Veteres avias tibi de pulmone revello
Persius, *Satires*

SECURED EXPECTATIONS VERSUS UNFORCED CHOICES?

Even utilitarians, it seems, cannot do without conscience. Bentham shifts moral philosophy's focus on the opacity of conscience toward a utilitarian manipulation of character formation. Since Foucault's analysis of Bentham's Panopticon in *Discipline and Punish*, he has become most familiar as a reformer of penal institutions. Critics have frequently presented him as someone who channels fantasies of subjection to sublime forces into institutionalized identifications of consciousness with a social structure. The differences of opinion among critics as to the psycho-socionomic function of Bentham's penitentiary suggest that his call for transparency in matters of solitary confinement is highly ambivalent. In a recent study, Janet Semple traces these ambivalences even back to the biographical complexities reflected in his two post-scripts to the letter on the Panopticon, as well as in some of the many unpublished manuscripts at University College London.[1] Considered in the light of Bentham's approach, Yorick's incarceration fantasies, in which the prisoner's Civil Death and the spectator's conscience fuse into a spectacle of mutual character-altering inspections, emerge as the transparent institutionalized form of Smith's theater of the sympathetic gaze.

72

What distinguishes the way Bentham isolates the prisoner from the public gaze most basically from the imaginative projections and identifications advanced by Sterne and Smith is of course his utilitarian premises. In an attempt to exorcise his contemporaries' premise of natural sympathy, in order to detach the everyday practice of sympathy from *a priori* assumptions about "natural" benevolence, Bentham calculates the rights, duties, and obligations of legal subjects in terms of the simple notions of pleasure and pain. Because of their irreducible status as "real entities," he interprets them as both genuine incentives for performance and liabilities for non-performance. Accordingly, he seeks to reformulate established law where its rules and procedures obfuscate those utilitarian realities.

One of Bentham's prominent targets in reformulating law is the practice of legal fictions (such as Civil Death or Substituted Judgment). He complains that this practice mystifies the operational necessities to which the representational constructs of those fictions are indebted – that is to say, he sees them as mystifying a ritual reproduction of judicial authority. Not only does Bentham merely acknowledge, as others did before him, that the concept of equity no longer informs the legal fictions practiced in England's equity courts. He also calls into question the power of legal fictions, traditionally ascribed to them, to revise shortcomings and inadequacies of the law *from within* the system of British common law. In short, Bentham calls for the reform of a legal system traditionally based on internal revision. He thus presents a different perspective from Sterne's sentimentalist preference for revision over reform, which I discussed in the previous chapter.

The reason, however, why Bentham's critique of legal fictions is important in the context of writers like Sterne is not so much that he dismisses sentiment as the foundation of all relations between law and human nature. While this is certainly true, it is far more important that Bentham launches an institutional critique against certain legal premises and practices established in the tradition of British common law. In this chapter, I hope to show two things: first, how both the critical importance of legal fictions and a utilitarian version of conscience collude in Bentham's effort to validate positive law – a notion of law that is posited with the implication that it may be changed despite the embarrassment of logical gaps occurring in the process; and secondly, what role institutionalization plays for him in his effort to maintain and preserve the validity thus achieved.

In contrast, Sterne makes use, across the institutional boundaries of law, of the revision-based function of the legal fictions practiced in common law. Bentham seeks to supplant one institution with another institution for the sake of a reform justified by an allegedly superior theory. In contrast, Sterne confronts the ritual character of legal fictions with that of commitments to sympathy. In the previous chapter, I demonstrated that Sterne does so in order to generate within the novel's institutional setting what both the legal system and sentimental spectacles of suffering fail to generate by means of self-revision. He generates a "remasculinized" sense of equity that he deems "proper" to shape ethical communities, yet that remains beneath the threshold of institutional reforms.

Nevertheless, both Bentham and proponents of moral sentiment such as Adam Smith can be said to operate along one continuum, which is to say that they address similar problems by means of different premises. In *The Theory of Moral Sentiments*, Smith suggests that incarcerated (civilly dead) felons ought to create a remorseful relation between the discovery and the acknowledgement of their guilt, and thus hope "by their death to reconcile themselves, at least in their own imagination, to the natural sentiments of mankind" (*TMS*, p. 173). The religious authority that formerly institutionalized the solitude of *civiliter mortuus* as an isolation in monastic retreat returns, under the auspices of moral sentiment, as an internalized authority that underwrites solitude as an isolation under inspection.

While Bentham does not start out from "the natural sentiments of mankind," he follows and expands Smith's theater of the sympathetic gaze by proposing to institutionalize the solitude implied in Smith's *forum internum* as the same concept of isolation that structures penitentiaries like the Panopticon. In this sense, Bentham's project, which he inherited from Helvetius and Beccaria, of "creat[ing] an artificial identity" for a "self-interested actor acting in the general interest," backed up by "a system of rewards and punishments,"[2] proves similar to Smith's "psychological theory." Both approaches explain

the expository mechanism underlying an emergent social system that eventually all but supplanted the emblematic, rhetorical, and ceremonial presence which for centuries had ritualized authority as public theater. In the new, narratively structured system, the site of enactment becomes private, mental, and individual; the medium of representation particular, factual, evidentiary; the mode of processing experience inferential, procedural, systematic. The means of representation, indeed the very fact of representation itself, become transparent, abstracted, inaccessible to direct apprehension.[3]

One crucial difference between Smith and Bentham, with respect to conscience's renunciation of illicit passions and pathological interests in the "interest" of an abstract ethical identity, lies in the answer to the question as to how this sacrificial logic may be used to establish social peace by means of localizing violence. On the one hand, the conscience embodied in Smith's Impartial Spectator projects guilt onto the actor only insofar as the aim of that projection, which is to guarantee a social pact, must not be revealed – neither to the individual nor to the community of individuals that are excluded from his or her particular internal trial – as the social function that the projection is to perform. This veil of ignorance, as it were, bars the subject of guilt from conceiving himself or herself as the very sacrificial victim (for the sake of social peace) which the religious sanctity of *civiliter mortuus* might have suggested as the focus of collectively projected guilt. On the other hand, the point of a utilitarian type of conscience is that it must make the individual's sacrifice acceptable to the extent that such a sacrifice prevents the expectations of the community from disintegrating.[4] In the terms of the internalized spectacle of the sympathetic gaze, the utilitarian version of Smith's Impartial Spectator transposes onto the actor the belief that the sacrifice made by an individual in the role of an ethical subject is indispensable to the common good insofar as it helps to maximize the utility of that good.

What Bentham shares with Smith is the notion of a choosing self whose concerns can be defined in abstraction from the concrete social worlds to which it belongs. These worlds are the object of what both theories of moral sentiment and utilitarianism will want to change once their theories are beginning to inform social practices. Those worlds are also the function of how each theory differently determines the choosing self's beliefs, desires, and expectations. Smith wants to show that, although certain features of existing society may be unjust or inexpedient, the basic social order deserves explicit or implicit acceptance. Bentham opposes the moral premises of such acceptance by introducing a radical scheme of social reconstruction linked to a particular view of personality and of social transformation. In the preemptive terms of reward and punishment, the utilitarian version of Smith's Impartial Spectator suggests to the actor that forgoing one's illicit passions and pathological interests is beneficial with respect to what may be received in return for that renunciation. Thus, the spectator implies that the very possibility for the actor to choose that benefit is a benefit in itself, the waiving of which would deprive the subject from participating in the utilitarian space of possible gains and losses.

More importantly, despite his discontent with the many obfuscations of utilitarian "realities," it cannot be in Bentham's "interest" to disclose to the actor(s) in his version of the *forum internum* one important problem. This problem is reflected in the actor's uncertainty as to whether the objects of illicit passions and pathological interests gain utilitarian significance prior to the legal and moral prohibition of those passions and interests. For while utilitarian conscience compels the subject to choose to withdraw from what is prohibited, it also obfuscates the problem that the very possibility of that choice comes into being only in the subject's act of withdrawing from what is prohibited.

One important reason for this is the fact that Bentham gives priority, as I will later demonstrate in more detail, to the security of expectations over the freedom of choices. By withdrawing from what is prohibited, the actor in this spectacle can only choose inclusion in the utilitarian community because what is prohibited is also designated as inaccessible in relation to the utilitarian distribution of attainable goods. The ultimate sanction in this scheme is of course that in case the actor chooses the unattainable (which is prohibited), he or she also loses the possibility to choose between the common interest and its unattainable-because-prohibited other.

Moreover, utilitarian conscience glosses over the problem that this choice is not only an imposed choice, as indicated, but also a reduced choice, first among attainable "goods," and then, when the choice becomes in fact apparent as an imposed one, between attainable and (alternatively) unattainable "goods." Those goods' values in exchange do not necessarily reflect any individual's actual estimation of their worth within what the utilitarian philosopher can only call a personal economy of illicit passions and pathological interests. The value of the utilitarian common good need not, in fact, have anything to do with why any particular individual is willing to choose it over what is prohibited in relation to it.

As a result, Bentham faces two crucial problems. First, the desire of individual "consumers" of the utilitarian good will vary greatly for any "commodities" that appear as "goods" in the utilitarian marketplace. These individuals will not always express the relative intensities of their desire or need for the use of a certain "good" in utilitarian terms of value. It is therefore important for Bentham that the definition of the wants which enters the utilitarian calculus be subject to restrictions. In other words, the complexity of ambivalent or conflicting desires must be transformed into quantifiable information about "given" desires. Bentham must define wants as virtually independent both of the economic institutions that may have contributed to causing them and of the relation of individuals' wants to what they imagine possible – a restriction which Georg Simmel criticized as justifiable only in purely isolated economic terms, because it neglects the expenditure of subjective energies, or "sacrifice,"[5] which he believed are no less necessary to satisfy desires.

The second problem follows from the first. The determining influence of institutional structures like the economy and the law, on the one hand, and the structure-denying impetus, for instance in fantasies of empowerment, to escape that structure or its determined transformation, on the other, only seem distinct factors in constituting individual wants. In fact, they often tend to overlap. This tendency becomes dangerous to Bentham's project whenever individuals actually experience the mechanism of an imposed choice as a reduced choice. The problem can then no longer be resolved merely by restricting the definition of wants to something given. For in such moments, individuals may actually experience their reduced choices in the form of a double bind in which they find themselves the more guilty the more they obey a utilitarian command of their conscience. As one consequence, they may be confronted with their own failure to reenact significant moments of unforced choice.

The unattainability of those moments of unforced choice is "accessible" only through modes of anticipation (or nostalgia) which prevent a projected experience of such unattainability from successful repetition. This problem is particularly striking when Bentham challenges, as I will show, the role of the judge in common-law and equity courts – not only as a mode of conscience externalized as an instituted office, but also as an ethical subject with respect to imposed choices. Utilitarian conscience operates contrary to the ideal order of British common law, which strives to successfully repeat principles in the successive application of precedents. Since its focus on a specific common good eventually implies an imposed choice, utilitarian conscience is likely merely to designate, in some traumatic fashion, the reemergent failure to integrate some unattainable core of an unforced choice. This is not to say that Bentham is unaware of the problem. He rather prefers to raise the question of imposed choices in different terms, namely whether they are necessarily unsatisfactory choices.

To maintain a plausible function of the law for utilitarian ethics, Bentham therefore decides to sail a course of secured expectations between the scylla of ritually reproduced judicial power and the charybdis of unstructured legal evolution. On the one hand, to repeat the decisions made by common-law judges in repetition of fundamental precedents, without putting those repetitions to a utilitarian test, would simply mean to render visible the specific deadlocks of judicial decision-makers as links in the chain of a historical necessity – the scylla of the "rocky" necessity to maintain judicial authority. On the other hand, Bentham cannot afford, in the light of his utilitarian premises, to surrender the necessities of how precedents come into existence to a flow of temporality which would render the event of a precedent as the charybdis of an epistemological abyss of unforced choices.

As a way of solving this problem, Bentham seeks to reformulate law to the extent that it reflects the utilitarian necessity to check the judiciary by means of a parliamentary legislation based on the utility principle. This is why Bentham gradually develops his critique of the common law into a claim for its abandonment in favor of legal positivism. However, it is not obvious that this gradual move toward legal positivism justifies his utilitarian premises in the same way that he uses utilitarian premises as a new foundation for the law. Significantly, Bentham must insist on reinstitutionalizing common law's premise of equitable justice as a publicly monitored repertoire of choices for utilitarian subjects. The success of his utilitarian project depends on institutional success. He is forced to exploit the institutional force of legal positivism in order to bridge the gap between, on the one hand, the spheres of illicit passions and pathological interests and, on the other hand, the more abstract notion of utilitarian interest.

In the wake of the criticism John Rawls launched against utilitarian thinkers[6] that they discount basic moral rights as subordinate to the maximized happiness of majorities, critics[7] argued that Bentham's utiliarianism disconnects his project from the liberal tradition. In contrast, recent criticism on Bentham has consistently been concerned to show how it may in fact be read as generating a discourse of distributive justice on the grounds that distributive justice provides a maximum of social well-being.[8] Regarding the relation between *individual* well-being and rights, Paul Kelly argues that

[t]he concern for security of expectations and the provision of the minimum conditions of subsistence are developed into two principles which form the basis

of Bentham's theory of distributive justice. The "security-providing principle" is a formal principle which determines that pattern of expectations which the legislator ought to secure in legislation and upon which the codifier ought to premiss his utilitarian code. The "disappointment-preventing principle" is Bentham's substantive principle of justice. It determines the ways in which the legislator may act in realizing an ideal utilitarian set of rules, while accommodating the expectation utilities which are derived from an existing system of rules. Because the right to property is the basic source of expectation underlying the "security-providing principle" the substantive principle of justice is largely concerned with extending access to property as the primary material condition of interest formation and realization, while protecting those expectations which are derived from the existing distribution of property rights.[9]

Like David Hume and other proponents of the common law in the eighteenth century, Bentham attempts to breach a modern gap between the protected rights to and the secured transfer of property. He seeks to frame a system of distributive justice that is supposed to maintain equitable justice in an increasingly commercial society. The problem that his theory faces (and attempts to solve) is how to account for the status and the equal distribution of rights and entitlements where considerations of maximized benefits for the greatest number would seem to overrule concerns of minorities. Unlike Hume, who bases distributive justice on customary rules, Bentham replaces the notion of custom by the utilitarian premise of interest formation, which by means of securing expectations is to bridge the moral and economical gap between the rights to property and the access to property. To show how this attempt is reflected in the ambiguity of his critique and rehabilitation of fictions, it will be useful to contrast Bentham with classical common-law theory.

COMMON-LAW THEORY: CUSTOM, REASON, SOLIDARITY

The classical theory of common law originated in a situation when the modern absolutist state emerged from feudalism as political power in England became more and more centralized.[10] Similarly, the Royal Court began to use law to shape modern society and its economy in the interest of the sovereign's political power. Common-law theory was established in order to counteract the spread of this centralized power to define what is justice and what is the common good. Friedrich Hayek explains that contrary to the political ideology of rationalist absolutism, common-law theory assumed that law is not created, but merely articulated by the legislator and the judge; statutes and decisions thus reflected the evolving nation's specific customs rather than universal rational principles.[11] According to John Davies' *Irish Reports* (1612),

> the *Common Law* of England is nothing else but the *Common Custome* of the Realme [. . . I]t cannot be made or created either by Charter, or by Parliament [. . .] but being only matter of fact, and consisting in use and practice, it can be recorded and registered no-where but in the memory of the people. [. . . English Law is] so framed and fitted to the nature and disposition of this people, as we may properly say it is connatural to the Nation, so as it cannot possibly be ruled by any other Law. This Law doth therefore demonstrate the strength of wit and reason and self-sufficiency which hath been always in the People of this Land, which have made their own Laws out of their wisedome and experience, (like a silk-worm that formeth all her web out of her self onely). [. . .] But, as it is said of every Art or Science which is brought to perfection, *Per varios usus Artem experientia fecit*: so may it properly be said of our Law, *Per varios usus Legem experientia fecit*. Long experience, and many trials of what was best for the common good, did make the Common Law.[12]

This sense of law as an "ancient collection of unwritten maxims and customs," contained in collective memory and "handed down by tradition, use, [and] experience," also informs William Blackstone's *Commentaries on the Laws of England*, published in 1765.[13] To prove whether an existing rule forms part of the law is, for Blackstone, to show whether custom has demanded to follow it (*CLE*, 1, p. 68). Since customs become legitimate to the extent that society at a given point in time publicly recognizes and practices them, customary rules will acquire legal authority to the extent that that society finds it just and reasonable to use them (*CLE*, 1, p. 67). Thus, common-law theory essentially connects the authority and validity of legal practices with a common sense of how society acknowledges that they are both appropriate and reasonable. According to this rationale, a rule or a decision can be considered appropriate if and only if its practice over time has authorized it to modify existing rules and thus become law. Tradition in this sense is, as suggested by Davies' "silk-worm that formeth all her web out of her self onely," a networking structure of communal practices, a self-transforming identificatory pattern for coalitions over time. Correspondingly, public actions ritually reenact, time and again, publicly recognized and accepted patterns of behavior, thereby confirming those continuities that bind community members in a social partnership.

Matthew Hale, who wrote his *History of the Common Law* one century before Blackstone, uses a classical metaphor to describe this particular notion of legal evolution, in which the sense of continuity with the past outweighs any desired identity of legal components over time: "the Argonauts' Ship was the same when it returned home, as it was when it went out, tho' in the long Voyage it had successive Amendments, and scarce came back with any of its former materials."[14] The discourse of common-law theory thus interprets, and helps to fashion, common law as a law immanent to the historical process in the course of which a society interprets and fashions itself.

The salient feature of that theoretical discourse is, therefore, the idea that customary law must be both reasonable and appropriate.[15] What is considered a principle in common law reflects reason not as an independent standard of validation, but as dependent on a practice of law that during an evolution of customs constitutes those standards which designate a consensus as to what qualifies as reasonable. Thus common law mutually adjusts rules and customs. Rules may change according to communal needs, while the community's participation in practices structured by such rules may again have repercussions on existing communal customs and expectations.[16] What qualifies as reasonable in such a scenario will depend on what counts as continuous with the past; and what counts as continuous with that past will depend on what qualifies as a reasonable legal analogy between past decisions and present problems. As a consequence, in order to affirm that the law is both reasonable and appropriate, each community member will have to share the conviction that everybody else accepts it too and acts accordingly. Such *rites of assent* are considered essential, in theory at least, for monitoring standards of insight or inspiration on the part of "solomonic" individuals in the decision-making process.

Judicial authority is supposed neither to create nor to transcend the authority of the law. In fact, common-law theory makes it almost seem as if only the case, and not the judge, could truly modify existing law. A judge is, according to Coke, merely *"lex loquens."*[17] His function lies, as Hale defines it, in "Expounding, Declaring, and Publishing [the law]."[18] His opinion serves, as Blackstone claims, to render the "most authoritative evidence, that can be given, of the existence of such a custom as shall form part of the common law" (*CLE*, I, p. 69). Consequently, since law and judicial opinion may at times differ from one another, rules and decisions must be considered open to reformulations. Of course, it is again the judges who are entitled to perform this task, provided that they pay sufficient respect to what Blackstone calls "the perfection of reason" (*CLE*, I, p. 71) – the tradition of precedents they consider to reformulate by means of putting presumably reasonable and appropriate opinions to the test of flexible adjudication. The need for reformulation arises especially in cases where the solutions needed in the present do not seem to match the decisions provided in the past. Therefore, Lord Ellsmere pointed out "that in *novo casu novum remedium est apponendum* [. . .]."[19] Common-law theory thus defines the repertoire of rules and decisions as a "grammar" of legal practices.[20]

One basic tool for seventeenth- and eighteenth-century judges to apply established law to new situations is the use of legal fictions. Blackstone argues that when social and economical changes began to affect established notions of property, judges needed to reformulate feudal law: "[Its] forms and delays were ill-suited to that more simple and commercial mode of property which succeeded [it]" (*CLE*, III, p. 268). They needed to reformulate it, he continues, not by means of legislative reform, but by means of "minute contrivances to accommodate such personal actions, as were then in use, to all the most useful purposes of remedial justice"; and those "contrivances" are to be understood as "fictions and circuities."

Blackstone defends what may seem like an embarrassment of contrived reformulation by using a simile whose function recalls the metaphor of the "Argonauts' ship" in Hale's discourse. For him, the common law is like a medieval castle, whose inhabitants must accommodate its labyrinthine interior arrangements to modern living conditions:

Our system of remedial laws resembles an old Gothic castle, erected in the days of chivalry, but fitted up for a modern inhabitant. The moated ramparts, the embattled towers, and the trophied halls, are magnificent and venerable, but useless, and therefore neglected. The interior apartments, now accommodated to daily use, are cheerful and commodious, though their approaches may be winding and difficult. (*CLE*, III, p. 268)

Old rules are replaced by new rules and practices, while the notion of change itself forms a permanent integral part of the repair-work that fuels the legal system's self-transformation. Relying on a process of dynamic self-transformation that absorbs external sources of control and interference – an idea that Bentham contrasts with the corruption of lawyers and judges – the law remains consistent, for Blackstone, with those ideas of reason and justice that members of the community share with respect to changes in the legal system. To the degree that change is noticed mostly after the fact, the importance of tradition structures change as continuity. Consequently, Blackstone sees common law as embodying, and embodied in, a sense of tradition rooted not in first principles but in practice.

Other seventeenth- and eighteenth-century common-law theorists use the same argument to integrate within their theories the political function of statutory laws, especially constitutional laws, issued by parliament.[21] Similarly, Burke insists that the validity of law depend not on the formal procedure of codification, but instead on a sense of collective solidarity "between those who are living, those who are dead, and those who are to be born."[22] He essentially conceives of self-reproducing collective solidarity in genealogical terms: "We wished at the period of the Revolution, and do now wish, to derive all we possess *as an inheritance from our forefathers.*"[23] Burke thus echoes Hale's opinion that the statutes issued by parliament may generate new rules but cannot create new law; for the practice of law to change, statutes first need to be accepted as continuous customs.[24]

Historians have pointed out, though, that the notion of collective solidarity was employed not only to respond to the constitutional crisis and the threat of centralized power, but also to challenge the monarch's extended prerogatives.[25] Common law thus enabled the rising class of merchants gradually (and somewhat secretly) to change feudal law. They are likely to have intended to secure their acquired property against both the aristocracy and democratic forces, binding them in solidarity while simultaneously limiting both the monarch's and the parliament's possibilities for reform.[26]

The reality of this ulterior motive adds an additional justification for the reason why common-law theorists cautiously resist natural-law assumptions about the contribution of reason to justice – so that informed readers may not reduce potential loopholes in their theories exclusively to socio-economical motives of control. Thus they generally argue that if common law is a networking structure of communal practices regarding what qualifies as appropriate and what qualifies as reasonable, reason can merely be an "artificial" concept.[27] Similarly, Hale cautions that reason is no principle external to law – that is to say, there is no such thing as "natural reason" – but instead a recognized tool to create analogies between concrete cases; reason ought to be considered a tool capable both of controlling the arbitrary nature of decision-making and of permitting the flexible application of rules.[28] Dissociating the artificiality of reason from any legitimation external to the legal system, he dodges criticism as to whether an artificial notion of reason that is restricted to concrete cases appears incomplete without any reference to general principles.

The aforementioned ulterior motive for common-law theorists to create a sense of collective solidarity thus helps to explain why they sometimes defended generalizations of reason in terms of practical and historically appropriate justifications, and why they had to defend them as being immanent in tradition-as-continuity insofar as reason could then be employed to mediate between general principles and concrete cases. Otherwise, the artificiality of reason could have made the theory look ambiguous, not necessarily because tradition and reason are said mutually to reformulate one another, but certainly because the notion of artificiality cannot itself be used to validate particular standards for reason. The concept of artificial reason leaves undecided, as far as loopholes in the theory are concerned, whether a law that defines particular standards for reason operates as the embodiment or as the vehicle of reason. While from the historical perspective of tradition-as-continuity the repertoire of standards appears to be self-transforming, a systematic perspective will reveal that the ambiguity of law as both the embodiment and the vehicle of reason contains two logically incompatible possibilities.[29] In the former case, the standards for reason may be justified through themselves, whereas in the latter case they require an external principle in order to be considered valid.

The origins of this problematic – that is to say, the question regarding the legitimate authority to determine valid standards of justice through the mediation of societal practices – lie in the response of common-law theory, as Postema explains, to the traditions of natural law, as represented by Thomas Aquinas, as well as positivism, as represented by Thomas Hobbes.[30] In Aquinas' *Summa Theologiae*,[31] *ius* represents a structure of social behavior either "naturally" based on communal agreements or "positively" based on the ruler's instituted law (1a2ae57.1–2), whereas *lex* is a precept defined on the basis of *ius*. (1a2ae90.4) While humans are destined gradually to discover the rational principles of *ius*, Thomas argues, laws issued by institutional authority are needed to express, prescribe, and maintain a rational order of social behavior to turn mere groups of individuals into communities. (1a2ae.90–95)

Within such a setting, the administrators of institutional authority and customs must ensure, by defining positive law and adjudication in relation to natural law, that justice, as Thomas understands it, remains a communal process which connects individual actions with interpersonal relations by means of focusing both upon common goals. (2a2ae57-62) Thus, it is essential for Thomas, first, that positive law complement natural law – also and especially with respect to Aristotelian *adiaphora*, or facts on which natural law holds no advice (2a2ae.57.2) – even though human beings are already endowed with the rational faculty of comprehending natural law; and second, that institutional authority – no matter whether represented by ruler or custom, but only if it performs its task of articulating the objective rational order of law – is supposed to guarantee public consensus on social interaction.

For Hobbes, such liaisons of law and reason render the validity of any authority problematic. To identify law with reason is to admit not only Coke's but also all other possible interpretations of reason.[32] Hobbes accepts only natural reason in matters of legal authority[33] – as opposed to conventions such as precedence, which he (like Bentham) considers merely subject to the natural reason of lawyers. This is why Hobbes claims that law must not be identified with the reason of individual citizens, nor with the artificial reason propagated by common-law theorists, but only with the sovereign's natural reason. In contrast, standards for reason – the good, the just, the reasonable etc. – cannot be found in nature but only in conventions that define a civil society.[34] While law becomes legitimate as a result of collective acceptance and voluntary subjection, Hobbes considers only individual reason as natural.

However, the impasse of religious authority which reduced the *forum internum* of individual reason to "a conscience without outside support" reveals, in Hobbes' view, "the authority of conscience in its subjective plurality [as] a downright *causa belli civilis*"[35] – an authority which he seeks to neutralize politically by declaring law the public conscience and distinguishing it from private opinions. Thus it is the anthropological "reality" of the state of nature, epitomized in the metaphor (and the real effects) of civil war, which informs Hobbes' assumption that law cannot "naturally" invest society with standards for authority: "[W]here every man is his own judge, there properly is no judge at all; as where every man carveth out his own right, it hath the same effect, as if there were no right at all."[36] Therefore, communal standards must be embodied, Hobbes concludes, in the sovereign's authorization of society as an artificial person – that is to say, in the representation of a single will.[37]

Hobbes contends that what makes a state a state are laws. The nature of laws is to warrant peace by means of preventing and curbing violence. Based on this assumption, the laws are supposed to revaluate the distinction between conscience and action *in foro externo*. Subjects cede to the sovereign their right not only to exert violence but also to remain in charge of their own actions.[38] The positive law issued by the sovereign represents the sole standard for reason, provided that the subjects' "natural reason" obeys the sovereign's specific ordinances, to the legality of which the subjects have given their general consent: "Law in general is not Counsell, but Command [. . .] of him, whose Command is addressed to one formerly obliged to obey him."[39]

This particular relation between natural and positive law marks precisely Hobbes' point of departure from the tradition of natural law. Whereas Aquinas considers even those facts on which natural law holds no advice as being under the influence of the same, natural law, this suggests for Hobbes simply that it is reasonable to obey it by way of general consent. Even where the laws of nature coincide with, or "contain" positive law[40], they cannot legitimize their own validity except through promulgation by the sovereign *in foro externo*. Only when given accessible content and when publicly enforced, "are they actually Lawes, and not before."[41]

Hale argues against Hobbes that the social mediation by means of law, as demanded by Aquinas, will best be achieved, not through the legislative activities of the sovereign and his representatives, but the rulings of common-law judges, who are better acquainted with the conventions and customs of existing social practices.[42] For the task of mediation depends on a given context of those practices. Therefore, analogies with famous past cases or compliances with tradition will always be more successful, Hale maintains, than to create a new rule, which needs to be contextualized in existing practices anyway before it can realistically guide individual action. Hale does not refute Hobbes so much as justify existing legal practice from a pragmatic perspective. Hale's main reason for obeying the law is his proposition that it effectively responds to concrete necessities. Common law is linked more intimately than Hobbes' alternative to common opinions and experiences, which in Hale's view can alone provide solutions to any given need for social mediation.

It is against the notion of Hobbes' individual reason, then, that the practice of collective tradition, which common-law theorists consider the "perfection of reason," gains its cultural significance. Since the practice of custom and precedent is immanent to the system of common sense, its agents or practitioners are unable to pass coherent judgments on its validity from an external vantage point. Practice constitutes and legitimizes artificial reason, according to this rationale, as long as its agents have always already been convinced that it is reasonable and just. Common-law theory is culturally significant insofar as Blackstone makes its assumptions an argument for freedom – a sense of freedom achieved through participation in a practice that expresses a consensus with respect to what the law is (*CLE*, i, pp. 73–4).

In such a public ritual, behavioral patterns are (re)enacted in order to affirm the continuity of that practice by emphasizing participation as constitutive of social relations. Whenever this ritual enactment of customs and their recognition is successful in ensuring the continued practice of those customs and their recognition, Blackstone finds evidence of the experience of freedom (*CLE*, i, pp. 17–20, iv, pp. 407–43). Wherever equitable justice is based on natural reason, freedom is in danger:

In so far as equity has any place in the law, Blackstone insists, it must be identified with the spirit of reason which *runs through the law*, the spirit in which all Common Law judges, if they are doing their job properly, approach the law (3 *Comm.* 429). But if equity is understood as a body of rational principles which stands in judgment of the law, it must be rejected. One major objection to the court of Chancery was that it purported to make its decisions, often abrogating proper decisions made in Common Law courts, on the basis of nothing more than appeals to "conscience," and "natural reason."[43]

Hobbes clearly takes issue with a notion of remedial justice that promises to undo previous instances of injustice in the sphere of adjudication merely by building the legal sytem on a continuity of self-revision. He does not dismiss equity, though. Rather, he demands that equitable adjudication, the theoretical model of which he sees embodied in Chancery, must operate like the sovereign wherever civil law holds no explicit advice – that is to say, a judge's proper understanding of equitable justice depends on "the goodnesse of [his] natural Reason."[44] Hobbes concludes that "I depart not much from the Definition of Equity, cited in Sir Edw. Coke [i.e. that Equity is a certain perfect Reason that Interpreteth, and Amendeth the Law Written . . .] though I Construe it a little otherwise than he would have done."[45] Upon this premise, he can in fact share with common-law theory a notion of equity-as-reason, which by means of bridging the gap of disorder and order between civil war and restoration transcribes the irrational as the frontier of politics.

For the Hobbesian function of politics is to identify injustice as a mode of violence that is antinomic to reason. Negating such injustice in the public space, the emergence of law defines civil society as a rule of law whose separation of violence and political power has to pay the price of reinstating structural inequalities among legal subjects. As political power oscillates between passions, reason, and self-preservation, Hobbes sees it no longer aimed at facing injustice as a mode of violence but at distributing power in the legal terms of remedial justice. The cycle of revolutions (and counter-revolutions), though, that *Behemoth* depicts as history continually haunts the legal apparatus that *Leviathan* devises as a rational state machine.

The state's monopoly of the exercise of power does become concentrated in a supreme institution, but it also constitutes the uncertainty as to how much it really differs from the very violence that it attempts to isolate as supreme injustice. For in order permanently to maintain peace, state power's reason-to-be must be always, as it were, to be at war with it as it enforces the power of law as a preemptive measure. It can only "make" history by ending, and thus excluding from law, history's anthropological narrative of the injustices inflicted in times of civil war. Thus, Hobbesian politics establishes and adjusts its rules of representation, power, and knowledge according to the "violent" avenues on which civility may be forced to lead civilization out of the state of nature.

In contrast, common-law theory does not actually separate the injustices exhibited in (the Hobbesian notion of) violence from the artificial reason intended to curb or undo them. The history of injustices inscribes itself into the continuity of practiced common law as a historical "trial." This test is supposed to prove that precedents of injustice may be redeemed, in a secular and somewhat conceptual manner, through the historicity of a self-revising "common progress." Within the scope of such self-revision, it is not unthinkable that interventions into given ethical codes may be transformed into a superior order of purposeful action, however unintentionally, unconsciously, or immorally the interventions themselves may have been performed. By proposing permanently to adjust principle and precedent, common-law theory can assert "common progress" with and against all evidence to the contrary, even against the "unreason" reflected in atrocious injustices.

Common-law theory's appeal to the power of continuity uses history to eliminate everything that seems irrational or contingent in the past injustices which may have gone undetected or unredeemed by law. Theoretical discourse thus helps to turn such contingencies into a ritual sacrifice that fuels the continuous process of sublimating injustices into

the legal institution of equitable adjudication. At the interface of common-law theory, politics and history meet in the idea of a ritual sacrifice
of a smaller good for the sake of a greater good – common progress.
Theory helps to implement specific unjust rulings, whose subsequent
revision as sacrifice redeems this internal corruption of the universal in
the particular, in the "superior" order of an autopoietic transformation
of customs.

Obviously, it is doubtful that such a scenario comes even close to
adequately describing eighteenth-century realities. Bentham clearly disagrees with the idea that history (as a tradition of unwritten law) proves
the convertibility of injustices into common progress. In fact, he puts on
trial, of all things, common-law theory's very implementation of injustices into allegedly superior orders of revised customs. He complains that
the exchange of functions between sacrifices and injustices is not as
reciprocal in practice as theory claims it is. According to his analysis of
the nasty remainders of that exchange, the existing legal system fails in
the attempt to let politics and history meet in the notion of progress – at
least unless accompanied by reformist institutions. More specifically,
Bentham exposes the relationship of judicial power and law-as-custom
as being non-reciprocal, the evidence of which is to be observed in the
"nasty remainder" that the supreme power of adjudication often cannot
embrace the claims for absolute justice and institutional equity without
committing institutional injustices in the name of custom-as-common-
interest.

The legal system must therefore become political in that it neither
merely negates nor entirely transforms, but instead represents injustice
and renders such representation publicly accessible. Otherwise, Bentham suspects, the injustices committed in the name of custom-as-
common-interest will remain compensated in mere supplements to
practiced law, for instance in tautologies such as *law is custom and custom is
law*. For these supplements tend to replace differences between justice
and injustice, in both theory and practice, by spectral images of public
enemies to the progress of common customs. To the extent that the
supplements are permitted to create such scenarios, Bentham concludes, they may also prevent legal subjects from effectively monitoring
judicial power. In order to call attention to the dangers involved in the
prevalent master narrative of principle and precedent, Bentham uses
the line from Persius's *Satires*, "I pluck the old wives' tales out of your
head [*lit.* lung]," quoted in the epigraph to this chapter, as the motto to
his own invective *Comment on* [Blackstone's] *Commentaries*.

THE UTILITY OF PRECEDENTS AND ESTABLISHED RULES

Against the backdrop of this general line of argument, Bentham develops his specific critique of the common law as he grounds law in utility. He proposes the notion of utility in order to solve a conflict endemic to common-law theory – the conflict between the acceptance of established rules and the violation of rules to secure concrete interests.[46] By refocusing the notion of utility from immediate needs to the maximized expectations of the greatest number (of community members), Bentham is thus able to extend the notion of justice from fixed to flexible standards. Only those conventions of general rules and practices will be considered just which structure the very expectations that promise the greatest utility for the greatest number within a given historical framework of expectable social mediation.

To follow established rules is therefore to conform to the law insofar and only insofar as such behavior maximizes the recognition of expectations that are covered by Bentham's extended notion of utility. In contrast, Blackstone requires that justice depend on established law (*CLE*, I, p. 55). The question arises, then, as to how the two notions of utility and conformity to established rules may be combined. On the one hand, Bentham insists, against common-law theory, that any particular or general nexus between justice and utility depend on a (positivist) concept which defines what qualifies as determined general rules or laws.[47] On the other hand, he does not make a decision as to whether whatever qualifies as just refers only to rules established through codification – that is to say, on the theoretical basis of legal positivism – or only to those rules that are based on maximized utility in cases where established rules and utility stand in conflict – that is to say, on the theoretical basis of utilitarianism. In *Principles of the Civil Code*, Bentham defines the utility of individual freedom, unlike John Stuart Mill in *On Liberty*, as the security of established rules (*Bowring*, I, pp. 297–364: pp. 322–6) This decision indicates the road he chooses to take in order to respond to such tensions between the theoretical premises of legal positivism and utilitarianism.

One important point in Bentham's *Principles of the Civil Code* that Mill does agree with is the "*redistributionist*" utility of "liberal conscience": "[Both] identified liberty with a good that cried out for some sort of just or justifiable distribution [. . .], far from being limited to the protection of property and contract."[48] Freedom, if considered natural, is of course possible without security, but the security of freedom which restricts human action is more valuable, to Bentham, for modes of social interaction other than in the state of nature.[49] As secured freedom can only originate in law, the latter must maximize security in order to create freedom. Standards of security are flexible because Bentham considers changes of law as immanent to the legal system. The restrictions to flexibility as defined by Hobbes, however, prove insufficient to Bentham's goal of minimizing potential insecurities. In addition, rights, privileges, obligations, and other social relations must be systematically connected with respect to security. He proposes that according to how (constitutive) "distributive" activities complement (regulative) penal activities in the task of organizing security, the legal system may be divided into civil/constitutional law and penal law.[50]

What allows Bentham to separate constitutive and regulative means of providing security is his central concern for property. Replacing the Lockean justification of property as a natural right (to be protected by government) by a cost-benefit analysis of its utility as a fiction, he grounds property in the advantages involved in securing the products of one's own labor.[51] In *Principles of the Civil Code*, he claims that it is expectations which motivate the treatment of property law as a part of civil law. In *Theory of Legislation*, as Alan Ryan explains, Bentham similarly defines property as a basis for expectation:

There are two sorts of expectations, those which exist prior to law or naturally, and those which are the creation of the law. The fact that law creates expectation is a source of happiness, and also a potential source of unhappiness. [. . .] The same thing applies to inheritance: before I inherit I have the pleasure of looking forward to my inheritance, and my parents have the pleasure of looking forward to my future enjoyment of their property. This possibility of pleasure is bought at a price, however, for if the pleasures of anticipation are sweet, the pains of disappointed expectation are particularly severe.[52]

Thus all rights and liabilities that the law grants and imposes on individuals are to be considered the normative property of those who are entitled to them (*Bowring*, I, pp. 307–8). Legal subjects must be protected against potential encroachments on the part of government as much as expectations must be secured with respect to other subjects' possessions. Bentham subsumes the distribution of legally defined entitlements and obligations among conventions and practices under civil law and, correspondingly, their enforcement under penal law. Whereas the constitutive function of law defines social and political relations on the basis of maximized expectations, the regulative function enforces rights and liabilities by laying down punishments (*Bowring*, I, p. 322).

Regarding the role of property, Bentham agrees with Hume that it ought to be based on utility. While Hume considers utility a human convention operating for the sake of general interest, Bentham treats it as an expectation operating for the sake of general interest. Despite their different premises, both Hume and Bentham discuss property, as Stephen Munzer points out, in terms of a notion of utility that does not necessarily "separate explanatory and justificatory functions":

[For Hume, u]tility in the sense of common interest explains how private property arises. And it justifies both the general institution of private property and specific rules of property law. Upon the first establishment of society, the cardinal rule is that people get to continue to possess whatever they currently possess. Thereafter, utility justifies rules pertaining to occupation, prescription, accession, and succession. Beyond that, people can always transfer property by contract. [. . .] Bentham, unlike Hume, explicitly defines property in terms of expectations. [. . .] If, as Bentham maintains, utility is the presence of pleasure and the absence of pain, then ceteris paribus utility will be promoted by securing persons' expectations with respect to things they possess. [. . .] Bentham offers both a theory of property and a reconstruction of the English property law of his day. He discusses ways of acquiring title, provides a theory of contractual exchange, suggests rules for wills and intestate succession, criticizes various forms of common ownership, and allocates risks of loss of property. Whereas Hume complacently endorses property rules deriving from Roman law and eighteenth-century Scottish law, Bentham examines his own legal system closely, even though many contemporary readers will find his proposals mainly cosmetic in character.[53]

Bentham shares with Hume the assumption that law and property are inseparable: "Property and law are born and die together. Before the laws, there was no property: take away the laws, all property ceases" (*Bowring*, I, p. 309). Similar to Hume's remarks on this subject in *A Treatise of Human Nature* (*T*, pp. 515, 527), Bentham conceives of property as a fiction because the relation that it creates and expresses between a person, a thing, and another person is purely conventional (*Bowring*, I, p. 308). He differs from Hume, though, in that he has property come into existence only through law: "Property is entirely the creature of the law" (*Bowring*, I, pp. 308–9). No recognition of "natural" needs or conventional agreements will suffice to secure the utility of property in terms of rights and liabilities; only when law performs this task will it also rise to what Bentham would like to see it become: "the most splendid triumph of humanity over itself" (*Bowring*, I, p. 309). Whereas Hume has the artificiality of law originate in informal conventions, among which legislation emerges merely as a late version, Bentham accepts law only when recognized by the legislator and thus excludes prelegislative customs from the sphere of valid law.

Bentham does not imply, however, that the legislator's fixed laws automatically prevent legal evolution. Fixed laws may be as effectively revised in terms of maximized utility as the expectations which they are to express must not be shattered (*Bowring*, 1, pp. 323–6). Thus the justification of property both arises from its own effects and serves to readjust them to the function of institutions that most effectively promote utility:

It is characteristic of utilitarian arguments that they are reversible; that is, since all justification rests on a consideration of consequences, a reconsideration of consequences will force a reconsideration of what is being justified. Moreover the malleability of human reactions allows utilitarians to ask whether the attitudes whose gratification or frustration determines how much happiness an institution produces are more or less the effects of the institution in question.[54]

The reversible nature of utilitarian justifications of private and public property generally informs utilitarian critiques of institutions, both legal and non-legal.

In *Comment on the Commentaries* and *A Fragment on Government*, Bentham launches his early institutional critiques and invectives against Blackstone.[55] He still endorses the common-law precept that established rules and decisions must be followed (*CoC*, p. 196n.2), even if an appeal to utility might at first suggest otherwise. Bentham cautions that whenever exceptions seem legitimate in novel cases, those exceptions should not be considered in terms of their utility but their analogy to existing law – that is to say, in terms of precedents (*CoC*, p. 197). Although later, in *Of Laws in General*, Bentham rejects the common law altogether, the ways in which the early Bentham here both agrees and disagrees with it are important to emphasize. For it is in these early writings that he first challenges the role of the judge in both common-law and equity courts. This particular "critique of judgment," in which Bentham analyzes judicial power at the intersection of utilitarianism and distributive justice, highlights the judge's role both as a mode of conscience externalized in an instituted office and as an ethical subject with respect to imposed choices.

According to Blackstone, one judge's past decisions must not bind another judge's present decisions. In order to keep decisions separate from legislation so that they merely serve to interpret the law, the judge will instead consider the principles on the basis of which those past decisions were reached: "*[T]he law*, and the opinion of the judge, are not always convertible terms, or one and the same thing; since it sometimes may happen that the judge may *mistake* the law" (*CLE*, I, p. 71). What makes the principles that inform decisions binding is the assumption that they form part of that sense of tradition-as-continuity which common-law theory uses to justify common-law practice. Any pattern of rule formation ought to be open to revision, according to Blackstone's model, even if a judge's former interpretation of a precedent already explicitly formulated the rule in question.

The early Bentham insists, against Blackstone, on adhering to established rules and, other than in his later years, on the idea of precedents. Based on these premises, he wants the judiciary to focus on the consequences of a particular decision rather than established rules. Against Blackstonians, who use the idea of precedents to privilege the past over the present, Bentham privileges the rule over the case to put on trial the impression of arbitrariness that he thinks Blackstone's judge-dominated law has created among the public:

The deference that is due to the determination of former judgments is due not to their wisdom, but to their authority: not in compliment to dead men's vanity, but in concern for the welfare of the living. [. . .] I know not that we owe any such deference to former times that we owe not to our own. I know not that we owe them any such deference as to suppose a reason for what they did, when none is visible. Sure I am that it is unnecessary to have recourse to any such deference to justify the adherence to this rule. Whether it never had a reason, or whether having once had a reason, that reason is now ceased makes no difference with respect to the reason we now have for adhering to it. (*CoC*, pp. 196, 203)

Bentham here differs not only from conservatives like Blackstone, but also from such progressives as Kames, who in his *Principles of Equity* of 1760 proposed, despite "introducing 'the principle of utility' into equity jurisprudence," that the task of legal reform be assigned to the courts.[56] In contrast, Bentham wants to see the legislative function more strictly separated from the judicial function. The legal changes caused by judges are not detrimental because a given discarded reason for adhering to a law becomes unreasonable or not, he argues, but because the fact that the reason for adhering to it is established as law precedes any distinction between reasonable and unreasonable: "[A] *new* Resolution, to break in upon a *standing* rule, is a practice that in good truth is big with mischief. But this mischief on what does it depend? Upon the rule's being a *reasonable* one? By no means: but upon its being a standing, an established one. Reasonable or not reasonable, is what makes comparatively but a trifling difference" (*FoG*, p. 409).

The underlying trope which makes this argument of Bentham's utilitarian is that a legislator's intentions in making laws should be, but in practice are not, considered his property. The legacy of such property should be, but in practice is not, exacted in the same way that heirs are expected to have a will exacted:

A Law is made: it is made to a certain end. The intention is manifest: it is to attain that end. It is improvidently penned: the effect is, that there is a case in which complying literally with its directions would not contribute to the attainment of that end. It is plain therefore that such compliance was not intended to be enforced at the time the Law was making. Exact it not, then, I say to the Judge: and to the citizen, suppose not that it will be exacted. To this case the law is not to be interpreted to extend. The words of a Legislator are no otherwise to be regarded than inasmuch as they are expressive of his will. [. . .] Change of circumstances may happen: but change of circumstances may be gradual: and may have happened in the eyes of some before it has happened in the eyes of others. The expectation of some men concerning the enforcement of the Law will not have followed the opinion concerning such a change in others. It is for them only to alter the course of expectation who first gave it its direction. [. . . A]nd to change their intentions to what it is conceived they ought to be, belongs to them only, and to no other person: for that other person who should do so would be himself the Legislator (*CoC*, pp. 115–16).

Hence Bentham's disregard for the equity courts that he finds operating in the 1770s (*CoC*, pp. 161n.2, 324–30). He does, however, sign a petition to Lord Chancellor Brougham in 1829, asking him to reduce the procedural rigidities, cost explosions, and procrastinations of trials in the Court of Chancery.[57] While he confronts the inefficiency and corruption exhibited in Chancery practices with the utilitarian "nondisappointment principle," which characterizes his own proposal for an "Equity Dispatch Court,"[58] he appears to tolerate its institutional status insofar as the practice of equity (i.e. pondering the revision of general rules) is guided by the principle of utility:

Unlike Blackstone, Bentham gave institutional expression to an essentially standard Aristotelian view of the role of equity (returning the rib of equity to the side of law from which it had been ripped by enterprising judges – [*FoG*, p. 395]). Equitable correction does not always call for revision of the general rule of law in question. For even the best and most just of general rules may yield injustice in some particular cases. Burke expressed well the Aristotelian dictum which lies at the heart of Bentham's theory of adjudication: "As no legislators can regard the minima of equity, a law may in some instances be a just subject of censure without being at all an object of repeal." Thus, there is a sharp difference between utilitarian adjudication within the shadow of the law and the "correction" of the law it may call for in specific cases, on the one hand, and legislative repeal, or interpretation of the law itself, on the other. These functions are kept separate, and responsible performance of each secured, by denying adjudicative corrective decisions precedential effect, by insisting on the absolute publicity of all decisions, and by designing a special process for "legislative" correction of the law by judges. Bentham believed that in this way he had protected the people from the dangers always posed by equity and the discretionary exercise of adjudicative power. It is often said that we are destined to be ruled either by fixed general rules, or by the arbitrary judgment of individuals (i.e. by laws or by men). Bentham rejected this dilemma, by rejecting the assumption on which it rests.[59]

Bentham's task, then, is to connect the principle of utility with principles of adjudication. If a judge, who upon applying an established rule in a concrete case has noticed a lack of utility, wishes to reform the law, he will only replace, according to Bentham, one defect by another and thus find himself in the sacrificial situation, as it were, typical of an ethical subject facing an imposed choice: "[P]artial amendment bought at the expense of universal certainty is but [. . .] that partial good thus purchased is universal evil" (*CoC*, pp. 223–4). The judge may want to make an exception from the established rule in question, without having to account for the insecurities that his decision introduces into the law. However, the law must be characterized by the continuity and predictability of its own application. In making the exception, Bentham contends, the judge will undermine public confidence in what is supposed to characterize the law:

A new Resolution made in the teeth of an old established rule is mischievous – on what account? In that it puts men's expectations universally to a fault, and shakes whatever confidence they may have in the stability of any rules of Law, reasonable or not reasonable: that stability on which everything that is valuable to a man depends. Beneficial be it in ever so high a degree to the party in whose favour it is made, the benefit it is of to *him* can never be so great as to outweigh the mischief it is of to the community at large. Make the best of it, it is general evil for the sake of partial good. It is what Lord Bacon calls setting the whole house on fire, in order to roast one man's eggs. (*FoG* [Preface], 409n.)

Having to balance the benefit to the parties involved in trials with the utility of his decision for the "community at large," the judge must also weigh the utility of applying a certain rule in a concrete case against the utility of adhering to established rules in general. While he must not sacrifice the public's expectation of utility to an inheritance of customs, he will have to consider his decision in light of the problem as to how significant the loss for the community at large would be if he were to make an exception to the established rule to honor the utility of a decision in favor of one party over the other. In theory, this ambiguity may only be resolved by an extended notion of utility – the "duty and interest junction principle"[60] – which Bentham privileges over any expectations based on the secured benefits for individual parties. In practice, the benefits of an exception to the established rule, which the winning party will enjoy, entail costs not only for the losing party but also for the community at large. For the exception made in that situation may shatter public confidence in the recognition of expectations concerning the validity of established rules.

The main problem Bentham sees in the nature of those departures from established rules is that judges are empowered to turn the exceptions they make into foundations for new rules and thus potentially for new laws. Judges are to adhere to established rules so that the borderline between the legislative and adjudicative functions may not be blurred by latent methods of judicial legislation. The expectation of utility and the predictability of adjudication thus meet in the notion of security, provided that the roles of the judge and the legislator remain institutionally distinct from one another. The legal system will be capable of mediating between subjects and institutions, according to Bentham, as long as security mediates between expectations and rules. As a consequence, the judge must not introduce new rules or make exceptions from old ones without considering the necessity of a public recognition that the greatest number of judges and laypersons would judge according to the same criteria of utility as he does. In other words, he must weigh the official and public dimensions of adjudication against one another.

To accomplish this balancing act, Bentham's judge must include in his assessment of utility the argument for adhering to established rules whenever he begins to make a decision. In the process of making that decision, he is supposed to personify the positions adopted by each of the parties that will be affected by his decision. Bentham wants the judge to determine which expectations may be the strongest by making him discover which expectation he himself would express if he were to adopt any given position among the parties involved in the case – and, ideally, among the public.

Why should decisions be uniform? why should succeeding ones be such as to appear the natural and expected consequences of those preceding them? Not because it *ought to have been* established, but because it is established. The intention to be established is apparent upon the face of the words: not to be the pretended knowledge of the Judge, or upon any private anecdote. The business of the Judge is to keep the distribution of valuables and of rewards and punishments in the course of expectation: conformable to what the expectation of men concerning them is, or if apprized of the circumstances of each case, as he is, he supposes *would be*. To do that he is to put himself in their place, and to pronounce from such lights, and from such lights only, as can appear to them. (*CoC*, p. 197n.c)

To the extent that the judge has to perform this task in each particular case, the principle of adhering to established rules will each time be put on trial as well. In theory, he is to submit, each time he determines expectations by means of personification, to the forum of public recognition Bentham's demand that judicial conformity with precedents coincide with the principle of utility. In practice, however, the determination of the parties' expectations will form part of the judge's effort to resolve conflicts between the parties through mediation before he may bring the dispute to the more formal trial stage. More often than not, there will be no recognized public interest in this early process of mediation. The mediation itself may therefore end up being carried on in private whenever necessary. And even if there exists such interest, Bentham significantly refrains from providing rules for how the judge ought to go about personifying this impersonal form of interest. Generally speaking, he does not seem to require that public interest be considered the interest of a third party to the case.

DON'T TRY THIS AT HOME! OR: CONTROLLING THE ACTIVATION OF UTILITARIAN CONSCIENCE

The judge's personification of the parties' expectations may be restricted to Bentham's generalized utilitarian notion of expectation, but it is to some extent left to the discretion of the judge's (supposedly utilitarian) conscience where he decides to draw the limits of such an expectation. Utility will have to guide him in balancing the security of executing the law with the various hardships that typically accompany the execution of the law. Once equipped with the "tools" of utility, he is expected to figure out whether the procedural costs of executing a law exceed the benefits of its execution. As Bentham puts it more succinctly in *The Rationale of Judicial Evidence*, the legislator's rules are "instructions" that must guide the judge's understanding but not manipulate his will (*Bowring*, vi, pp. 563–4). The very danger, however, that the judge's will may in fact be manipulated – depending on whether the prescriptive status of the code is interpreted in terms of parameters or determinants of judicial decisions – testifies to a tension in Bentham's model between the demands for flexibility and security of formal rules.

Odd as it may seem in the light of Bentham's general aversion against the practice of legal fictions, this premise recalls the judge's personifications in the legal fiction Substituted Judgment, crafted by Bentham's near contemporary Lord Eldon, which was discussed at the end of the previous chapter. By means of this legal fiction, we remember, a judge could imaginatively substitute someone's judgment. His decision substituted for the missing will of an incompetent as soon as the label "incompetent" marked the incompetent as inarticulate according to the requirements established by the court.[61] From 1816, the Lord Chancellor in Chancery could extend his authority to administer the fortunes of incompetents into the judicial realm of equity and impersonate their "donative intent" such *as if* they possessed right reason. The authority with which judges in equity courts might move from administered to substituted rights put parts of the judiciary in a position to grant money by circumventing principles of property transfer. They often did not have to account for the reasons why an incompetent was to be considered less alive and his or her fortune more or less in need of protection.

Bentham's notion of an ethical subject in relation to the judge is obviously far different from that of an incompetent in relation to the judge. But there is a striking similarity betwen the two modes of a judge's take on rendering equitable justice. Just as Substituted Judgment suggests that the judge has access to the unarticulated intention of an incompetent, and that the incompetent has had a genuine intention capable of being substituted by the judge, the utilitarian conscience of Bentham's judge is supposed to be capable of impersonating the intentions of ethical subjects, whether they are parties in a given case or belong to the public, whose general expectations must inform the judge's motives in making a decision. This odd similarity casts some doubt on the coherence of the vantage point from which Bentham launches his vehement critique of legal fictions. Coincidentally, it recalls the fact that Bentham's life-style proved similar to Eldon's, even though the inventor of Substituted Judgment belonged to "the traditional system of arcane lawyer's law":

[Eldon] did everything that Bentham's father had hoped that he would do: after Oxford and a successful career at the bar he ended up as Lord Chancellor. Eldon said that success at the law could only be achieved by one who would "live like a hermit and work like a horse": such was the effort needed to master the precedents. Bentham conspicuously lived like a hermit and worked like a horse for all his long life: such was the effort needed to try and change a class of lawyers fed by precedent.[62]

The judge's utilitarian "obligation" to impersonate the parties' expectations is also related to Bentham's premise of a quantifiable "psychological hedonism."[63] The obligation to impersonate implies, for the purposes of judicial decision-making, a (rather questionable) degree of equality among subjects with respect to their expectations. For that reason, Bentham believes that the judge's role-play is capable of measuring the relative intensity of expectations more effectively than Blackstone's notion of artificial reason: "How have stood the stocks of Pain and Pleasure upon such a disposition of things as the determination in question is calculated to bring on? This is the question, stated indeed in the most general and comprehensive terms, which a Judge ought to put to him upon the occasion of every fresh case" (*CoC*, p. 199). Thus the principle of the judge's adhering to established rules may continuously be put on trial. But the utility of that principle *as such* remains on Bentham's agenda, even as he later moves from revising to abolishing the common law, complaining that it altogether impedes the utilitarian determination of legal standards.

To direct his action to the general expectations of both the parties involved and the public, the judge will have to control his own motives. In *Draught for the Organization of Judicial Establishment*, Bentham writes, "Under the auspices of publicity, the cause in the court of law, and the appeal to the court of public opinion, are going on at the same time" (*Bowring*, IV, pp. 305–406: p. 316). In order to see such control implemented, Bentham wants the judiciary to be hierarchically structured in terms of authority and responsibility.[64] Its representatives should be prepared, as Bentham argues in one of his *Papers Relative to Codification and Public Instruction*, to comment on the reasons why the application of a particular law benefits the citizens governed by that law; even a "well-disposed judge" may have to be "subjected to accusation at the hands of part of his fellow-citizens [. . .] to justify him in the sight of the whole" (*Bowring*, IV, pp. 451–533: p. 492).

Legal sanctions alone, however, are not sufficient to accomplish this goal because they would merely secure compliance with the utility of expectations. In addition, self-imposed moral sanctions are needed, as he claims in *The Rationale of Judicial Evidence*, to involve a degree of private ethics sufficient to internalize social morality as public conscience and thus hold a judge both liable and accountable with respect to his motives *(Bowring,* vii, pp. 326–7). The judge's motives, like those of every other office-holder, are likely to be basically focused upon the advancement of his private good, but his concern for self-respect will always also depend on his public recognition as an honorable and principled official.[65]

This line of reasoning also explains why Bentham conceives of sympathy itself as a moral sanction. In the Appendix to *Nomography,* he contends that, "were it not for the operation of this sanction [sympathy or benevolence], no small portion of the good, physical and moral, which has place in human affairs, would be an effect without a cause" *(Bowring,* iii, pp. 231–95: p. 292). Only the internalized gaze of the public eye will make the judge effectively virtuous. And, as Bentham points out more generally in *Introduction to the Principles of Morals and Legislation,* an imposition of moral sanctions governed by the internalization of public opinion is likely to succeed in putting sympathy in the service of utility *(Bowring,* i, pp. 36–8).

The judge's concern for self-respect is therefore to a considerable extent the effect of having to represent an institution and properly to internalize the liabilities and accountabilities he inherits by being appointed to his office. On the one hand, his conscience is supposed to operate exactly like that of every ethical subject. On the other hand, the ritual of institution that is his assignment sanctifies, as it were, an arbitrary boundary between himself and all the other ethical subjects who were not appointed and whose expectations he must, *qua* assignment, attempt to personify. By making the underlying reasons for his decisions publicly accessible, as Bentham's theory demands, the judge will also make himself known and recognized for the difference between himself and those who recognize him. Bentham domesticates, as it were, that difference as an institutional boundary. Thus it appears that his own motivation is not guided by an interest in decentralizing legal power or politicizing judicial authority.

It is, in fact, in the nature of that difference that the ritual of instituting judicial power can, despite Bentham's system of utilitarian checks and balances of it, influence the representations which the unappointed have of that power. More importantly, such ritual institutions can influence those representations of judicial power in ways the unappointed themselves cannot. Feeding on the utilitarian production of recognition for his office, the judge will maintain that difference, even in those cases when the assignment transforms the very representation he has of himself, and the behavior that a utilitarian conscience makes him feel obliged to adopt in order to conform to that representation. Bentham seeks to constitute judicial identity as acting in keeping with, not only a certain nobility of utilitarian convictions, but with the competence, legally speaking, of one's assigned judicial rank, defined in the related terms of privilege and duty.

The appointment to his office signifies to the judge his presumed utilitarian identity by expressing it simultaneously to the ethical subjects who are supposed to recognize him. To the extent that he accepts the sacrifices implied in the preservation of privilege, the judge will feel obliged to comply with the status of the specific function designated by Bentham to ensure adjudication on a utilitarian basis. Bentham clearly wants the judge's subjective aspirations regarding the performance of that function to depend on the public recognition of an assignment that both accords privileges and imposes duties. The cost-benefit analysis behind this rationale suggests that the judge is invested in the same office which he himself has appropriated. This motivational feedback loop serves to prevent the sacred security of utilitarian expectations from being desecrated by pathological interests and desires.

Consequently, one might argue that there is yet another function involved in ensuring adjudication on a utilitarian basis. This function may be that the judicial institution serves to discourage, for the sake of secured expectations, any attempt to transgress the boundary of recognition that separates the judge's utilitarian conscience from the ethical subjects' conscience. Maintaining that institutional difference will, besides the codification of law in the process of parliamentary legislation, contribute to the stability of the legal system. The role of codification may in fact be intimately connected with the institutionalization of this particular difference. For the efficacy of institutionalization will be the higher, the more the ethical subjects, for whom the ritual institution of judges is performed by the authorities, are disposed, by being accorded sufficient public access to codified law, to receive it as something that meets general expectations. At the heart of Bentham's interest in ensuring the security of expectations lies, therefore, the search for a method that structures ethical subjects' dispositions to the extent that they become durable.

This strategy of Bentham's, however, raises the question as to how the institutionalization of the difference between the judge's and the subjects' conscience relates any *concrete* invocation of conscience to the ensured security of expectations. For Hobbes, conscience is still a space of interiority granted the individual, though not the legal subject, by the sovereign's proclaimed moral neutrality, due to the need for a lasting peace. Only in Hobbes' postwar times do institutions begin to tolerate conscience as a non-actionable eruption of selfhood, which its observers can merely acknowledge and respect with a sense of stunned tolerance but cannot put on trial as far as its content is concerned. By Bentham's time, the moral doctrines of Enlightenment have already repoliticized morality through the authority of conscience and, as a result, collapsed the Absolutist separation of private individuals and public subjects: "To the extent to which the initial situation, the religious war to which [the Absolutist] State owed its existence and its form, was forgotten, *raison d'état* looked like downright immorality."[66] In the light of Bentham's preference of security over freedom with respect to expectable choices, however, the individual's freedom to invoke a moral authority of utilitarian conscience in the political context does not necessarily serve the legitimacy of conscience *as* such an authority. Instead, it may perform an entirely different function.

Bentham starts out on the shoulders of a problem that Enlightenment thinkers typically have with assigning to each individual the freedom of conscience, namely that under this premise law and conscience tend to go separate ways and thus begin to parallel the separation of law and ethics. Wherever the freedom of conscience exists, institutions will respect the individuality of expressions of conscience, but also refuse to accept conscience as binding in terms of suprapositive law. For if suprapositive (and thus suprainstitutional) law exists, the question will arise as to why such law would need conscience to reflect it in many different individual ways. The freedom of conscience thus implies a necessary departure from its traditional (religious) attachment to normative truth. Truth, law, and conscience continue their existence as separate avenues toward binding decisions but cease to be used for purposes of their mutual legitimation.

What remains the core of conscience, however, is that the ones who appeal to it also subject themselves to the danger not only of restricting their possibilities of action but also of threatening stable features of their personalities (which permit identification over time) by confronting them with too many of those possibilities. The freedom of more or less unlimited possibilities for invoking one's conscience may threaten the security of identifying the integrity of one's personality with utilitarian character. Conscience thus remains a site of supreme adjudication, but at the same time also challenges the limits of utilitarianism's very cost/benefit calculus of general interest by which it is supposed to be activated.

Hence the necessity, for Bentham's purposes, to domesticate this aspect of conscience – that is, conscience as a potential enemy to the formation, by legal means, of utilitarian character – by situating it precisely in the institutional difference between judicial authority and ethical subjects. Bentham institutes the judge's utilitarian conscience not simply as a mirror function of the ethical subjects' conscience; the former also serves to compensate for the latter's deficiencies. For if the judge is considered subject to an internalized pressure to make his decisions in conformity to general public expectations, the effect on ethical subjects may well be that their freedom to fall back on conscience will not so much encourage as spare them from actually having to invoke it.

Bentham subjects the complexities of commercial society to a utilitarian principle. Insisting on general expectations, he cannot any longer ascribe precise individual expectations to forms of behavior that used to be based on institutionalized roles. To the extent that individuals find themselves confronted with an increasing number of alternative expectations with respect to their personalities, Bentham must design utilitarian conscience as relatively indifferent to individual character formation, thus minimizing potential discontent over asymmetries between achieved and ascribed roles. Too many alternatives are likely to overwhelm the capacity of a conscience that works toward individualizing a personality which at the same time variously identifies with "higher authorities."

By assembling the functions of a judge's and an ethical subject's conscience in the utilitarian conscience of the judiciary, and by institutionally separating this complex from the individual conscience of ethical subjects, Bentham compensates for the complexity of responsible actions. For these actions would turn detrimental the moment individuals had to subject all possible consequences of those actions to their conscience. Alternatively, utilitarian conscience, secured by institutional difference, serves Bentham to prevent individuals from being urged into situations where their conscience may actually turn against them. In *The Rationale of Judicial Evidence*, he demonstrates the utility of how self-confrontation emerges as a confrontation of evidence in the courtroom and how self-representation *in foro interno* becomes the presentation of arguments for others in institutionalized *fora externa*.

Bentham must of course insist that ethical subjects remain ethical subjects. Yet he is likely to achieve that goal, not by submitting the matter to a test of individual conscience, but by norming the options according to which ethical subjects make their choices. One such normed variable is the institutionalized difference, in terms of conscience, between judge and ethical subject. The subjects will certainly expect the judge to submit his decisions to the test of general expectations. At the same time, Bentham seeks to enable them to internalize the institutionalized difference between judges and themselves, which they are unable to choose, as something impersonal which does not determine their individual personality formation. They may at all times put that difference to the test, but in Bentham's utilitarian model, institutions are not supposed to exert any pressure on individual conscience actually to do that.

Institutions will be even less likely to provide means for the individual parties affected by controversial exercises of judicial authority to argue their claims by making appeals to higher principles according to conscience. Bentham reduces the equitable function of making appeals to the authority of individual conscience to the form of an argument that specific expectations have in some way been frustrated or defeated. To stabilize this utilitarian version of appeals is equally to destabilize ways for parties, acting in the name of the public, to hold the judiciary accountable for any principles in their practices and policies which differ from that of utility. While utilitarian conscience is supposed to maximize the accountability of those who hold judicial power, it seems to minimize the role of individual conscience in actively participating in debates over that power. For Bentham, the principle of utility clearly must not be endangered by the "irrational" influence of moral sentiment. Disagreement according to conscience ought to be reducible (which of course it is not) to conflicts of individual interests – that is to say, to conflicts of utility.

To make his model work, Bentham cannot simply rely on individual personalities highly capable of identifying with the complex utilitarian order of things. Rather than guaranteeing that individuals must be permitted to listen to their conscience, he must have an interest in protecting the utilitarian network of public roles for ethical subjects, which might otherwise collapse under massive crises of individual conscience. In other words, he must have an interest in avoiding situations where individual conscience disengages ethical subjects from their participation in the utilitarian project.

Where individual conscience has caused unlawful behavior, the judge's utilitarian concience is supposed to balance conciliatory and adjudicative decision principles in terms of a cost/benefit analysis based on general expectations. Before he can consider the limits of the particular sacrifice that conscience-driven individuals may be required to make, the judge has to determine whether the individuals in question, who have to face the consequences of their choice among alternative actions according to conscience, have adequately been measured by the number of possible alternatives not taken by them. To save the equitable call of conscience for utilitarianism is to replace the truth of its voice by the utility of its function.

Bentham indeed wants to save equity for utilitarianism, albeit in pronounced separation from its traditional (Aristotelian) vehicle – that is, in separation from the practice of legal fictions in common law, "specifically the arbitrary suspensions of a [state] power already arbitrary, identified by Blackstone in pardons and equity."[67] We have already seen, however, that the equitable aspect of a judge impersonating the parties' expectations oddly resembles the mechanism of legal fictions such as Substituted Judgment. In the remainder of the chapter, I will demonstrate how this duplicity is reflected in yet another duplicity: Bentham's early critique of legal fictions and later rehabilitation of fictions in general.

LEGAL FICTIONS AND JUDICIAL AUTHORITY

Bentham's arguments for legal reform were directed against an unsystematic and often reactionary use of penal law to curb crimes against property. In eighteenth-century England, statutes instituted to protect the social hierarchy were frantically applied to contain what were considered threats against existing structures of property distribution. What Blackstone dismissed merely as a number of unreasonable excesses of parliamentary legislation, Bentham interpreted as common law's very own limitation.[68] As the body of law was being shaped in part by parliamentary legislation and judicial production of rules, in part by the solicitor-general, barristers and conveyancers (specializing in the transfer of real estate), corruption sometimes invaded the judiciary's sphere of relative autonomy.

Legal subjects were punished for crimes of whose existence they remained unaware to the extent that they could not afford legal counsel.[69] A practice of law based on deterrence, obfuscation of rules, and the aforementioned hard-to-grasp principle of immanence began to define legal subjects in terms of subjection,[70] creating suspicions that ulterior motives for that definition remained clouded by a veil of technical rules and mysterious procedures.[71] The blatant lack of protection against malpractice rendered Blackstone's apology for flexibility in adjudication highly spurious.

In this context, Bentham claims that Blackstone and other theorists are masking this truth about the common law as a mystery in order to legitimize the activities of the courts (*FoG*, p. 410). The inconsistencies between common-law theory and practice, as well as within theory itself, that he undertakes to expose, all come down to a fallacious relegation of reason, insofar as reason stands in conflict with specific private views on it, to natural-law arguments about issues "that all men are agreed about" (*CoC*, p. 159). Instead of having to subject their justifications of decisions to a consideration of public expectations, judges are free to ground the motives for those justifications merely in their own private ideas about what all private persons presumably share. It is in such a potentially private legitimation of judicial practice that Bentham identifies the source of the many manipulations of law in his time. Consequently, he focuses his critique on the medium of those manipulations – legal fictions.[72]

For Blackstone, legal fictions are responsible for creating the flexibility with which rules may be adapted to changed circumstances. In this sense, they are instruments of "remedial" justice. For while they help to preserve valuable old forms, they simultaneously effect changes in the law that reflect new social, economic, and political needs – concerning for instance the effects of an antiquated property law in times of commercial society. Thus legal fictions also maintain the (Aristotelian) corrective function of justice (*epieikeia, aequitas,* equity) against the rigid letter of the law.

[Judges] wisely avoided soliciting any great legislative revolution in the old established forms, which might have been productive of consequences more numerous and extensive than the most penetrating genius could foresee; but left them as they were, to languish in obscurity and oblivion, and endeavoured, by a series of minute contrivances, to accommodate such personal actions as were then in use to all the most useful purposes of remedial justice; and where, through the dread of innovation, they hesitated at going so far as perhaps their good sense would have prompted them, they left an opening for the more liberal and enterprising judges, who have sat in our courts of equity, to show them their error by supplying the omissions of the courts of law. And since the new expedients have been refined by the practice of more than a century, and are sufficiently known and understood, they in general answer the purpose of doing speedy and substantial justice, much better than could now be effected by any great fundamental alterations. The only difficulty that attends them arises from their fictions and circuities; but, when once we have discovered the proper clue, that labyrinth is easily pervaded (*CLE*, III, p. 268). And these fictions of law, though at first they may startle the student, he will find upon further consideration to be highly beneficial and useful: especially as this maxim is ever invariably observed, that no fiction shall work to extend an injury; its proper operation is to prevent a mischief, or remedy an inconvenience, that might result from the general rule of law. So true it is, that *in fictione iuris semper subsistit aequitas.* (*CLE*, III, p. 43)

For Bentham, legal fictions are an image of the common law's corruption. They represent to him such an abuse of legal language that no single use of legal language can create and secure expectations anymore. For one, legal fictions turn flexibility into idiosyncracy as they fail to render an account of motives for the justifications used in the process of adjudication. More importantly, they conceal the fact that they supply the judiciary with a degree of legislative power that both exceeds constitutional premises and causes an increase in judicial corruption along with the exploitation of unprotected legal subjects: "A fiction of law may be defined – a wilful falsehood, having for its object the stealing [of] legislative power, by and for hands, which could not, and durst not, openly claim it, – and, but for the delusion thus produced, could not exercise it. Thus it was that, by means of mendacity, usurpation was, on each occasion, set up, exercised, and established" (*FoG*, p. 509).

In such a scenario, legislators, judges, and lawyers conspire to establish, by means of legal fictions, an ominous legal monopoly whose validity rests, as Niklas Luhmann pointed out in a more general context, on the tautological circularity of the law's normative and cognitive functions: "Decisions are legally valid upon the basis of normative rules because normative rules are valid only when implemented by decisions."[73] For Bentham, subjects end up incapable of protecting themselves against injustice, of claiming and exercising their rights, and of performing their duties in good conscience: "A sort of partnership was thus formed [. . .] having for its object the extracting, on joint account, and for joint benefit, out of the pockets of the people, in the largest quantity possible, the produce of the industry of the people. Monarch found force; lawyers, fraud: thus was the capital formed" (*FoG*, p. 509).

Bentham implicitly dissociates an acceptance of legal fictions from a consensus on equity. Suspicious about the confluence of their functions, which used to define the entire Aristotelian tradition, he attacks their practice in common law, alleging a lack of transparency and utility. The rigidity of equity courts in employing legal fictions has no longer (if ever) got anything to do with "remedial" justice. Thus Bentham considers this practice even worse than that of blindly adhering to established rules. Not only is it not useful with respect to expectations but also incomprehensible to the public. Mere conformity to the practice of legal fictions, which Blackstone demands, will not stand the test of plausibility with respect to a consensus on equity.

It is not entirely clear, though, whether this critique is based on sufficient knowledge about concrete manipulations. Ogden notes about Bentham's claim, in *The Theory of Fictions*, to substitute "Fictions, Equity, and Interpretation" by "Candour – in relation to fact, Clarity, in the practice of nomography, and Codification, in the interests of the greatest happiness": "Though legal fictions are only a particularly obvious form of linguistic compromise, it is commonly implied that Bentham's objections to their use was based on ignorance" (*ToF*, pp. cxiv-v).

Nevertheless, Bentham insists that the law's foundations need not only, as common-law theory has it, be sought in oral traditions but may also be discovered in legislative acts. Thus the law itself may create conformity to the law and does not necessarily depend on expressions of common practices.

Modes of conduct for the first time of their appearance, single modes of conduct are legalized: and thence flows indeed a custom of observing modes of conduct of the like sort. But is this custom a custom from consent? With reason precisely equal it might be said, that the custom of observing statutes was a custom flowing from consent and thus this much magnified property by which the Common Law is to be distinguished from Statute, is a property that belongs to both. (*CoC*, pp. 332–3)

Hence he can argue that common law confounds forced agreement with spontaneous "assent." This is why Blackstone's reasons for grounding the law in "assent" will always reproduce that ambiguity instead of resolving it: "The fallacy lies in the abusive application of the term 'assent': in the giving to a uniform course of action according to a Law, after that Law is passed, and punishment threatened for the breach of it, that same name '*assent*,' as is given to an express declaration of the concurrence of the party's will with the Law before its passing" (*CoC*, p. 221). If foundations of legitimacy may always already be a product of manipulation on the part of the judicial elites, attempts at censuring manipulation will suffer an impasse.

Resenting such a development, Bentham contends, "For my part, I know not for what good reason it is that the merit of justifying a law when right should have been thought greater, than that of censuring it when wrong. Under a government of Laws, what is the motto of a good citizen? To obey punctually; to censure freely" (*FoG*, p. 399). It is this very possibility "to censure freely" that the practice of legal fictions is barring. In *Nomography*, he points out, "A rotten egg or a rotten apple is quite as necessary and conducive to the stability of a bridge for the convenience of its passengers, or of the edifice in which justice, or what is called by that name, is to be administered, as fiction, legal fiction, ever can have been or ever can be to any good work that may be attempted with it" (*Bowring*, III, p. 242).

Bentham illustrates this impasse in censuring manipulation with various examples of legal fictions. Those subjected to what he calls "*ex post facto* law" and "dog law"[74] learn about the crimes they committed, in construed absence of rational obedience, once they are punished for them, like dogs, whose punishment is justified by what they should not have done. Next to the fictions of the social contract, rights, duties, and privileges, Bentham frequently cites a fiction concerning property, which formalizes the political semantics of the body, death, inheritance, loss of civil rights, and "corruption of blood" as Civil Death – the same Civil Death[75] that makes its entry, as discussed in the previous chapter, into Sterne's *A Sentimental Journey*. In *Nomography*, he complains,

The corruption ascribed by the lawyer-branch of the flash-language, to the blood of those whom, on this or that occasion adverse fortune has placed on the losing side in a contest between two candidates for the faculty of sacrificing to the fancied felicity of a single individual the real happiness of twenty or a hundred and twenty millions – as a specimen of this nomenclature, with the atrocious tyranny involved in it, will afford to all posterity a melancholy proof of the state of corruption in the hearts of those who have given creation, preservation, and extension to that tyranny, and in the understandings of the deluded people who could remain unopposing victims to it. [. . .] In the aggregate mass of the blood of the whole population, not a drop that was not [. . .] in a state of corruption, actual or eventual, according to the system of physiology established for the benefits of most religious kings, by learned lords and learned gentlemen. (*Bowring*, III, p. 273)

Elsewhere, Bentham underscores his aversion to the practice of Civil Death and its sinister genealogical implications:

[By the use of legal fictions, t]he state of law is rendered more and more incognoscible. By wrapping up the real dispositions of the law in a covering of nonsense, the knowledge of it is rendered impossible to the bulk of the people – to the bulk of those whose fate depends upon it. What meets their eyes is gross and palpable nonsense: a man dead and alive at the same time; a dead man and a live man the same person. (*ToF*, p. 148) The English lawyers, to justify the confiscation of property in certain cases, have [. . .] imagined a corruption of blood which arrests the course of legal succession. A man has been capitally punished for the crime of high treason; his innocent son is not only deprived of his father's goods, but he cannot even inherit from his grandfather, because the channel by which the goods ought to pass has been corrupted. This fiction of a sort of political original sin serves as a foundation to all this point of law. But why stop there? If in fact the father's blood is corrupted, why not destroy the vile offspring of corruption? Why not execute the son at the same time with the father? [The editor adds:] The lawyers are always reasoning upon fictions, and giving to those fictions the same effect as to realities. They admit for example, *contracts* which never have existed; and *quasi contracts* which have not even an appearance of existence. In certain cases they admit a *civil death*, in others they deny the *natural death*: such a dead man is not dead; such a living man is not living. A person who is absent is taken to be present; a person who is present is regarded as absent.[76]

Manipulations of equity by such ominous uses of legal fictions have made the common law, and specifically the practice of equity courts, too rigid. Bentham concedes, however, that the element of security that he would like to see reflected in adhering to established rules – "universal good" at the expense of "partial evil" – may introduce even more rigidity into the adjudicative process. In *Of Laws in General*, Bentham argues that a judge's rational sensibility in impersonating the misery of others must, for utilitarian reasons, not degrade into procedural technicalities. Significantly, the way Bentham phrases that argument is more reminiscent of the moral sentiment of sympathy that Hume expresses in *A Treatise of Human Nature*, than of utility.

Familiarized with the prospect of all those miseries which are attendant on poverty, disappointment, and disgrace, accustomed even to heap those miseries on the heads of those by whom he knows them to be unmerited, [the judge] eases himself by habit of the concern which the prospect of them would produce in an unexperienced mind.[77]

The need for flexibility and the necessity of exceptions to rules are likely to create once again the very tension between the security of laws and the sensibility for utility in concrete cases which equity was traditionally employed to reduce.

Legal fictions, however, instead of providing the security desired, create but an arbitrary *simulacrum* of equity. In Bentham's opinion, they turn the maxim of strict adherence to established rules into obscure manipulations of precedents beyond the reach of public censure. To him, the contradiction between an adherence to established rules and an arbitrary use of legal fictions seems in fact typical of common-law practice. A judge can justify the use of both by calling on principles from the same legal system. Therefore, Bentham eventually attacks the very foundation on which that contradiction rests – common law itself – and wants to see it replaced by a system of codification that integrates the discrepancy between binding and flexible rules in terms of public censure.

Hence his premise that law must first and foremost consist of general rules – instead of concrete adjudication – which need to be formulated in order for them to gain authority.

A law is a discourse – conceived mostly in *general*, and always in *determinate*, words – expressive of the will of some person or persons, to whom, on the occasion, and in relation to the subject in question, whether by habit or express engagement, the members of the community to which it is addressed are disposed to pay obedience. This is the only plain and proper sense of the word: in this sense the object of which it is designative is a *real entity*. In every other sense, it is figurative and improper; the object of which it is designative is a mere *fictitious entity*; and every discourse, in which the reality of it is assumed delusory. (*Chrestomathia, Bowring,* VIII, p. 94) A rule of law must be predicated of some certain assemblage of words – It never can be predicated of a bare assemblage of naked ideas. It is words only that can be spoken of as binding: because it is words alone that are producible with certainty when occasion comes for any individual to be bound. (*CoC,* p. 259n.a)

In the final analysis, however, the premise of formulated rules can, in relation to the premise in common law of use-as-custom, only compete with the latter in making an effort to gain authority. As a matter of fact, the positivist arguments that Bentham uses to refute Blackstone's defense of *lex non scripta* resemble the very "method of criticism he himself regularly condemned in Blackstone and other natural law writers. This was the attempt to overcome undesirable laws by dismissing them as 'not law.'"[78]

This is why Bentham needs to add yet a better argument against the fluctuating rules of common law than the mere accessibility of written law. In order to avoid any emergence of arbitrary authority, he argues,

[t]here is only one way in which censure, cast upon the Laws, has a greater tendency to do harm than good; and that is when it sets itself to contest their validity: I mean, when abandoning the question of expediency to contest the

right. But this is an attack to which old-established Laws are not so liable. As this is the last though but too common resource of passion and ill-humour; and what men scarce think of betaking themselves to, unless irritated by personal competitions, it is that to which recent Laws are most exposed. I speak of what are called *written* Laws: for as to *unwritten* institutions, as there is no such thing as any certain symbol by which their authority is attested, their validity, how deeply rooted soever, is what we see challenged without remorse. A radical weakness, interwoven into the very constitution of all unwritten Law. (*FoG*, p. 402n.e)

The public standard for valid rules must also determine the criteria by means of which the validity of rules itself may be determined – that is to say, it must determine the criteria for a codified designation of rules. Bentham assigns to codification the function of coordinating social interaction, while adjudication serves to adjust that coordination to the concrete cases of individuals.

FROM POSITIVISM TO INSTITUTIONALIZATION

Despite his early critique of arbitrary judicial authority regarding legal fictions in the 1770s, *The Theory of Fictions* – a collection of essays and notes, the first draft of which was written in 1814 – plays an important role for Bentham's legal and political theory.[79] Bentham here connects legal positivism with empiricist epistemology. He argues that justifications of the validity of law by the principle of utility require an empirical foundation. Such a position creates, as Wolfgang Iser explains in his analysis of Bentham's argument, a "gulf [. . .] between cognition and usage," necessitating a rehabilitation of fictions against the same empirical tradition whose "epistemology" Bentham is not willing to sacrifice:[80]

Bentham adheres to empirical epistemology, but with his affirmation of fiction he eliminates the disparaging connotations that were still inherent in Hume's concept. Against this background, legal fictions change into warning signals that a fiction must always be known as such, and hence must never be reified; furthermore, Bentham's self-experience allows him to see the imagination as the source of fiction.[81]

Bentham's critical position on the limits of cognition means "pursuing empiricism to one logical end" (p. 117). Such an argument isolates his early critique of fictions from the context of legal and political theory as well as practice. For in that particular context, legal fictions perform functions, as we have seen, that are different from "warning signals" against empirically "reified" "fiction" (p. 116).

In the context of his legal and political theory, Bentham's rehabilitation of fictions must also match his demand that the validity of rules and their criteria, even if now unavoidably fictitious, be publicly accessible and comprehensively codified. Only those ordinances and sanctions which fulfil this particular requirement in "relation" to real entities can form part of the material necessary to construct a legal system: "[A power, a right] together with duty, obligation, and a multitude of others of the same stamp, being of the number of those fictitious entities of which the import can by no other means be illustrated than by showing the relation which they bear to real ones."[82]

Customary rules, in Bentham's view, do not fulfil that requirement. Considered in epistemological terms, they do not refer to "real entities." As ideas projected by judges who by means of precedent create analogies to ideas previously projected by former judges, customary rules merely structure and restructure a system of references in which customs branch out as "fictitious entities." In order to generate authority for that system, judges delude legal subjects into believing that it is founded in "real entities" – that is to say, they showcase the "fictitious entity" named custom as a "real entity." On the basis of the very epistemological problems which caused him to rehabilitate fictions, Bentham can still find himself in a position to criticize common law by debunking its premise of custom.

To demonstrate that fictions are indispensable, Bentham outlines a system of hierarchically ordered fictitious entities, whose existence depends on language (*ToF*, p. 15). By engaging in them, human understanding can inferentially or perceptually access a complex of indubitable real entities, which may include such incorporeal substances as God, angels, or minds (*ToF*, pp. 7–10). A process of abstraction (*ToF*, pp. 126–36) leads from real to fictitious entities – for instance to rights, duties, penalties, licenses, and judgments. Bentham describes these particular examples of fictitious entities as derived (*ToF*, pp. 38–9) from a second order of fictitious entities – quality and modification (*ToF*, pp. 27–8) – whose existence is feigned by human understanding in order to establish discourses on real entities (*ToF*, p. 114). Understanding and language thus conspire to create a system of fictitious entities that organizes a structure of real entities according to pragmatic-utilitarian (instead of *a priori*) criteria and simultaneously allows for interventions into that structure. To feign a reference to real entities is as delusive as it is indispensable to attempts at meeting general expectations concerning access to real entities. For Bentham, there exist no conceivable alternatives to the utility of feigning, as far as acts of organizing and intervening into the structure of real entities are concerned.

Moreover, Bentham subjects the criteria for interventions into the structure of real entities, which understanding and language "collaborate" to organize, to questions of legitimacy and validity. First, he distinguishes between necessary fictions – necessary in the sense that they necessarily refer to real entities – and useless "fabulous" fictions – useless in the sense that they may be discarded without great loss, because they generate ideas without correlatives on the level of real entities. Secondly, he divides "fabulous" fictions into the harmlessly deluding fictions of poets and the harmful fictions used by priests and lawyers for reckless or insidious purposes (*ToF*, pp. 17–18). Bentham validates any such fiction only as a "deception that has been seen through" in the first place – a deception that "contrary to epistemological expectations [. . .] endows fiction with multiple usage."[83]

To be sure, a "deception that has been seen through" is a criterion that extends to both useful/necessary and useless/fabulous fictions. Thus one might object that "seeing through" appears itself to be undecidably caught between necessary usage and "fabulous" manipulation. For Bentham admits, when in Appendix VIII of *Chrestomathia* he refers to this notion of "seeing through" as a *"key-presenting, or special contrivance-indicating principle,"* that "it is only in the way of fiction that when applied to any operation, or affection of the mind, anything that is said is either true or false" (*Bowring*, VIII, p. 174). To what extent, then, may the undecidability between necessary usage and "fabulous" manipulation distort the integrity of "seeing through" as a *"contrivance-indicating principle"* – a principle which Bentham cannot do without in declaring fictitious entities indispensable? One might further object that Bentham should have (he did not) even fictionalized language – to which he believes fictitious entities owe their existence – in order to account for the possibility that usage and manipulation often cannot be neatly separated.

But Bentham refuses to let this undecidability collapse the distinctions between useful/necessary, useless, and fabulous fictions, which were already indispensable premises in his early legal and political theory. He maintains those distinctions on the basis of his assumption that real entities themselves are not subject to "seeing through," while their predication is. In the light of this assumption, his point is not inconsistent because it specifies the particular aspects of "seeing through" that fictitious entities may refer to. He can, in fact, comfortably distinguish between the beneficial and detrimental usage of fictions as long as the particular aspect of usage/manipulation remains separate from the aspects of predicating, accessing, and qualifying real entities: "For Bentham it is not a matter of eliminating fiction but of eliminating particular uses of it."[84]

Only on the level of usage/manipulation, Bentham claims, do the distinctions between useful/necessary, useless, and fabulous fictions need to be applied: "What is meant here is, not that no such fictions ought never, on any occasion, to be employed, but that to the purpose and on the occasion of instruction, whenever they are employed, the necessity or use of them should be made known."[85] He can make his early critique of legal fictions compatible with his later revaluation of fictions as such by pragmatically interpreting the former as a "reminder of [the latter's] misuse":

Bentham calls [legal fictions] *"encroachment* or *imposture"* [*ToF*, p. 122], because legal practice suppresses awareness of their fictitious character and takes them for realities. Fiction must always be known as such if it is to be capable of manifold usage, for this would not be possible if fiction coincided with something that preceded this usage. Bentham attributes the reification of legal fictions to the craftiness of lawyers, but they could not maintain their authority for long if their suppressed understanding of what fiction is like did not have another, perhaps even more powerful, sustaining force: its success. This elevates fiction into a self-sustaining reality. Bentham developed his critique of fiction by way of law partly because of the certainty that this type of fiction was discourse-dependent, and partly because legal fiction, which was always known to be fictitious, embodies only one special instance of fiction. In his attempt to initiate a turnabout in the assessment of fiction, Bentham had to have recourse to the inherited denunciation of fictions as deceit, lies, and delusions in order to outline the indispensability of a construct that had no foundation in re and that could be legitimized only by what its application was meant to achieve – not an easy undertaking for a positivist. What the legal fictions had obscured, he wanted to lay bare: fiction's dependence on discourse and its resultant generalization.[86]

This is not to say that Bentham's general revaluation of fictions dismisses as irrelevant the effects of their concrete "misuse" that may in fact have been witnessed as conspicuous deceptions. In his legal and political discourse, fictitious entities such as rights and duties continue to play an important role in determining and making publicly accessible the legal structures which constitute social and political relations.

As soon as rights and duties appear as laws systematically arranged in and through language, they correspond to fictitious entities that qualify *as* "laws" those "facts" which already qualify real entities in legal terms. Bentham's positivism thus causes his notion of fictitious entities qualifying real entities to modify the classical notion of *qualitas*. The latter is treated, in the Aristotelian tradition, among arguments about *what* happened (or *status definitivus*) – that is, the question under which "law" a "fact," *if* it actually happened (or *status coniecturalis*), may be subsumed – and *why* it happened (or *status qualitatis*) – that is, whether the action in question may be equitably justified or exculpated, against the letter of the law, by appealing to exceptional circumstances.[87]

Fictitious entities which qualify real entities as facts (in legal terms) belong to Bentham's category of "existence": "Existence is a quality, the most extensively applicable and at the same time the most simple of all qualities actual or imaginable" (*ToF*, p. 49). In contrast, fictitious entities which qualify those facts as falling under certain laws belong to Bentham's category of "fictitious qualities" – that is to say, they belong to those fictitious entities whose task it is to qualify facts pertaining to the fictitious entity "existence."

Necessity, impossibility, certainty, uncertainty, probability, improbability, actuality, potentiality – whatsoever there is of reality correspondent to any of these names is nothing more or less than a disposition, a persuasion of the mind, on the part of him by whom these words are employed, in relation to the state of things, or the event or events to which these qualities are ascribed. [. . .] Quality is itself but a fictitious entity, but these [i.e. necessity, impossibility, certainty etc.] are all of them so many fictitious qualities. They do not, as real qualities – they do not, like gravity, solidity, roundness, hardness – belong to the objects themselves to which they are ascribed, in the character of attributes of the objects to which they are ascribed; they are mere chimeras, mere creatures of the imagination, mere non-entities. Yet, non-entities as they are, but too real is the mischief of which some of them, and, in particular, the word *necessity*, have been productive – antipathy, strife, persecution, murder upon a national, upon an international scale. (*ToF*, pp. 50–1)

Some of these "fictitious qualities" – that is, necessity, impossibility, certainty etc., which qualify "facts" as falling under certain "laws" – are only falsely (or "fictitiously," in the manipulative sense of a "deception that has been seen through") ascribed to those fictitious entities which qualify events as "facts." For in the process of qualifying already existing qualifications, they have caused considerable "mischief." According to the sections on "Deception" and "Fiction" in *Constitutional Code*, "mischief" on the level of government breeds the danger of "misrule" (*Bowring*, IX, pp. 76ff).

Bentham's verdict on the causes of such "mischief" is specifically concerned with corresponding practices in common law. Its representatives consciously ascribe, or are at least aware of such a practice, "fictitious qualities" to fictitious entities. But they do not seem to account, in publicly accessible form, for the reason or reasons why a particular validation of "fictitious qualities" ascribed to fictitious entities ought to be binding. The concrete "mischief" caused by a specific common-law practice of fictions – however indispensable the latter may have turned out to be in philosophical terms – consists in a *customary* silence, on the part of judges and lawyers, about the epistemological gulf opening between law and fact.

Bentham's solution to such "mischief" lies in a rationalized production of evidence from the conditions under which real entities are presented. *The Rationale of Judicial Evidence* is considerably influenced, as Postema argues, by premises which also inform his *Theory of Fictions*. Bentham defines evidence as the presentation of an "evidentiary fact" to a judge – a presentation intended to generate in the latter the persuasion about another, "principal fact," which is necessary for the decision, while the "evidentiary fact" itself may only contribute degrees of probability or improbability.[88] The probability of qualities ascribed to "facts" thus depends on those participating in the production of evidence from registered acts of perception and inference.

The production of evidence itself, however, should not be based on customary laws of association. In opposition to theories of moral sentiment, Bentham prefers to subject to a more rational evaluation, by means of "measuring the shortfall from full confidence," the degrees of persuasion that probability or improbability express about a "principal fact":

Bentham emphatically rejects the view that belief or persuasion is formed simply as a brute or intuitive response to experience. He calls this "nonsense psychology" or "nonsense *pisteutics*" and lumps this heresy together with "nonsense ethics" (moral sense and moral sentiment theories) which he excoriates (e.g. in Chapter 2 of *Introduction to the Principles of Morals and Legislation*). (He attacks Hume for falling into this heresy after seeing the Utilitarian light; *The Rationale of Judicial Evidence, Bowring*, VI, p. 240n*.) All of these heresies rest on the irrationalist "principle of sympathy and antipathy." The mistake both in ethics and "pisteutics" is that the view short circuits the process of rational formation of judgments in light of experience (and utility). This process takes "thought and talent," he insists, not mere sentiment or the propensity to believe.[89]

The complexity involved in the process of revising degrees of persuasion reflects Bentham's effort to optimize rational judgment in the service of collective utility. Hence his refusal, after *The Theory of Fictions*, to count a delusion without a subsequent misdecision among those conditions which exclude evidence. In *The Rationale of Judicial Evidence*, he argues that the danger of deception is not a proper ground for the exclusion of evidence, because an exclusion of evidence merely on those grounds provides no security against misdecisions.

> Misdecision is the word to be used in this place, not deception. Why? Because in misdecision consists the mischief, the only mischief. Suppose deception, and yet no misdecision, there is no real mischief: suppose misdecision, yet no deception, the mischief is as great as if deception had been the cause of it. (*Bowring*, vi, p. 386)

(Deceptions caused by judges, however, seem not to be included here.)

Utilitarian conscience and rehabilitated fiction are offshoots of two related problems, each involving conflicts between flexibility in adjudication and security of expectations threatened by institutionalized forms of corruption. Bentham responds in each case with a measure of reinstitutionalization. The first conflict emerges from the aforementioned problem of how to save conscience for utilitarianism. How can Bentham keep the equitable function of conscience intact, in order to monitor and eventually dismantle the judiciary's corrupt conscience in using legal fictions for manipulative purposes, while at the same time restricting any individual activation of conscience, in order not to put at risk the desired security of expectations? His solution is institutionalization. Utilitarian conscience reinstates, as I have argued, the authority of conscience as a conciliatory and adjudicative function of utility. On the one hand, it is supposed to bind the judge to the "call" of utility, as far as the parties subject to his decision (and, ideally, public opinion) are concerned. On the other hand, it is supposed to prevent the ethical subjects' individual conscience from activating actual debates over assessments of personal conduct when a dispute arises.

The price, however, of dissociating the utility of conscience's function from the truth of its "voice" is a degree of unpredictability largely incompatible with Bentham's claim for secured expectations. Unpredictability arises from the problem that the number of possible functions of utilitarian conscience exceeds the judge's task of internalizing an external law identified as utility. If what used to be an external law turns into a function of its anticipated internalization, then the spheres of the internal and the external can no longer be taken for granted as already formed. To treat utility as still being a purely external law then would come dangerously close to treating its customary forms of internalization as precedents. Accordingly, underwriting adjudicative motivation with utilitarian conscience involves an instability that is typical of all "higher authorities" faced with situations where increasingly contingent relations between truth, freedom, and utility challenge concerns for the security of expectations. For in those cases, "higher authorities" must operate along and across the borders of the very customs and interests which activated and shaped them.

The second conflict emerges from the problem of how to preserve the political function of opposing the practice of legal fictions in common law within a general system of their rehabiliation on pragmatic grounds. How can Bentham keep the equitable function of this particular articulation of critique intact, in order to maintain a utility-based distinction between the legitimate usage and illegitimate manipulation of fictions, while at the same time securing the pragmatic function of fictions in general, namely to generate a reality of predication in relation to real entities which does not exist prior to the employment of fictitious entities? Again, his answer is institutionalization – this time an institutionalization, according to function, of related discourses on the dissociation of fiction from delusion.

His method of positivist classification allows Bentham to divide the maxim of "seeing through" deceptions into different discursive tasks: predication, access, qualification, and usage. Predication transforms the conditions under which understanding and language relate to real entities from diverse fantasmatic epistemologies into one pragmatic necessity to generate presence. Access creates a relation between fictitious and real entities that incorporates motives for predication into modes of generated presence. Qualification establishes connections between real entities and the forms of evidence ascribed to them by means of relating "evidentiary facts" to "principal facts." Finally, the political distinction between usage and manipulation helps to sustain the functional distinction between securing expectations according to utilitarian conscience and securing judicial power in the ritual reproduction of customary rules. By classifying his demystification of delusions, Bentham seeks to elevate what appears to be the contingent usage of fictions into an evidence-providing authority. This authority operates along and across the limits of the very critique of legal fictions whose epistemological aporias eventually activated and shaped his general revaluation of fiction.

Utilitarian conscience and rehabilitated fiction may respond to the same problem – that is, how to combine the security with the flexibility of rules. But their different institutional consequences in adjudication and positivism perpetuate rather than solve that problem. Bentham wants to see his concept of adjudication, partly embodied in utilitarian conscience, complement his concept of legal positivism, partly embodied in the classification of demystified delusions as formally identified rules. Ideally, public expectations ought to be reflected in legislation, and not in the patterns that emerge from the judiciary's activities. If they do, however, emerge from those patterns, then expectations will focus on precedents instead of the code.[90] And if in fact public opinion comes to justify a judge's deviation, for utilitarian reasons, from established rules, then the expectations arising from that very justification are not unlikely to develop separately from other expectations that are merely reflected in the code.

One might argue, therefore, that expectations will not merely occasionally, but perhaps even frequently exceed the limits of codification and extend into the various contexts within which the public interprets how judicial decisions meet or disappoint existing expectations. Moreover, the expectations fashioned by public interpretations of court activities may result in a reshuffling of expectations regarding legislation. The judge's utilitarian conscience is supposed to take into account public expectations concerning the law. But the positivist premise implies that legal subjects should not derive their expectations from the consistency of the judicial understanding of the law's objectives over time, while they are nevertheless entitled to have access to it.

Conversely, while the judge's utilitarian conscience must consider public expectations, it is still a conscience in the traditional sense of an internalized "higher authority" not bound to strict adherence to the code. This concession of Bentham's leaves it rather vague whether utilitarian considerations are supposed to define or merely guide the judge's conscience. Under which conditions will that conscience also be encouraged to turn against the pressures for a consistency with decisions over time and among different courts? Under which conditions will it also be encouraged to turn against the institutionalized pressure to conform to utilitarian considerations? Even a utilitarian conscience cannot escape the functional instability arising from the problem that these conditions may be altogether arbitrary.

The possibility that the very activation of utilitarian conscience depends on this instability could cause it to operate on ethical grounds which may well exceed the confines of utility used by Bentham to define adjudication. This unintended double bind in Bentham's model, which entangles the solution and perpetuation of problems, challenges his claim for the security of public expectations concerning the legitimacy of the legal system. The complexity of disputes resists the positivist classification of social situations in terms of individual conflicts of interest. And the complexity of disturbances in modern life resists Bentham's identification of an allegedly achieved consensus on utilitarian principles with the complexity of positive law in commercial society.

Although Bentham is far from treating this problem successfully, he brings to our attention the critical role that institutionalization plays in legitimizing positive law apart from inherited customs and long-standing practices:

[. . .] Bentham's position accommodates in other terms much of what preoccupied Locke and Kant. There is nothing "special" about the embodiment of the labour of one's body and the work of one's hands in external objects. First occupancy, first possession by working, taking or whatever, can all found a title by reference to the general objects of law and the nature of property. There is no emphasis on our wills, no emphasis on our standing as uniquely free moral agents. A common-sense understanding of ordinary human needs and wants, and a common-sense acceptance of everyday ambitions underpin the theory. Institutions do not express human capacities, and they are not to be understood by reference to the hidden purposes of history. A positivist view of law allows the theorist to stand back and enquire how well or badly the legal recognition of various interests in things of value will promote the several elements of the utilitarian goal.[91]

Bentham's measures are not untypical of Western political systems early in the nineteenth century in which the alterability of the law, especially concerning alleged inactivity on the part of legislators, has become incorporated into public expectations. Standards in positive law are now measured by the validity of political impediments to the alterability of the law. An early symptom of this development is Hale's and Blackstone's legitimation of "judge-made law" by means of absorbing the indeterminacy of judicial decisions into the interpretation of customs as precedents.

Bentham is convinced that the question as to how the flexibility and security of rules may be combined has begun to structure social expectations. At the end of the eighteenth century, the daunting task of legislating legal change, as Luhmann has pointed out, becomes a major cultural challenge in Western societies: "Law has to be institutionalised as alterable over time without impairing its normative function."[92] Consequently, the legal problematic of effecting such an institutionalization is coming to be considered as fundamentally interconnected with other spheres, for instance the economic.

Bentham does indeed notice that the institutionalization of law as an alterable entity in commercial society, as suggested by classical common-law theory, causes changes in the law to accelerate. For the changes in some areas cause changes in other affected areas simply because corrections have become necessary as a result of the initial changes. These changes subsequently accelerate a change in the expectations concerning the flexibility and security of expectations and express this accelerated change of expectations as a problem for which the idea of an organic change of inherited customs appears insufficient. As a result of more complex expectations, more topics become subject to legal dispute, which in turn necessitates the institutionalization of the changing functions of legislation and adjudication. Parameters of this institutionalization are the needs to respond to different conflicts emerging from the tension between security and flexibility.

For Bentham, institutionalization has become inevitable to the extent that the possibilities available to legislation and adjudication in common-law theory and practice fail to cover the scope of changing, conflicting, or disappointed expectations in the concepts of custom and precedent. He holds out the method of positivist classification as a promise, claiming to guarantee the minimum of generalization needed to stabilize expectations. On the basis of such a generalization, the subjection of individuals to their "subjectivation" in the gaze of the public eye and the substitution of utilitarian consensus for the renunciation of illicit passions and pathological interests can be made mutually to define one another, without taking recourse to the mechanism of the legal fictions Civil Death and Substituted Judgment, in order to ensure stabilized expectations. Generalization requires that the law, irrespective of its concrete content, applies to different cases, which in turn requires an anticipation both of the future consent of third parties and their behavior in the case of disappointed expectations. To institutionalize these anticipations, Bentham suggests, is to make unfulfilled expectations outlast moments of disappointment.

CHAPTER 4

Aporias of retribution and questions of responsibility: the legacy of incarceration in Dickens's Bleak House

One of the causes of the delusion which attributes to the higher orders of pre-eminence in relative moral aptitude, i.e. in effective benevolence, is the association by which men are led to regard a man's benevolence as being in proportion to his benificence.　　　　Bentham, *Constitutional Code*

The costs had absorbed the whole case, all the fortunes involved. And so the fantastic fog of Chancery is dispersed – and only the dead do not laugh.
Nabokov, *Lectures on Literature*

OUTLASTING DISAPPOINTMENT UNDER POSITIVE LAW

In *Bleak House*, Dickens revisits, more than in any other of his novels, the complexity of expectations that is at the center of Bentham's project. He shares with Bentham a sense of disappointment about the complex ways the common law is practiced. However, while his text[1] displays a high degree of formal complexity, Dickens does not, generally speaking, allow the reader to diagnose specific social problems of complexity, which the text depicts, as symptoms of an identifiable cultural crisis.

Among Dickens's novels, *Bleak House* stands out because of the unique way it combines encyclopedic density with formal innovation, engaging in semantic and, to a degree, semiotic problems of order and coherence. By means of a specific formal disintegration in terms of length, density, and closure, the text participates in, and is meant to influence, symptoms of what many of Dickens's contemporaries perceive as the role of the law in social and psychological disintegration. However, their perception of unconnected symptoms of disintegration on the level of responses to legal practices may already express a defensive mechanism. They feel already forced to guard themselves against what one might call an arbitrary distribution of disappointment in the context of unsecured commercial and moral expectations.

Therefore, Dickens raises but -- unlike Bentham – does not attempt to answer the question whether the existing practice of law is responsible for or merely reflects an experience of disappointment across the classes. *Bleak House* may instead be said to cross-examine variations of this question: how are Victorians to connect the complexity of expectations with political, social, or cultural discontent when the complexity in question fundamentally complicates any articulation of crises, let alone solutions to them?

Bentham sees a crisis in the traditional function of common law to limit the sovereign's legislative action. John Stuart Mill reiterates this sense of crisis by deploring the continued inertia of traditional legal mechanisms. The alterability of the law, which Bentham bases on utility, has begun to affect the status of calculable expectations in Victorian society. The inertia of legal mechanisms now appears to be the very reason why in many cases legislators failed to meet society's expectations.

According to John Stuart Mill's judgment, "[t]he incongruity of such a mode of legislating would strike all minds, were it not that our laws are already, as to form and construction, such a chaos, that the confusion and contradiction seem incapable of being made greater by any addition to the mass."[2] Mill may merely articulate his contemporaries' observation that the alterability of "our laws" does not structure their expectations the way they anticipated that it would. But his statement also reflects some discontent over the experience that the public has not been rendered access to the legislative and adjudicative assessments of expectations.

In *Representative Government*, Mill demands an extension of the franchise in order to redefine politics apart from civil society's existing conventions, for instance the proportional representation of property. Yet at the same time, he remains skeptical about the utilitarian value of politically representing the motivations and interests of the people as social facts, which his father James Mill advocated in his *Elements of Political Economy* of 1820. Instead, he seeks to dissociate interest from purely social determination. As Catherine Gallagher explains, Mill expects national institutions not only to describe but also to instruct the electorate as to how the political process should be used to represent the public, and not merely the accumulated "motivations that drive civil society."

His proposed Parliament would not correspond to any empirical social reality but would, rather, directly express, by distorting what is, that which ought to be. Mill, it turns out, wishes the state institution to represent value *to* the population. According to his essay, the state represents value, first, by so constructing its institutions that they should teach the population what it should want instead of passively mirroring what it does want. By adopting Mill's plurality scheme, for example, the state would stand for no present social fact but for a normative value to be realized in the future [. . .]. The state, then, in the very workings of its institutions, would not mirror the desires and ambitions of the population, but instruct the population about what its desires and ambitions should be. Value, in Mill's essay, thus becomes a set of normative propositions that are not arrived at by accumulating facts.[3]

Mill's position, Gallagher concludes, betrays some unexpected affinities with Matthew Arnold's argument, in *Culture and Anarchy*, that if the extension of the franchise is not to result in a disintegration of society according to class conflicts, the state must become the representative, not of social facts, but of a value-based notion of culture in terms of intellectual cultivation.[4] The desire, expressed by two otherwise very different political advocates, to remove the mutuality between politics and culture "from any dependence on a God above or a social world below"[5] emerges as a mirror-function of the growing desire in mid-Victorian England to get in on the (re)distribution of means to access institutions that are in charge of negotiating public expectations.

The sense of a lack of access, which Mill exemplifies by drawing on the inertia of legal mechanisms, may simply be due to the fact that many of Bentham's proposals in this regard were not actually implemented. It seems more likely, though, that both Bentham and the proponents of classical common-law theory created new problems in the wake of the ones their models had been meant to solve. As one result, the Representation of the People Bill of 1865-66 split the Liberal party and divided the proponents of the utilitarian tradition. Furthermore, the Judicature Act of 1873 divided the judiciary over the question as to what institutional role equity courts should play.

Both Bentham and the proponents of classical common-law theory treat the alterability of the law as necessary in order to coordinate expectations in an increasingly commercial society. However, while in this process more topics become subject to litigation, the increasing complexity of the law tends to impede the chances for reform where reform is needed. For it has become less obvious, or more obscure, what kind of law it is – or if so, how it is applied and executed – that in a given courtly procedure does not meet certain expectations. Moreover, the increasing complexity of conflicting expectations, once they are articulated, does not necessarily reflect any utility that may arise from the complexity of laws. Gerald Postema's *obiter dictum* that Bentham's utilitarian positivism is a "political debate *stopper*"[6] equally applies to the *rites of assent* endorsed in classical common-law theory.

In the historical context of this problem, to complain about a lack of access to the law's mechanisms and, not unlike Bentham, to call for a higher degree of transparency in applying and executing it is not necessarily to reduce its complexity. Calls for reform may simply trigger new changes in the process of the legal system's self-revision. More importantly, the validity of laws resulting from such changes will tend to be more provisional as growing changes in terms of legal reform become absorbed into the system's process of self-revision. Given the double trouble of an accelerated alterability of the law and the increasingly ephemeral status of reformist changes, basic and radical reforms are less likely to happen. As the ephemeral status of reforms becomes absorbed into the law's accelerated alterability, expectations concerning palpable effects of reforms will be left more and more disappointed. Similarly, expectations concerning the law's function to secure expectations will be frustrated.

As a result, public confidence in the traditional expectation that laws apply to different cases over time will be shaken. The normative aspect of law concerning expectations is that it can be considered a formalization of trust by means of guaranteed licences and sanctions. Instituted law implies that formalized expectations will not be given up in cases of disappointment. But as soon as societies inscribe alterability into the normative dimension of law, expectations may be compromised, depending on how much the interest in accommodating rules to needs exceeds the interest in preserving the stability of expectations. This effect is due to the conflictual functions of expectations. On the one hand, expectations demand that the law change ever more rapidly in order to coordinate changing expectations. On the other hand, they are also a means to encourage or pressure authorities to institute or change laws in order to stabilize existing expectations or, to use the jargon of classical common-law theory, customary anticipations.

In relation to the public's shaken confidence in the law's task to combine the security and flexibility of rules, the complexity of the law no longer sufficiently reflects expressions of disappointed expectations. Consequently, individuals are more likely to blame the disappointment they suffer with respect to their expectations on the legal system. Those who administer the law's complexity appear to dodge public expectations regarding the security and flexibility of rules. In many cases, though, it takes more than corrupt lawyers and judges to effect a disappointment – at least as far as the disappointment about the security of individual expectations is concerned. This complicity of unfulfilled expectations with the complexity of alterable positive law leaves it undecided whether disappointment concerning the law's function to stabilize expectations is an arbitrary by-product of legal evolution or the inevitable response of individuals to an alleged conspiracy to ritually reproduce the legal elites' authority. However, even an awareness of that undecidability cannot undo the general impression among Dickens's contemporaries that the existing practice of common law fails to make unfulfilled expectations outlast moments of disappointment.

According to both Bentham and classical common-law theory, all citizens are subject to the law in the sense that the latter coordinates their expectations, or customary anticipations, by means of generalization. Where the law fails to prevent disappointment about its own effects, Dickens depicts such disappointment as frequently resulting in an isolation of subjects from other subjects. Some insist on individually claiming their economic, moral, and sentimental expectations in the form of legal expectations. Dickens frequently portrays them as absorbed and isolated in their will to resist disappointment about courtly procedures, which they remain subjected to but are in no adequate position to comprehend. Some manage to counterbalance the inscrutability of legal practices with the sense of coherence provided by family or philanthropic action. Dickens frequently portrays them as isolating, more or less successfully, local enclaves of autonomy from experiences of more global disappointment. In both cases, disappointment about the law forces subjects to decide whether, and if so, in what ways, they want to choose between readjusting and perpetuating their expectations in the face of disappointment.

The characters of *Bleak House* sometimes make themselves immune to this structure, which determines their choices, and sometimes render it problematic. They react in either imposed or chosen isolation to how they feel the legal system affects and infiltrates their private lives. But the sometimes contradictory way they both readjust and perpetuate their lives reflects the way the alterability of positive law allows for differentiated contradictions of readjusted and perpetuated expectations to co-exist. The characters challenge, but for the most part do not break with, the utility of their own subjection to the law.

Such behavior reflects the way the alterability of positive law requires the fiction of a consensus that the law apply to everybody as well as the social isolation of those who openly dissent. Yet while all characters are subject to the law, whether or not they consent to (or are aware of) this fact, few consent to the way positive law generalizes the complexity of expectations. Participation in court trials seems limited, in their cases, to roles that require a representation of themselves as reasonable, responsive, and cooperative. They feel disappointed about the way the Court of Chancery expects them to be willing to convert actions and harms into accounts and claims, to specify claims according to procedural and discursive conventions, and to accept the court's questionable decisions without organizing protest.

Dickens expresses this degree of limitation by troping the anonymous disappointment of some characters as an isolation in legal terms. I am going to argue that in those cases, the legal fictions Civil Death and Substituted Judgment, whose formalization of confinement I discussed in the previous chapters, make their reentry into Dickens's text. One paradoxical effect of this troping is that while these characters implicitly consent to principles of subjection, subjectivation, and civil society, they either are treated as, or feel like someone guilty of turning against those principles. In various ways, which I will explore in detail, their conscience not only reproduces the characters' turn against themselves as subjectivation's reason-to-be. Troping those characters' isolation in legal terms also pushes conscience to a limit where its withdrawal from the authority of the law challenges the very space of possible gains and losses in which the system of distributive justice allows conscience to operate.

Dickens's use of conscience differs from Sterne's and Bentham's in that he interprets its fragility as the conceptual limitation of a system of distributive justice that cannot account for itself by adopting a position beyond itself. The circular logic with which Chancery justifies its own principles of distributive justice is tautological: Equitable jurisdiction is valid because it is valid. "Tautologies are distinctions that do not distinguish," Niklas Luhmann notes. "They are always based on a dual observation scheme: something is what it is."[7] I will show how Chancery's tautologies contrast with the paradox that conscience both is part of the system of distributive justice and allows it to be challenged from a temporary outside position.

Dickens does not resolve that paradox. Instead, he relates it to a problem that lies at the heart of the legitimacy of positive law. The problem is that its increasing alterability has made positive law more dependent on the mechanisms of its internal transformations and less dependent on the established values, institutionalized customs, and explicit expectations of civil society. For Victorian citizen-subjects, this means that mid nineteenth-century British law does not encourage *more* debates on the consequences of subjection to the extent that its own relative autonomy relies *less* on an indoctrination of subjects with ideologies that encompass their lives.

For Dickens's characters, this problem becomes visible only in its effects. Despite the complexity of positive law, the necessity remains, in all their attempts at preventing disappointment, that the law be applied as it was laid down. The increasing complexity of the difference of those two functions would be meaningless without their initial connection in the concept of equitable justice. Yet the legal and ethical meaning of equitable justice has itself become so complex that any proof concerning the question as to whether instituted law best solves a problem can be nothing but hypothetical.

As to that part of the problem which is not visible, Dickens merely suggests, by means of strategically withholding information from the reader and thus thematizing invisibility, that courts of equity, the very institutions that are supposed to render equitable justice, avoid the institutionalization of political conflict as part of an acceptable formation of expectations. On the one hand, courts are to adopt, but not problematize, the hypothetical nature of instituted law as a premise that makes the concrete decisions of an equity court judge, or applied law, possible in the first place. On the other hand, actual relations between principles and precedents have become an ever more complex matter. All the more has it become difficult for citizen-subjects to determine whether a judge's particular decision concerning their accounts and claims *interprets* or *creates* rules for applying the law(s) in question.

COMPLEXITIES AND COMPLICITIES: LEGAL PRACTICES AND THE NOVEL

The incarceration trope in *Bleak House* is a consistent form of response, on the part of many characters, to invisible but palpable problems arising from the complexity of positive law and the complexity of expectations. In performing this function, it is related to, by way of contrast, the London fog, a trope suggestive of the inscrutability of both legal practices and expectations. The incarceration trope figures forth a disintegration of the particular in relation to a nebulous nexus, or more general context, that officially no longer includes but somehow continues to implicate it. Critics analyzing its function in Dickens's texts have frequently followed in the wake of Michel Foucault's analysis of individualization through discipline in *Discipline and Punish* and Louis Althusser's thesis on the "interpellation" of the subject by ideology.[8] They have also drawn on Jacques Lacan's remarks[9] on modern subjectivity's various renunciations of the symbolic order. Some have read Dickens's tropes of incarceration as a correlative of interpretive aporia. Others have used them to call for responsibility in reading and cultural criticism. Against the backdrop of its different appropriations, it seems useful to locate that trope in, and identify it in relation to, Victorian discourses on equitable justice that are most relevant to *Bleak House.*

These discourses are law and philanthropy. Within the context of the legal reforms initiated by Bentham and the Evangelical activities of Exeter Hall, the incarceration trope gains its profile. Regarding the law, Dickens employs it in order to comment on the practicability of legal security. Regarding philanthropy, Dickens employs it in order to comment on the promise of an institutionalized relief from misery in return for character formation. As I indicated, the same legal fictions that I discussed in *Tristram Shandy* and *A Sentimental Journey*, Civil Death and Substituted Judgment, foreground and specify the incarceration trope in *Bleak House.* We remember, both legal fictions enact displacements or exchanges of intention, which in turn connect metaphorical death and judicial influence on inheritance and bequest rules. Philanthropists practice the same, albeit inverted displacements of intention as they set out, in their donation rituals, to bless the wretched and poverty-stricken independently of their will. The legal fictions confront metaphorical death with literal inheritance and bequest. The donation rituals isolate the wretched and poverty-stricken from their will to remain in a position that allows them to return or refuse the sometimes questionable legacy of philanthropic gifts. Both legal fiction and ritual here rely on incarceration as a trope and thus reveal formal affinities to the incarceration trope in *Bleak House.* However, the tropes in literary fiction, in legal fictions, and in donation rituals reflect different objectives with regard to what each respectively is made to address as a crisis of expectations.

My argument will therefore focus on the ways those three "institutions" "exchange" the incarceration trope among one another as they employ it in separate ways. *Bleak House* depicts a variety of misery apparently extending across the classes. Most characters universalize their experience of misery by anticipating an ineluctable reversal of the injustice they spot in many different but equally unsuccessful ways. Two

Enlightenment-born institutions, a legal system controlled by parliamentary legislation and a philanthropic movement backed by theories
of moral sentiment, appear to be corrupt and their promises either lies
or illusions. Dickens articulates certain legal and ethical aporias of
expectations as the problematic legacy of Enlightenment-born institutions. Such an articulation, however, also occurred within those very
institutions, particularly along with the legal reforms inspired by Bentham's observations on distributive justice and benevolence – for instance his remark from *Constitutional Code* in the epigraph to this chapter[10] – and the institutional self-critique advanced by Wilberforce and
Shaftesbury in their writings on philanthropy. Dickens thus participates
in a culturally typical articulation of misery in the legal-ethical complex,
however, without simply building, as Michael Bell argued, a "Fieldin-
gesque" "social ritual of fiction"[11] upon a projected intimacy with his
readers' feelings.

   The prominent plotline in *Bleak House* – Esther Summerson discove-
ring the illegitimate circumstances of her unknown parentage -- is
interwoven with numerous other plots, which ramify through ominous
implications of characters and actions in the Chancery case of Jarndyce
and Jarndyce. Esther's disfigurement from small-pox and her acceptance of John Jarndyce's marriage proposal on the basis of the false
assumption that the physician Allan Woodcourt is not in love with her
impede her progress from Jarndyce's ward to Woodcourt's wife. While
she becomes the Lord Chancellor's ward of Chancery, together with
Ada Clare and her cousin Richard Carstone, it is John Jarndyce who
personally looks after all three of them. Ada and Richard get married,
but Richard eventually dies as a result of his futile efforts to bring the
case to a favorable end. Similar to Esther's progress, Caddy Jellyby, the
daughter of incorrigible philanthropist Mrs Jellyby, gets married to
junior dance instructor Prince Turveydrop, and Trooper George gets
reunited with his mother, housekeeper at Chesney Wold, the Lincolnshire estate owned by the aristocratic Dedlocks.

   The Chancery case causes many characters to die in its process,
which contrasts their and Richard's fate with that of Esther. Claimant
Gridley dies from his painful frustration about the case's endless procedures. Disturbed rag-and-bottle dealer and self-appointed alternative
Lord Chancellor Krook dies from "Spontaneous Combustion." Crossing-sweeper Jo, who accidentally becomes implicated in the case, dies
from the effects of disastrous sanitary conditions in Tom-all-Alone's, the
slum adjacent to London's Inns of Court district. Esther discovers her

mother, Lady Dedlock, dead at the gate of the paupers' graveyard, where her lover, Captain Nemo, lies buried, having died from an overdose of opium. Lawyer Tulkinghorn, manipulator of many lives affected by the case, ends up being murdered – however not by Lady Dedlock, as omnipresent detective Bucket finds out, but by her former maid Hortense. Against all odds, the case is actually closed when toward the end of the novel the court discovers that the estate at issue has been swallowed up in legal costs.

Criticism has usually presented Dickens's relationship with the law as characterized by confrontation rather than affinity. As far as his relation to Bentham is concerned, that confrontation for the most part refers to utilitarian, and not necessarily legal theory. Yet while school master Tom Gradgrind, a major character from *Hard Times*, certainly reflects the stereotype of an inhumane Benthamism, critics argued that Dickens is not as uncomfortable with utilitarian ethics as is commonly assumed.[12] What distinguishes him from Bentham in a more fundamental sense is the way he looks at the role of the law as contributing to a crisis of expectations. To understand the reasons for that difference, it seems useful to review a few biographical and historical data.

Having worked as a law clerk and court reporter, Dickens was familiar with the legal system, ever since in the 1820s his father was incarcerated for debt. In the 1830s, 40s, and 50s, he found himself in a controversial context of legal reforms, which for the most part were inspired by Bentham's writings. The fact that in the 1850s he complained, in *Household Words*, about reprehensible court practices indicates how slowly reforms were turned from theory into practice. *The Pickwick Papers* and *Bleak House* address this complaint by focusing on the Court of Chancery – the nation's highest equity court and an institution whose representatives had for the longest time been resisting submission to reforms.[13] In 1844, Dickens himself went to Chancery to sue some publishers for plagiarism and breach of copyright regarding *A Christmas Carol*. During that law suit, he personally experienced the legendary slow and ineffective procedures in matters of legacies, trusts, disputed wills, and wardships. Although the court ruled in his favor, Dickens had to pay more in legal bills than he was able to collect in damages.

As it had been for Bentham in the late eighteenth century, Chancery was for Dickens a symptom of ubiquitous corruption in the legal profession. Krook's "Spontaneous Combustion" in *Bleak House* certainly suggests more radical responses to this problem than the reforms proposed by Bentham, yet only in a postrevolutionary form. For Dickens suggests that Carlyle's use of imagery of spontaneous combustion to characterize the *ancien régime* before the revolution[14] bears little or no consequence after 1848/49. This fantasmatic option of a legal system going up in flames merely results in another casualty at the expense of Chancery's continued resistance to institutional revision.

When Dickens attacked Chancery in *The Pickwick Papers, Bleak House*, and *Household Words*, he did not stand apart from the process of Bentham's reforms. His own critical voice joined others, which since the late 1820s had made such attacks topical[15] – although *Bleak House* does of course not exhaust itself in its topicality.[16] Dickens's articles in *Household Words* and his portrait of an emaciated Chancery inmate in *The Pickwick Papers* were in line with the accusations previously launched by a series of articles in *The Times*. As one writer complained, "To the common apprehension of Englishmen the Court of Chancery is a name of terror, a devouring gulf, a den whence no footsteps return."[17] *Bleak House* proved to have considerable influence on the Chancery Procedure Act and Suitors in Chancery Relief Act of 1852, the Common Law Procedure Act of 1854 and the comprehensive Judicature Act of 1873.[18]

Chancery was originally instituted to counterbalance, in matters of legacies, wills, and trusts, the work of juries in common-law courts, which dealt with such crimes as theft, robbery, or murder. The court would reach a verdict according to principles of equity after considering written evidence in the form of affidavits – such as Nemo's document in *Bleak House*. The Lord Chancellor was supposed to protect the parties, in the absence of a jury, from any exaggerated rigidity in reading the letter of the law, particularly in situations where there was no precedent or where a common-law court was powerless against influential claimants.

In the course of the nineteenth century, Chancery created such an inscrutable network of procedures and precedents that more and more people complained about legal abuse and lawyers' profits.[19] If a party challenged a will like that of Tom Jarndyce in *Bleak House*, the estate at issue would be turned over to Chancery until a decision was reached. In the preface to his novel, Dickens mentions that the production of affidavits, which the Lord Chancellor would during long sessions read to the parties, as well as the hearings of witnesses and litigants raised administrative expenses to a degree often incompatible with the initial value in dispute. The original idea to hear all parties to the case occasionally turned into a bureaucratic monster. Public opinion gradually began to question the Lord Chancellor's authority to invent new "writs" in order to meet cases not justly settled by precedents. He eventually lost that authority in the Judicature Act of 1873 when common law and equity were institutionally united and the greater part of premises for judge-made law was replaced by statutory law.

Bentham's attack against the legal fictions in common law was refueled by the work of reform commissions from the 1830s to the 1850s. This discussion was so topical that Dickens was familiar not only with the customary practice of legal fictions, but also with Bentham's, Mill's, and George Graham's critique of that practice.[20] Dickens apparently shared Bentham's opinion that both legal fictions and the fictions operating in social interaction are ambivalent with respect to the question how much good they may do. But Dickens did not necessarily consider his own literary fictions, which Bentham would have labeled "fabulous entities," equally ambivalent. Instead, he would probably have agreed with Bentham's position in *The Theory of Fictions*. He universalized fiction and at the same time called attention to various uses and abuses of fictions which caused legal and ethical problems. However, Dickens would not have shared Bentham's unequivocally disparaging judgment on theories of moral sentiment. Finally, each took a different view on affinities and incompatibilities in the cultural interaction of law, ethics, and literature.

The practice of Chancery, which characters in *Bleak House* see as the symptom of a crisis of expectations, is not identical with that crisis which characters across the classes experience as misery in material and "spiritual" terms. As a journalist and activist, Dickens propagated reforms as solutions to crises. While *Bleak House* promises little hope for the success of reforms, the novel does not suggest a dismissal of responsibility, not even of naive notions of poetic justice.[21] Death remains omnipresent and challenges the novel's fairy-tale ending. Either death affirms the legal system's power to end human life or it marks the threshold toward utopian alternatives. Esther's and Woodcourt's inheritance of the new Bleak House hands down to further generations the inherited act of naming, and thereby (re)creating the potential problems of, an ominous legacy. Dickens thus makes it obvious that the genealogy of crises concerning expectations stands in direct proportion to a legal and ethical imperative to alleviate misery.

The impact that early instalments of *Bleak House* had among the reading public suggests that the novel, like legal reforms, in some way participated in the project of alleviating misery. The reforms focus on legislative change. The novel focuses on revising existing notions of crisis by means of revising, as I will later explain in detail, narrative conventions such as closure and perspective. Both the law and the novel are cultural forms of narrative,[22] even though it may seem that while the law happens to be one of the novel's main themes, novels are not exactly the facts that legal narratives use as their themes. If the novel participates in working on a problem that is also the target of legal reforms, the law can no longer simply be considered an object of the critique of complex expectations articulated by the novel.

The two discourses intersect in the medium of legal fictions, whose largely invisible but noticeably corrupt practice is *Bleak House*'s central topic. Defended by Blackstone, legal fictions are also the object of Bentham's early invectives. While Bentham in his later years rehabilitates fiction in general, the duplicity of its usage and manipulation that he maintains in his philosophical discourse continues to suggest legal fictions as dangerous procedures. Legal fictions are also duplicitous in *Bleak House*, as I will show, insofar as Dickens not only criticizes their practice but also uses their mechanism to structure his narrative. According to classical common-law theory, we remember, legal fictions perform judge-made revisions of the legal system by circumventing legislation. They are considered the vehicle of a conservative transformation of common law, which Bentham finally wants to see replaced by codification. Dickens's literary fiction might be considered a medium for making the corrupt practice of legal fictions transparent, if it did not also resemble their conservative function of solving adjudicative problems apart from legislative efforts. To describe the role of Civil Death and Substituted Judgment in *Bleak House* is to reevaluate the ways the novel is implicated in the legal practices it explores.

The narrative opacity that Dickens employs in *Bleak House* suggests links between opacity as such and notions of crisis whenever expectations are supposed to be coordinated by means of their representation. Based on the absence, or inaccessibility, of Tom Jarndyce's original will, the characters implicated in the case – most notably Richard, Esther, and Miss Flite, who expect an outcome in their favor – begin to connect and organize the isolated details of information they have available. In doing so, they repeat and thus expand, at least up until half way through the novel, the law's effect of implicating other characters in the process of connecting isolated details. Early on, Dickens suggests a connection between the spheres of law and family in the role of the Lord Chancellor, who promises to look after his wards Esther, Ada, and Richard *in loco parentis*.

Both narrators, Esther and a detached third-person voice, occasionally refer to the notion of connection and thus encourage readers to make connections for themselves. Apparently, positive law must respond to certain pressures arising from various sorts of social separation in seventeenth- and eighteenth-century Europe – also affecting the family – which Philippe Ariès associated with "the Cartesian revolution of clear ideas."[23] To the extent that human separation continued to affect traditional norms of inheritance into the nineteenth century, judges and lawyers will also have felt challenged to revise their own inherited means of adjudicating conflicts of inheritance and bequest.

As the number of possible connections increases, so does the number of problems which characters face as they discover that actual connections between isolated details of information are opaque. Soon *Bleak House* seems about more than the public's weariness of existing legal practices that degrades Chancery to Krook's rag-and-bottle shop. In the satire on the parliamentary crisis of the early 1850s ("Lord Boodle, Lord Coodle. . ."), Dickens is also concerned with problems of political representation. Moreover, he addresses the question as to how social problems may be represented that emerge in the radical distance between the economic and hygienic "misery" in Tom-All-Alone's and the estrangement of aristocratic character from aristocratic status in Chesney Wold. Finally, in the stylized discussions of freedom and determination between John Jarndyce and his parasitical poet-houseguest Harold Skimpole, the novel focuses on Carlylean problems of how to ascertain inherited cultural values against the experience of modernity.

The more Dickens's characters respond to such problems, the more the problems themselves appear to be interrelated. Crises in political representation, in the mediation between the classes, and in the legitimacy of cultural values seem to affect one another. Yet the contingency of their connections defies identifications of one single crisis – identifications that claimants are likely to make as they change their roles from courtroom observers to philanthropic activists or family members. Many characters resemble one another in that they feel threatened by crises they may have invented by themselves – Leicester Dedlock, for instance, by the parliamentary crisis in political representation; philanthropist Mrs Pardiggle by her social distance to Jenny, the brickmaker's wife; and George the Trooper by the uncertainty as to how free or determined his actions really are.

Those who pass the general verdict that Chancery's corruption is reflected in an intended opacity of its monstrous practices identify the

inaccessibility of Tom Jarndyce's original will with the origin of a
general crisis. Dickens shows, however, that such diagnoses are themselves already responses to disappointed expectations. For instance, he
suggests Lady Dedlock's and Captain Nemo's affair as the origin of
Esther's disappointed expectations. To the extent that readers are
moved toward a position where they feel encouraged to connect different "origins" of crises, the assumption of a single origin falls back into
opacity.

Post-Foucauldian critics have read the characters' (and sometimes
the narrators') assumptions of a crisis against the backdrop of more
general thematic and representational aporias. Those critics frequently
see the articulations of crises in the discourse of both narrators implicated in a more general eighteenth- and nineteenth-century form of
discourse that Foucault characterized as discipline.[24] Building on his
premise that during the Enlightenment period language ceased to be a
unified medium to depict and create worlds, Foucault demonstrated
how Enlightenment institutions may be said to "produce" individuals –
"produce" in the sense that those individuals are compelled to define
themselves by internalizing the discipline to which institutions like the
law have so far subjected them only externally. Post-Foucauldian criticism of *Bleak House* has often generalized this argument, which Foucault
made against the "repressive hypothesis," into an analysis of how this
particular novel is implicated in the cultural processes of constructing
realities contemporaneous to Dickens's literary production. David A.
Miller, for instance, argued that the "Discipline in Different Voices,"
which impersonally emerges from institutions like Chancery on a global
level, frustrates (or turns into aporias) the characters' and the first-
person narrator's efforts to act responsibly on a local level.[25]

Such readings tend to reduce the relationship between institutions
authorized to control discourses and individuals defined by the internalization of discipline to a double bind between impersonal villains and
individual victims. This double bind appears to (re)produce a nexus of
authority and knowledge in modern societies. Critics who advance such
readings resemble many of Dickens's characters. They already interpret
cultural and narrative opacity in terms of a specific crisis. They recapture the effect of interpretive aporia, which Dickens generates by having
characters fail in criticizing irresponsibilities they believe to have been
caused by Chancery, as an indication that as critics they must not fail in
criticizing the conspiratory workings of discipline unearthed by
Foucault. As a result, the interpretive challenge of cultural and narrative

opacity appears merely to reflect a sophisticated but despicable nexus of capitalism and a crisis of representation.[26]

In contrast, it should be noted that institutions of law and philanthropy are often also concerned to revise, on the local level of their own discourses, irresponsibilities they may have caused on a more global level. Bentham's ambiguous view, for example, on the actual uses and abuses that define the practice of legal fictions can in fact be considered an instance of the law's reflection on aspects of its own irresponsibility, even if he then again insists on the positive qualities of discipline to reduce or limit the damage inflicted. Instead of reducing interpretive aporia concerning responsible action to the idea that discourses on responsibility are generally implicated in a reproduction of authority, it seems both more accurate and more useful, as Bruce Robbins points out, to acknowledge *Bleak House*'s diversity of responses to aporia.[27] To give accounts of that diversity is to avoid oversimplifying the relation between responsibility and irresponsibility in Victorian culture.

As we will see, a number of characters who refuse to rely on consolation when faced with aporias – for instance Gridley, Krook, Richard, and Lady Dedlock – displace exemplary grief with various activities of suffering. Along with other characters who in contrast manage to survive, they generally insist on making their lamentation continuous with the sharpness of their feelings, but hesitate to universalize the latter into exemplars fulfilling the requirements of established norms. Dickens presents their feelings as singular cases that constitute passionate events instead of objects of interpretation. Being for the most part inept in handling the rules of positive law, they substitute improvised actions for representations of rules. Thus they respond to the law's lack of extrinsic criteria for truth and justice, as well as its inefficiencies and inequities, with an agility of practices that may allow them to take advantage of sudden circumstances in order to seize the initiative in times of crisis. Such a type of activity, or "practice," preserves ways of making differences for the subject, who acts in defense of the particularity of personal experience but whose body is inscribed with the law's instrumentality and its sentences.[28] Practice opens up possibilities, expectable but not predictable, to voice and proclaim the singularity of suffered injuries within the networks of norms and generalized expectations, whose authority has supplemented the subject's voice of practical vigilance.[29]

The complicity of the characters' actions and desires with the complexity of positive law can thus be explained as more or less successful "tactical" defenses of practice.[30] Eagleton claims for sympathetic imita-

tion in the eighteenth century that, "[t]o mime is to submit to a law"[31] –
for instance the law of "Production of a Commodity-Text."[32] In contrast, the voices of many characters in *Bleak House* replicate, but do not
necessarily submit to, a substitution of the law's mutuality of principles
and precedents for voices assumed coincident with practice: "The
sound of the body becomes an imitation of this part of itself that is
produced and reproduced by the media – i.e. a copy of its own arti-
fact."[33]

Positive law derives its authority, in the eyes of the characters, from a
circularity of reason and historical appropriateness in the reinterpreta-
tion of principles through precedents and the adjustment of the security
and flexibility of rules. Yet rather than countering the law's communicative regime of perpetuating and adjusting expectations, the characters' practice can be said to reenter it in order to make differences within
it. These differences may in turn set off new differences between forces
within the system. In fact, they may redistribute among legal subjects
across the classes expectations concerning the probability and improbability of change, and thus encourage power to circulate in a non-
transitive way.[34]

Specifically, those characters who feel that being "locked" into the
Chancery case amounts to a form of death-in-life – that is to say, those
who use a psychological metaphor of Civil Death – can be said to make
very complex differences. I hope to show that they make themselves – to
use the jargon of those post-Foucaulian and post-Lacanian critics whom
I was referring to – "other" to the "symbolic order" of an "Other,"
whose law they identify with Chancery's practice of equity. These
characters' formal position is one of an explicit "other within" their own
culture. Similar to the ambivalent power of the semiotic to diffuse "social
effect[s] of the relation to the other"[35] that a culture's symbolic order has
established, they sometimes act subversively and antagonistically, sometimes petrify into deadly forms of narcissism and fetishism.

This ambivalence determines the relationships between these characters' subjective exclusion from and subversive inclusion in the symbolic
order. To be sure, anyone or anything can in principle occupy the
position of the Other as symbolic order. But the binary oppositions they
set up between oppressive forms of distributive justice, on the one hand,
and equitable forms of domestic or redemptive justice, on the other,
figure the law as the primary Other. In their view, the law infiltrates all
other agencies or orders that occupy positions of otherness, be it the
other in terms of class, the irrational, the incompetent, or the uncanny.

These characters are perfectly capable of seeing themselves as always implicated in that which they choose to oppose. Nevertheless, they are frequently presented as failing to resist seeing political contestation in terms of a pure transcendence of contemporary relations of power. By foregrounding the metaphor of Civil Death as an ambivalent articulation of death-in-life, Dickens urges his readers to refigure this structural position of exclusion. He seems to endorse what Judith Butler proposed as a "constitutive outside," an irrecuperable form of practice which casts the force of negation "as a future horizon [. . .] in which the violence of exclusion is perpetually in the process of being overcome." Butler claims that this "constitutive outside" "illuminate[s] the violent and contingent boundaries of the normative regime [. . .] through the inability of that regime to represent a fundamental threat to its continuity."[36] Similarly, Dickens employs the metaphor of Civil Death as an ambivalent vision of the political that sometimes borders on, sometimes exceeds the conventional political ideals of distributive justice, including the representability of expectations and the egalitarian sharing of benefits and responsibilities.

THEMATIZED PERSPECTIVITY

The literary notion of the fantastic plays an important role for the various responses to aporia in *Bleak House*. If what Dickens, in his preface to *Bleak House*, calls the "romantic side of familiar things" (*BH*, p. 43) is identified with Freud's notion of the uncanny,[37] cultural and narrative opacity will appear to form conspiracies with local enclaves against discipline. Law and philanthropy will then turn into Enlightenment inequities and Esther's sentimental forms of self-discipline into a transference of traumatic experience. As a modality of the uncanny, the fantastic in literature will suggest narrative crisis as an index of pathology for the opacity of positive law.

However, the feeling of unknowability in nineteenth-century cities such as London or Paris may have already rendered the nexus of urban details as a nexus of illusions, reflected only in the anxieties and projections of those who populate them. Dickens shares with Walter Benjamin's *Arcades Project* the sense of "phantasmagoria" as one crucial effect of modern urban reality.[38] "Phantasmagoria" is a form of reification – a de-realization of subjects and objects from their relations to economic realities as well as past and present, for which Benjamin also cites Dickens's texts as examples.[39]

The urban disintegration of social existence caused by nineteenth-century commodity culture corresponded, according to Benjamin's *The Origin of German Tragic Drama*, to the seventeenth-century Baroque use of allegory. Benjamin demonstrated how this use of allegory served to reduce a sense of ruin and fragmentation concerning social existence to the melancholic disconnection of signifier and signified in the emblematic features of the death's head. More recently, Paul de Man recontextualized, in *Allegories of Reading*, Benjamin's notion of allegory as unreadability. Drawing on de Man's interpretation of Benjamin, Jeremy Tambling argued that the various narrative aporias in *Bleak House* suggest a use of allegory that not only disables the epistemological demands of literary realism but also explores the diversity of impossibilities to resist modernity.[40] It is in this sense that Dickens's use of the fantastic goes beyond a mere articulation of the uncanny. He can be said to connect it with the aforementioned role of practice in affecting normed probabilities and improbabilities of change.

Dickens's "romantic side of familiar things" often generates alternative worlds without simply yielding to cultural norms of how to generate alternatives to existing expectations. Whenever that occurs, the characters' responses to their experience of legal opacity need not necessarily be considered pathological. To be sure, the characters remain the captives of their own fictions with respect to what they consider "homely." However, the "prisons" they have generated for themselves do not always have to result in a submission to frustration, even though for some they do. To the extent that Dickens uses the fantastic to create *changing* alternative worlds, he enables characters who feel metaphorically incarcerated by the legal system – a feeling sometimes represented by the image of Miss Flite's captive birds (which recalls Yorick's captive starling in *A Sentimental Journey*) – to modify experiences of global aporia.[41] The fantastic in *Bleak House* both articulates the uncanny and generates changing alternative worlds. Building on this duplicity of the fantastic, Dickens manages to mitigate the almost Gnostic dualism according to which characters appear as resisting evil and as tempted by, or conspiring with evil.[42]

As he explores this duplicity, Dickens multiplies perspectives on the law's complexity without letting them converge. This means that the text does not merely serve to counteract, complement, or improve the worlds to which it makes reference with respect to what they appear to be lacking. Instead, by insisting on the disjunction of multiplied perspectives, Dickens encourages readers to be suspicious about normed solutions to crises. He structures that multiplication by means of juxta-posing the two narrative perspectives. While Esther focuses on the private and "homely" character of her memories, the third-person narrator addresses something uncanny, which appears not only to penetrate the workings of Chancery but also to connect all characters from Jo to Leicester Dedlock. The uncanny thus contrasts with private memory, "returning" unexpectedly and, it is suggested, unpredictably. Dickens thematizes perspectivity whenever homely memories and the uncanny emerge as being different from one another. Such an articu-lation of the uncanny as private memory's other can be called fantastic insofar as it both suggests and withholds the representation of an uncannily global nexus of isolated local perspectives on the complexity of expectations.[43]

Thematized perspectivity thus emerges as a specific feature of Dick-ens's literary realism, which fulfils two functions. First, to thematize perspectivity is to demarcate the discursive perspectives employed to organize those worlds of social disintegration that the novel is concerned with. Chancery's version of common-law adjudication becomes the "uncanny" condition of a corrupt legal system. Generally speaking, nineteenth-century common law is not defined in terms of codification and in this sense not formulated as discourse. Hence Dickens's refusal even to attempt to control its transformations by means of one single narrative perspective. Instead, he introduces additional perspectives such as the critique of institutions and philanthropy.

To thematize perspectivity is therefore to suggest the common law as an opaque nexus of multiple perspectives. For instance, by having John Jarndyce periodically complain about the legal elite's manipulations of fictions and equity, Dickens recalls the genre of critical essays that the reading public identified with Carlyle's invective against Chancery in *Past and Present*, as well the anti-Chancery campaign launched by *The Times* since the summer of 1851. Similarly, philanthropist Mrs Pardiggle owes her aggressively benevolent methods of fundraising to those of the Catholic Oxford Movement of Pusey and Newman, which Carlyle, in *Sartor Resartus*, denounced as Christian dandyism. Other characters who act like dandies are the fashion-obsessed aristocratic guests at Chesney Wold, whose party affiliations in turn establish a connection with alleged bribery in Parliament. Moreover, the catastrophic hygienic conditions in Tom-All-Alone's, as well as the association of St. Martin's Graveyard, where Captain Nemo lies buried, with a sense of illness and infection that, in the case of Esther's infection with Jo's small-pox, extends across the classes, refer to discussions about the urgency of health reforms, which Dickens propagated from the late 1840s – especially after the Tooting "baby farm" scandal of 1849 when 180 orphaned children died from cholera. And finally, Mrs Jellyby's "telescopic philanthropy," a form of benevolence exclusively directed towards problems abroad, opens a perspective on the missionary blindness of Evangelical philanthropic institutions like Exeter Hall for domestic misery – a blindness that Dickens, following Carlyle, actively criticized.[44]

The second function that thematized perspectivity fulfils is to transgress the limitations of single perspectives in the course of their multiplication.[45] Specific legal abuse in Chancery metonymically extends to institutional abuse on the part of Carlyle's Christian dandies in the Oxford Movement and the aristocratic dandies involved in bribing members of parliament. Reverend Chadband's philanthropic blindness in the light of Jo's failure to articulate himself in response to the rhetoric of edification delivered to him metonymically extends to the Coroner's ignorance regarding Jo's incapability to answer his questions about Nemo's death in a correct and comprehensible way.

On a more abstract level, Dickens metonymically relates questions of how to distinguish between necessary and unnecessary forms of philanthropy to the way Bentham insisted on a distinction between useful and detrimental fictions. To transgress – rather than merely demarcate – discursive perspectives is to initiate changes in how perspectives serve to organize worlds of social disintegration. Transgressing discursive norms is important for Dickens to the extent that he can thus articulate, by means of rotating perspectives, a complexity of crises that appears to resist discursive topographies of it.

The way Dickens suggests that a sense of opacity affects all classes as symptoms of a crisis may be called the novel's social dimension. On the one hand, he focuses the problem of social disintegration on how characters perceive the common law as undergoing a crisis in terms of its validity among legal subjects. On the other hand, he represents the complexity of disintegration as a multiplication of perspectives on how to organize the expectations disappointed by it. The strategic absence of coordinated perspectives on what constitutes Chancery's validity thus indicates the sense of a lack with respect to what makes social norms binding.

Compared to the perception of such a lack, any multiplication of perspectives on the complexity of positive law will render this absence of coordination as exceeding the controllable familiarity of norms, and therefore uncanny. Thematized perspectivity serves to articulate this very problem. On the one hand, characters like Esther, Richard, or John Jarndyce are permanently looking for ways to recapture uncoordinated social norms. On the other hand, Dickens calls into question, by refusing to let perspectives converge, the moral basis of their question as to how the disintegration of norms may be recaptured.

Dickens unfolds this problem of uncoordinated social norms in terms of law and philanthropy. Both are part of what characters experience as a crisis of opacity. Their experience of that crisis causes them to call for internal revision in both legal and philanthropic institutions. As discourses which are already supposed to translate the necessity for revision into practical solutions to specific problems, both law and philanthropy appear to be insufficient, treacherous, or corrupt. Regarding the necessity for revision, law is expected to be impartial and philanthropy disinterested, but both fail in attempting to meet that expectation. What they are supposed to achieve on an institutional level – a sense of equitable justice according to their respective definitions of the term – turns out to be what is actually excluded by them. A pretext of altruism seems to cover up institutional interests. What they inofficially exclude, or fail to do justice to, is thus paradoxically domesticated in their discourses as that which they pretend to live up to. Whenever that which is excluded by them seems no longer domesticated, it remains vague how law redresses injustice and how philanthropy alleviates misery.

Positive law embodies a transformation of rules for the coordination of norms. This transformation sometimes occurs so fast that humans interpret themselves as the targets of human-made rules. The most prominent victims of such self-interpretations are Lady Dedlock and Richard Carstone. Their tragic deaths reintroduce a moment of familiarity into the uncanny procedural circularities ("the law is the law") by means of which Chancery seems to perpetuate its authority. Legal norms operate, whether or not they stand in need of revision, as the condition of actions like Lady Dedlock's and Richard's. Thus they also contribute to the sense of crisis experienced by other characters. Whenever legal norms cause unpredictable actions like Lady Dedlock's escape from Chesney Wold or Krook's Spontaneous Combustion, they appear to have effects just as nature does. At same time, Dickens clearly articulates that they should not have those effects, because the injustice or misery caused by them stands in need of revision.

In this context, Dickens's presentation of the effects legal norms have on legal subjects highlights the self-serving quality of positive law, as well as its manipulation by different interest groups, represented for instance by lawyer Tulkinghorn or Leicester Dedlock. As cultural complexity has increased, so has the pressure of social problems which the law is expected to vent. By employing norms as negative signals, Dickens seeks to activate his readers' potentials to respond to, and perhaps negate, some of the ways in which positive law operates.

In contrast, philanthropy represents a contemporary position to alleviate misery.[46] To the extent that philanthropy institutionalized and popularized some of the positions advanced in eighteenth-century theories and novels of moral sentiment, Dickens renders it favorable. To the extent, however, that it neglects the sphere of domestic problems, as in the case of Mrs Jellyby's "telescopic philanthropy," Dickens renders it contradictory. Philanthropy appeals to a public conscience about social misery, but not to the necessity also to alleviate that misery at home. This contradiction is an historical index of how contradictory expectations collided with demands for social action.

The seemingly futile "mythopoetic creation of a general social conscience based upon feeling," for the sake of which Dickens "adapts the sentimentalist inheritance",[47] is based on a tension between different responses to such contradictions. As Nabokov put it, "The costs had absorbed the whole case, all fortunes involved. And so the fantastic fog of Chancery is dispersed – and only the dead do not laugh."[48] In this statement, he aptly expressed how Dickens's ironic sentimentality frequently vacillates between comic and grotesque moments. By means of this vacillation, Dickens formally connects the conflicts between, on the one hand, how law redresses injustice and how it serves to simulate altruism and, on the other hand, between how philanthropy raises conscience on a global level and how it serves to alleviate misery on a local level.

The instability of those positions allows Dickens to undercut any exclusive identification of social action with specific social norms. As a result, he is in a position to render visible the problematic of norms as such – that is to say, restrictions with respect to human action. Furthermore, he can cross-examine norms of property transfer and realities of inheritance by presenting both in varying contexts. If considered achievements of the Enlightenment period, law and philanthropy are valid in the sense of normative discourses. Dickens suggests, though, that if one considers them as nineteenth-century institutions that have specialized in administering certain social norms, they must be, given the new necessity to revise the procedures of corrupt institutions, activated in new ways as well.

While the vacillation between comic and grotesque elements enables such a new activation of law and philanthropy, Dickens also insists on a sentimental mode of presenting misery in order to augment the effects of that activation. The common metaphor of England's two separate nations suggests an abyss between classes. This image articulates the very structure of a society questioning the validity of its legal and moral norms. Dickens illustrates that structure in the various ways characters have internalized a sense of communicative isolation. Not only is Tulkinghorn frustrated by Jo's sociolect when he interrogates him. For the most part, Lady Dedlock and Esther fail in communicating their respective needs – forgiveness and recognition – to the other person. So do Richard Carstone and John Jarndyce when it comes to explaining what specific crisis of legal norms it is that each thinks necessitates measures of revision. Barriers in the process of communication emerge as symptoms of a general failure to validate social norms.

If Dickens had wanted to communicate that failure in a sentimental mode, then sentimentalism would have merely served to underscore the fact that England's two nations fail to coexist both in reality and in the novel – even though the 1850s saw practical, and the 1870s legislative improvements in the fusion of common-law and equity courts as well as statutory law and precedents. Nevertheless, Dickens cannot do without the utopian remainder of some social vision. For him, something needs to be done in order to stimulate forms of action that help to reduce misery.

As soon as he has characters verbalize that utopian remainder, however, utopia returns as an affirmative norm. For instance, the norm articulated by Esther suggests that only the poor are capable of acting humanely, while everybody else has already become "denatured": "There were many little occurrences which suggested to me, with great consolation, how natural it is to gentle hearts to be considerate and delicate towards any inferiority. [. . .] Why, what had I to fear, I thought, when there was this nobility in the soul of a labouring man's daughter!" (*BH*, xxxvi, p. 562). "[N]obility in the soul[s]" of the poor is a metaphor for transcending the gulf between classes. Misery seems to Esther so pervasive that hope needs to be affirmed. In a Rousseauesque manner, she appeals to what she believes are the very basic human affects that will help her and her fellow beings to overcome the isolation of classes.

For the third-person narrator, utopianism originates in a symbolic notion of misery that unites those who are separated: "What connexion can there be between many people in the innumerable histories of this world, who, from opposite sides of great gulfs, have, nevertheless, been very curiously brought together!" (*BH*, XVI, p. 272). Misery thus extends from poverty to boredom. Consequently, property relations do not simply represent deprivation or happiness but different forms of the same symbolic misery. The third-person narator suggests various forms of illness (Esther, Charley, Richard, Leicester Dedlock, Mr Smallweed, Jo, and Jenny's family) as metaphors for such misery. To be sure, physician Allan Woodcourt's art of healing seems to epitomize a utopian form of philanthropy, which can actually cure misery as if it were a non-symbolic illness. However, Esther's sentimental discourse already reifies such utopian philanthropy as an affirmative norm: "I know that from the beds of those who were past recovery, thanks have often, often gone up, in the last hour, for [Allan's] patient ministration. Is this not to be rich?" (*BH*, LXVII, p. 935).

The aforementioned social dimension of *Bleak House* consists in an assembly of various unconnected structures within which people co-exist: Chancery, the police, detectives, the family, the class structure of separation, and the social structure of a bourgeois code of morals defined by "nobility in the souls of the poor." Whenever these structures connect, their hidden components surface and create uncanny effects. What used to be familiar about them when considered separately from other such structures then begins to surprise. It is not the class structure, but the unfamiliar forming an integral part of the familiar, which for Dickens defines Victorian realities.[49] Realities which force the familiar and the unfamiliar into copresence exceed familiar perspectives on them. They apparently require unfamiliar forms of representation. Dickens's deformation of the representable with his strategy of thematized perspectivity serves to articulate the unfamiliar as an offshoot of incoherent norms. Reality as a whole seems unrepresentable. But it still requires responses to the realities of "misery" and unvalidated social norms.

Dickens organizes this deformation of representation by letting his two narrative perspectives alternate. For the sake of narrative continuity, Esther restricts the presentation of her knowledge to one sentimental perspective. The less involved third-person narrator rejects such a restriction. Their diverging perspectives thus generate gaps in the narrative sequence, portraying the novel's social dimension as something that frequently exceeds the perspectives projected on it. As opposed to Esther, the third-person narrator must do without sentimental continuity, yet has more options for rendering the unfamiliar as something surprising. Esther reduces her memories to continuity. Her narrative counterpart accumulates detailed descriptions that in turn generate more opacity in terms of the discontinuity of events. Esther engages less in the complexity of legal norms and expectations than in what may be called a combination of self-discipline and altruism. It is only detective Bucket who eventually uncovers various contradictions in Esther's ways of responding to complexity.

Both narrators, however, relate to the characters' experience of opacity by means of minute description. Thus they both perpetuate rather than reduce, probably contrary to their intentions, the effect of unconnected and isolated details. Esther accommodates details to the needs of continuity. The third-person narrator evokes something unappropriable. Whenever thematized perspectivity forces the accommodation of details and the evocation of something unappropriable into copresence, the unfamiliar begins to characterize the normative aspects of a society whose actions exceed attempts at controlling or accommodating the unfamiliar.

To create this particular effect, Dickens uses different strategies. He frequently withholds information about what motivates characters and how events are related. He presents false leads, as for instance in the case of Tulkinghorn's murder, where Hortense is found to be the murderer only after George was considered the main suspect. Using the twists and turns in every new instalment to prolong suspense, Dickens also mirrors the detective reader in characters like Guppy, who has rather inquisitive inclinations but whose private motives often prevent him from finding anything.

To represent society as a Chancery case is to suggest its social dimension as excess. For to enact society's complex expectations as a law suit which obfuscates aspects of reality is to suspend those "natural" attitudes towards expectations which the official discourses on legal norms advocate. Hence the possibility for Dickens to highlight the fantastic as that which expresses what is unfamiliar with respect to institutions in the normative social world (law, philanthropy, the police, the family). What these institutions have in common is that they insist on reducing complexity to familiar continuities. While Esther's optimism renders the unfamiliar marvelous, her marriage at the end of the novel renders the marvelous predictable. The uncanny itself, and not merely the response to it, emerges as something human-made.

In response, Dickens manages to create a therapeutic effect that differs from Esther's optimism. In contrast to the utopian remainder of humanitarian humanism suggested by the many dark visions of *Bleak House*, he seems to remain optimistic about society's chances to work through the home-made effects of what surprises in the midst of the familiar. Characters are acting upon the "double contingency" that "being able to hold firm expectations of another person involves presenting to that person also a pattern which provides similar firmness of expectation."[50] For this purpose, Dickens employs the ambiguity of real and imagined isolation, which defines a number of prominent characters that I will examine, to show how individuals respond to an increasing pressure of incompatible expectations.

LAW AND CRIME

Optimistic reductions of complexity alone, as well as the mere recognition that opacity may be home-made, cannot undo institutional corruption. Chancery continues to combine "respectability" with "[t]he one great principle of the English law [. . .], to make business for itself" (*BH*, XXXIX, p. 603). For this reason, lawyers Kenge and Vholes – the latter being Richard's attorney – refuse to abolish those rules which provide them and their colleagues with administrative authority and, as a result of the fees raised, enormous revenues. Alluding to the threatening impact the case of Jarndyce and Jarndyce has had on several characters involved in it, the third-person narrator ironically remarks "that [such] changes are death to people like Vholes" (*BH*, XXXIX, p. 605). When eventually the whole estate is found to have been swallowed up by costs and fees, Kenge identifies Chancery's practice of legal fictions with the very respectability that Bentham reprehended in his invectives against Blackstone. Kenge explains to Allan Woodcourt

that this has been a great cause, that this has been a protracted cause, that this has been a complex cause. Jarndyce and Jarndyce has been termed, not inaptly, a Monument of Chancery practice. [. . . On] the numerous difficulties, contingencies, masterly fictions, and forms of procedure in this great cause, there has been expended study, ability, eloquence, knowledge, intellect, Mr Woodcourt, high intellect. For many years the – a – I would say the flower of autumnal fruits of the Woolsack – have been lavished upon Jarndyce and Jarndyce. If the public have the benefit, and if the country have the adornment, of this great Grasp, it must be paid for in money or money's worth. (*BH*, LXV, p. 923).

While Dickens here clearly suggests such legal practice as a profitable nexus of power and secrecy, within the novel's narrative panorama he insists, by insinuating that the details presented may be synecdoches in relation to an unrepresentable whole, on an undecidability between a home-made opacity regarding expectations and a conspiracy of lawyers and judges. For instance, the first two chapters, "In Chancery" and "In Fashion," share a certain sense of Protean mutability, which however is not rooted in nature, as in Proteus, but in artificial principles of the common law: "Both the world of fashion and the world of Chancery are things of precedent and usage" (*BH*, II, p. 55). The worlds of fashion and common law connect, in the eyes of the narrator, in some sort of a secret agreement or contract that helps silently to stabilize the power of aristocracy and legal elites – just like that silent "partnership" between "[m]onarch" and "lawyers" which we remember Bentham was determined to expose: "Monarch found force; lawyers, fraud: thus was the capital formed. [. . .] Whatever was the fraud thus practised, partners on both sides found their account in it: interests of both provided for of course."[51]

Secret mutability, however, is only one among several other metaphors of opacity. The fog around London's Inns of Court and the searing heat during the long summer vacation connect Chancery's secluded practices with the Dedlocks' isolated privacy on their estate Chesney Wold, "deadlocked" in a sultry haze forming after endless rainshowers. The sultry haze around Chesney Wold in turn recalls the sultry night Krook dies from Spontaneous Combustion, and Krook's dusty rag-and-bottle shop recalls the dust in Tulkinghorn's office.

To the extent that Dickens assembles details to insinuate an anonymous conspiracy, the characters who protest against their exclusion from the powers of justice begin to resemble one another in their isolation and anonymity. Whether they are drop-outs and objectors, or victims and martyrs of Chancery, it is their resistance which ironically seems to keep a corrupt legal system running. Tom Jarndyce's suicide in a London pub – apparently already an expression of revolt against something unknown to the reader – triggers the litigations about his will. For the parties involved, the will amounts to a curse, while the legal profession considers it a goldmine.

Tom's ominous legacy is also Richard Carstone's curse. For Richard is led to believe that Chancery's many victims are precedents for the "case" of his own life – the epitome of a monstrous Manichean antagonism.

[Richard] passes under the shadows of the Lincoln's Inn trees. On many such loungers have the speckled shadows of those trees often fallen; on the like bent head, the bitten nail, the lowering eye, the lingering step, the purposeless and dreamy air, the good consuming and consumed, the life turned sour. This lounger is not shabby yet, but that may come. Chancery, which knows no wisdom but in Precedent is very rich in such Precedents; and why should one be different from ten thousand? Yet the time is so short since his depreciation began, that as he saunters away, reluctant to leave the spot for some long months together, though he hates it, Richard himself may feel his own case as if it were a startling one. [. . .] But injustice breeds injustice; the fighting with shadows and being defeated by them, necessitates the setting up of substances to combat; from the impalpable suit which no man alive can understand, the time for that being long gone by, it has become a gloomy relief to turn to the palpable figure of the friend who would have saved him from this ruin, and make *him* his enemy. [. . . It] is a justification to him to have an embodied antagonist and oppressor. Is Richard a monster in all this – or would Chancery be found rich in such Precedents too, if they could be got for citation from the Recording Angel? (*BH*, xxxix, p. 612)

The Manichean polarity Richard creates between the legal profession and its "victims" results from what he suggests as an ominous reduplication of precedents over time. Dickens exemplifies such paranoic polarities in characters like Gridley and Krook, but particularly in Richard.

Richard's "antagonists" become the more threatening, the more he and the other objectors and drop-outs, who feel excluded from the legal system's benefits, begin to accept the problem that they can recognize their antagonists only by way of speculating about their plottings. Like their opponents, the excluded objectors and drop-outs thus connect details in the form of plots. Richard surmises that what Chancery presents him with may falsely resemble that which is really happening. Therefore, he becomes suspicious that such a dissimulation could be meant to prevent him from seeing what is actually going on. But he also seems to feel that this assumption is the same as the one on the basis of which his antagonists – provided they exist according to his Manichean polarity – wish Richard's paranoia operates – namely, that the discourse of law enacts doubles of what is really happening.

Richard's very intention to win against Chancery defines his own defeat. To protect himself against Chancery's staged doubles of what is really happening is to use the notion of "enemies" in order to define the possibility that a latent nexus of isolated details forms a structure of victimization. Thus he ultimately intends to justify the reality of his own suspicions. He crafts an identity for himself whose function is to maintain and preserve a Manichean polarity between objectors and their antagonists. This reduplication of suspicion may be slowed down only by eventually suspending any belief in such identities – that is, by addressing the paranoic structure itself. But Richard fails to replicate his antagonists' voices and simultaneously to deflect the purpose of that replication, as proposed by de Certeau,[52] from any formation of target-able identities. Consequently, he becomes at least as much a victim of his internalized Manicheanism as he believes himself to be a victim of Chancery's plottings.

In theory, law aims by its accumulation of practical wisdom through the inherited expectations of precedent and immemorial usage of rules to privilege the customary and the usual. In practice, it fosters the incalculable possibilities arising from the arbitrariness of an unfor-mulated body of cases. Attorney Vholes fails in trying to comfort his client Richard by advocating the benefits of the customary. Richard openly insists not only on an artificial but also "impatient" replication of his attorney's strategies to comfort him and thus makes himself vulnerable.

"A good deal is doing, sir. We have put our shoulders to the wheel, Mr Carstone, and the wheel is going round."

"Yes, with Ixion on it. How am I to get through the next four or five accursed months?" exclaims the young man, rising from his chair and walking about the room.

"Mr C," returns Vholes, following him closely with his eyes wherever he goes, "your spirits are hasty, and I am sorry for it on your account. Excuse me if I recommend you not to chafe so much, not to be so impetuous, not to wear yourself out so. You should have more patience. You should sustain yourself better."

"I ought to imitate you, in fact, Mr Vholes?" says Richard, sitting down again with an impatient laugh, and beating the Devil's Tattoo with his boot on the patternless carpet. [. . .]

"Mr Carstone, you are represented by –"

"You said just now – a rock." (*BH*, xxxix, pp. 607, 609)

Richard here attempts to usurp his attorney's power by projecting his own criticism in the place of the force he contemplates. By having Vholes call himself a "rock" (*BH*, xxxix, p. 608), Dickens somewhat associates Richard with Job, who wishes his complaint were a message carved on a rock and supposes a reader capable of speaking that complaint aloud. Richard similarly projects the possibility of his re-demption into such a face-to-face encounter between himself and other victimized characters, who are supposed to appropriate the force of the original "carving" of pain and suffering, to internalize it, and then express it as their own. Yet as he aspires to create some sort of a subjective continuity between objectors, he eventually mistakes this sublime expression of pain and suffering for a force independent of the subjective exchange of energy among "victims." Thus he can be said to mistake the sublime event for something representational – contrary to Kant's *caveat* that it cannot be made subject to mimesis.[53] Instead, he prefers to see it merely as a struggle between "victims" to articulate personal suffering in the first person, as well as a struggle between attorney and client to speak out for or against the power of law.

Richard turns himself into a hypersensitive detective who disconnects the law from the aspects of certainty and tranquillity that Vholes associates with the routines of everyday life. He assumes that the Hobbesian morality of lawyers – wolves concealed as humans – is the darkest of conspiracies that he must disclose. In this sense, he in fact works in the name of the law, in order to restore the reign of its principles of equity. Ironically, this objective causes him to act like an adventurous law-breaker in relation to what he perceives as officially recognized, and thus legal, conspiracies. What excites Richard in the early stages of this undertaking – that is, before suffering begins to define his excitement – is the pathos with which he is able to combine the subject-positions of the outlaw and the self-appointed judge in matters of equity. In comparison to this pathos, the lawyers which he targets as criminals appear like indolent bureaucrats and careful conservators of boredom. The true adventure, which renders all the other jobs that he rejected a waste of time, is the defense of the law itself – as if every other particular crime were a petty crime.

Richard's attempt at challenging the rules of established law reveals, in an almost Hegelian sense, that the opposition between the law and its transgressions repeats itself inside the evolution of positive law itself. Yet he refuses to accept this revelation to the extent that he begins to understand that he cannot help but disclose it. He learns from the behavior of judges and lawyers that the validity of the law they administer rests on the general assumption that what makes law universal is its opposition to crime. Since such a notion of law would be an empty scheme unless filled with the content provided by particular crimes, the law will change according to how it reconciles changing definitions of crimes with its universal opposition to crime. This process, Richard believes, also reshuffles the relations of principles and precedents in the "case" of his own life. What makes a crime a crime depends on the way positive law generates from the strangeness it ascribes to particular crimes its own validity as the institutionalized normality of universalizing crime. He suspects that the law determines the negative force of a particular crime according to how it universalizes crimes in order to define its own validity.

More importantly, it appears to Richard that positive law results, in the final analysis, from the dominant views on how particular crimes are said to negate the universality of the law. He concludes that law dominates crime when it converts all individual crimes into mere particular crimes. What he experiences in Chancery epitomizes for him an abstract law without particular content, a law that is generally opposed to crimes but also itself a supreme crime in that it dominates, in the absence of public debate, the rules for naming absolute contradictions between law and crime. By emphasizing the universal at the expense of the particular, Richard recognizes, Chancery fails to live up to its institutional task – to protect the very particularity of exceptional circumstances Blackstone identified as the law of equity, "which is thus defined by Grotius, 'the correction of that, wherein the law (by reason of its *universality*) is deficient.' . . . There should be somewhere a power vested of excepting those circumstances which (had they been foreseen) the legislator himself would have excepted."[54]

To the extent that he decides to align his personal interests with a "corrective" restoration of equity, Richard remains trapped in a struggle with his own cynical wisdom that the power of positive law fundamentally remains a form of radical "violence." He must obey its "force" regardless of his subjective appreciation. What Richard experiences but fails to articulate as "something rotten in law," regarding the universalized relation between law and crime, is essentially what Jacques Derrida, in his reading of Walter Benjamin's "Critique of Violence," calls a "differential contamination" between the positing and conserving of legal authority:

[T]he very violence of the foundation or position of law (*Rechtsetzende Gewalt*) must envelop the violence of conservation (*Rechtserhaltende Gewalt*) and cannot break with it. It belongs to the structure of fundamental violence that it calls for the repetition of itself and founds what ought to be conserved, conservable, promised to heritage and tradition, to be shared.[55]

Other characters perpetuate the Manicheanism of Richard's expectations even to the point where they believe they are helping him. John

Jarndyce, for instance, suspects the legacy of the case to be so threatening that for him death outweighs the false benefits of resistance: "'Rick, Rick! [. . .] don't found a hope of expectation on the family curse! Whatever you do on this side the grave, never give one lingering glance towards the horrible phantom that has haunted us so many years. Better to borrow, better to beg, better to die!'" (*BH*, xxiv, p. 393). Incidentally, Richard at one point wishes he were dead (*BH*, xlv, p. 677), because he feels his life has been "'ruined by a fatal inheritance'" (*BH*, lx, p. 881). Nevertheless, he rejects John's advice and thus ironically finds death by challenging, not avoiding the "phantom." John's recommendation perpetuates Richard's Manicheanism in that it antagonizes the family curse with the promise of redemptive death.

By juxtaposing Richard's and John's gothic interpretations of the case, Dickens can examine the psychology of apocalyptic overtones exhibited in his characters' experience of the uncanny. Readers are already familiar with the figure of apocalypse from the way Miss Flite associates the Lord Chancellor's Great Seal of England with St. John's vision of the broken sixth seal in *Revelations* VI 12. In making such a comparison, she juxtaposes the earthly injustices of metaphorical incarceration with a liberation from Jarndyce and Jarndyce in redemptive death (*BH*, iii, pp. 81–2, v, pp. 98, 104–5, xiv, p. 251, xxxv, pp. 553–4).

When it turns out that the estate in dispute has been swallowed up by costs, Richard issues one last cry of sick pain before he collapses in silence: "On being roused" by Allan, who finds him "sitting in the corner of the Court [. . .] like a stone figure," "he had broken away, and made as if he would have spoken in a fierce voice to the Judge. He was stopped by his mouth being full of blood [. . .]" (*BH*, lxv, p. 924). From that point on until the moment he asks Ada and John for forgiveness (*BH*, lxv, pp. 925ff), he no longer claims justice under a known law. Until the language of Esther and his other comforters tranquillizes his inarticulate pain by means of a sentimentalist code of sympathy, he no longer measures his ruin inside a narrative of success and failure, nor attempts to render his experience in a probable form in order to normalize it. His choking voice leaves no room for articulating the precedents of suffering and consolation that his comforters are later going to construct for him. In the eyes of his observers, he even threatens to scramble the axiomatic systems of appeal in a singular and uncoded form of insurrection, quite similar to what Gilles Deleuze and Felix Guattari call "schizo-flow."[56]

For this brief period, Richard retreats from all codes of redemption and lapses into what Julia Kristeva calls an "asymbolia" of mourning: "[A]ll translatability [has] become impossible. Melancholia then ends up in asymbolia, in loss of meaning: if I am no longer capable of translating or metaphorizing, I become silent and I die."[57] Richard's collapse occurs precisely at the point where he can no longer translate loss into communicable forms. Nor can he choose a refuge from a circular logic of legal practices justified through themselves – a logic with which Chancery appears to protect the authority of the norms it enacts.

Gridley's redemptive death and Krook's Spontaneous Combustion are two other examples of how Dickens connects the paranoic antagonism between the initiated and the excluded with the antagonism between phantoms of death-in-life and redemptive death.[58] Gridley ultimately seeks redemption from the suffering over injustices he believes Chancery inflicted on him. Krook's more radical gesture of resistance recalls Tom Jarndyce's suicide. Krook attempts to escape the very business of judges and lawyers that he ironically represents as a self-appointed alternative Lord Chancellor. Nonetheless, his death articulates only one among many other instances of how the "family curse" that John cautioned Richard about extends across generations and classes. To the extent that he operates as the real Lord Chancellor's double, he merely modifies Richard's Manichean antagonism between objectors and their "enemies."

Eventually, Krook's death connects Tom Jarndyce's ominous legacy with the inheritance he himself leaves behind for the Smallweeds. In fact, when they take over his shop, in the absence of a will that would determine proper legal succession between Krook and his only sister, Mrs Smallweed (*BH*, xxxiii, pp. 519–23), they exhibit and perpetuate the same sarcastic obsession with other people's belongings that they themselves reprehended in him as well as in Guppy and Weevle. And they continue to do so until Bucket unearths from the piles of Krook's unburnt documents a new will which favors Smallweed and forebodes the end of the case (*BH*, lxii, pp. 894–901).

Lady Dedlock's family curse goes back to yet another antagonism between life and death – an antagonism that is associated with both Richard's and John's, as well as Tom Jarndyce's curse to the parties to the case. The Dedlock family legend of the "Ghost's Walk" suggests this antagonism as a cross-generational exchange between life and death: "'I will die here where I have walked. And I will walk here, though I am in my grave. I will walk here, until the pride of this house is humbled. And when calamity, or when disgrace is coming to it, let the Dedlocks listen to my step'" (*BH*, VII, p. 141). Lady Dedlock is possessed by the curse of Chesney Wold, but cannot possess it or own it as her own property. She cannot claim or enter upon this particular inheritance, which makes its appearance in the form of a labyrinth full of ominous connections and resonances: "A labyrinth of grandeur, less the property of an old family of old human beings and their ghostly likenesses, than of an old family of echoings and thunderings which start out of their hundred graves at every sound, and go resounding through the building. A waste of unused passages and staircases [. . .]" (*BH*, LXVI, p. 931). The Dedlocks' "ghostly stories" eventually also hit upon Tulkinghorn, who sought to gain profit from the family curse, "with a deadly meaning" (*BH*, XLVIII, p. 721). Thus the family curse of Chesney Wold can also be associated with the practice of legal fictions, which Blackstone likened to a "gothic castle," whose "inferior apartments, now accommodated to daily use, are cheerful and commodious, though their approaches may be winding and difficult"(*CLE*, III, p. 268).

Esther in turn interprets the disquieting legacy of her parentage, whose facts she initially withholds from the reader, as a labyrinth of resonances from the "Ghost's Walk." Unrelentingly staging self-nega-tion and self-sacrifice, she projects her mother's sense of guilt onto herself: "[. . .] my echoing footsteps brought it suddenly into my mind that there was a dreadful truth in the legend of the Ghost's Walk; that it was I, who was to bring calamity upon the stately house; and that my warning feet were haunting it even then." A force beyond the scope of her memory keeps pulling her back to the curse: "Seized with aug-mented terror of myself which turned me cold, I ran from myself and everything, retraced the way by which I had come [. . .]" (*BH*, XXXVI, p. 571).

Together with Ada and Richard, Esther is a "ward in Chancery." Being part of the case as the Lord Chancellor's ward exposes her to the equally uncanny legacy of the proceedings themselves. What the Lord Chancellor promises her in the homely terms of institutional protection is always on the verge of turning into metaphorical incarceration – "'incarcerated" in the very case that is supposed to guarantee her rights (retroping the mechanism of Civil Death), and subjected to the paternal judgment of the very Lord Chancellor who is supposed to protect the exercise of her judgment (retroping the mechanism of Substituted Judgment). The wards are in continuous danger of becoming puppets in

Chancery's procedural games with fictions. This is why Miss Flite compares them to her caged birds (*BH*, xxxv, p. 555) and, in doing so, emphasizes the incarceration trope: "'I call them [i.e. her birds] the Wards in Jarndyce. They are caged up with all the others'" (*BH*, LX, p. 875). To be a "ward in Jarndyce" is thus to be metaphorically incarcerated with respect to claiming Chancery's legacy of distributing equitable justice – a legacy dispatched, commissioned, and dictated to the case's parties in uncanny ways, while to external observers Jarndyce and Jarndyce seems merely about private claims to property, intended to "bring home" an inheritance.

WHAT IT MEANS TO INHERIT A LEGACY OF PROPRIETORIAL EXCHANGE

We remember that in Civil Death, real incarceration connected metaphorical death with a forfeiture of inheritance due to "corruption of blood." We also remember that if a potential testator had no capability or right reason to articulate an intention concerning his or her will, Substituted Judgment entitled the equity court judge paternally to administrate both the fortune and the intention underlying that will. It is thus not hard to see how closely the practice of legal fictions was associated with what was considered a controversial practice of property transfer.

Sparsely mentioned in the books of feudal law, the rules of property law became a bone of contention along with the expansion of national trade. Blackstone, for instance, treated property in terms of natural law, but the transfer of property purely in terms of civil law (*CLE*, II, pp. 6–8, 12–13). He argued that increasingly complex property relations required a more complex application of legal fictions, as opposed to legislative simplicity, that would be capable of accounting for the complex relationship between civil liberty and the security of property (*CLE*, III, pp. 266, 325–7, 423–4). We have already seen that Blackstone, by emphasizing this line of argument, dodges the question concerning moral justifications of legal complexity, which is so crucial for Bentham.

Perrin v. *Blake*, a property case lasting from 1758 to 1777, can serve to illustrate some of the typical problems that questions of property transfer caused in common-law practice.[59] At first, the court followed the testator's intention, "'that none of my children shall sell or dispose of my estate for a longer time than his life.'"[60] Whenever intentions were formulated as ambiguously as in this case, the courts usually constructed the testator's intention in his or her favor. However, if an intention's technical flaws turned out to be unlawful to begin with, the courts tended to apply standard rules to perpetuate the certainty of property law. "Unfortunately in the case of English law, these standard rules for interpreting devises had been formulated as part of the elaborate web of legal fictions through which the courts had gradually extended the individual's power to alienate property. As a result, they were enormously complex and technical, if not entirely unintelligible to the uninitiated."[61] The "rule in Shelley's case" was such a rule, which was initially applied in *Perrin* v. *Blake*. "According to that rule, the son received the estate as a tenant in tail in possession. He thereby enjoyed effective power to alienate the estate as he pleased, in violation of the testator's intention to limit his powers over the estate to his own lifetime."[62]

The "rule in Shelley's case" had its origin in the idea to prevent the evasion of feudal dues. From the sixteenth century it was used to interpret rules that helped to facilitate the alienation of property. Initially, it prevented the testator's intention in *Perrin* v. *Blake* from being effected. When the case came before King's Bench in 1769, Chief Justice Mansfield decided against Shelley's rule and for the testator's intention. Blackstone, however, when in 1772 the case came before Exchequer Chamber, where he was a judge in the court of Common Pleas, reversed Mansfield's judgment, pointing out the precedents that stood against that decision.

In terms of these arguments the decisions of the two courts occupied rather narrow legal ground. What was disputed was whether the testator had recorded his intentions with sufficient clarity, both courts accepting that if this had been achieved, the intention was to override the relevant rule of construction. But in support of their rulings, the two courts also addressed other questions. They raised more general issues regarding the relationship between precedents and principles, and highlighted the divergent implications of an historical understanding of England's legal inheritance.[63]

The questions concerning property transfer in *Perrin* v. *Blake* thus also represent "England's legal inheritance." The validity of how judges formed legal rules appeared to depend on whether principles or precedents were given preference in the process. Such a vacillation simultaneously defined the reformist and conservative positions of Mansfield and Blackstone. At the bottom of this particular problem of property transfer was the question as to whether the common law was in need of reform or sufficiently flexible.

If Lieberman is right in describing this question as "England's legal inheritance," then any application of rules concerning the legal problematic of bequeathing and inheriting property emerges as a way of troping the tensions underlying the official administration of that problem. Civil Death and Substituted Judgment exemplify that very troping of inheritance. Their mechanisms do represent the inherited tensions underlying the administration of rules for property transfer. But they may also be used as tools to influence and manipulate the problems of "England's legal inheritance" – the tension between principles and precedents. Like Civil Death, Substituted Judgment brackets certain rights, particularly those concerning the transfer of property, and specifically by means of substituting intentions. The metaphorical death of real incarceration in the case of Civil Death corresponds to the suspended right, in the case of Substituted Judgment, legally to enter upon an inheritance. The substitution of rights is the effect of a metaphor, which translates actions by proxy into an exchange of intentions and literally affects, in the course of that operation, legal premises of property transfer.

The observation that these legal fictions are both causes of and responses to legal and ethical problems of property transfer becomes even more important when compared to another observation. Both common-law theorists such as Hume and positivists such as Bentham considered legal notions of property to be crucial for the exercise of justice. In Hume and Bentham, Blackstone's opposition against Mansfield in terms of "England's legal inheritance" of principles and precedents "returns" on the level of legal theory.

Hume describes justice as rules which define property. For him, justice has to establish and guarantee the stability of all social interaction. That stability rests on the stability of possession of material goods and precedes all criminal law.[64] He supports this point, which itself is not particularly convincing, by a double premise: first, sympathy is the basic principle of all passions; and second, custom and opinion are the two basic principles of the formation of judgment in social interaction.[65] In *Principles of the Civil Code*, Bentham similarly believes property to be inseparable from law. He believes property to be an accepted fiction in the sense of an artificial and conventionally defined relation between persons and a thing. For him, that fiction is identical with established expectations, not merely maximized utility (*Bowring*, 1, pp. 308–9). Civil law creates definitions of such expectations where they are missing or secures and corroborates expectations by clarifying, codifying, and making publicly accessible the ones that already exist (*Bowring*, I, p. 323). Hume insists on criteria for the usage of legal conventions, such as custom and opinion, that may be historically differentiated. In contrast, Bentham requires legislation to effect a more just distribution of affluence according to established expectations (*Bowring*, I, pp. 312–16).

Along the lines of Bentham's argument, Mill believes that the power of bequest, as opposed to the right of inheritance, derives from the idea of private property founded on labor. This idea, which for Mill does not include donations or transfers at death, requires restrictions in the interest of distributive justice.[66] Therefore, he argues that even the power of bequest could be limited if its exercise conflicts with the interests of utility or social welfare, to which end he thinks property ought to be only a means, but not itself the end. As a consequence, he is concerned to limit the right of inheritance.[67] He prefers that the law restrict, not what a person might bequeath, but what anyone should be permitted to acquire by bequest or inheritance.

The problem of property transfer in legal discourse, which Mill discusses in terms of inheritance and bequest, emerges in Dickens's literary discourse as the aforementioned ethical symptom of a crisis of expectations. Both discourses are concerned with the literal transfer of property. This concern is reflected in the philosophical (Hume, Bentham) and practical (Blackstone, Mansfield) debates, on the one hand, and the battle of interpretations over Tom Jarndyce's will, on the other. Both discourses are also concerned with metaphorical notions of property transfer. That second concern is reflected in the battle over the validity of principles and precedents in the formation of legal rules, on the one hand, and the association of a mysterious legacy of England's Bleak House – the two nations – with wills and family curses, on the other.

In their judicial discourse, Blackstone and Mansfield emphasize the literal dimension of property transfer. They do so in order to translate theoretical problems into practical solutions. In his literary discourse, Dickens focuses upon the impact of property transfer as a trope. He does so, for instance by suggesting a case as a curse, in order to interweave symptoms of a legal crisis with a crisis in terms of expectations. Nonetheless, at no point does Dickens disconnect the trope of property transfer from its legal "sources," for instance when Richard's metaphorical view of the case as a curse causes him even more legal consequences, or when detective Bucket "seems imperceptibly to establish a dreadful right of property in Mademoiselle [Hortense]" (*BH*, LIV, p. 797). Numerous characters in *Bleak House* are legally connected in terms of debt and credit.[68] Furthermore, this connection extends to the nexus of legal and sexual tensions in marriage contracts.[69] Dickens certainly does not satisfy the ethical imperative to solve these problems legally. But he also refuses to detach the crisis of expectations from the crisis in legal practice.

After the Great Exhibition of 1851, property became more exhibition-ist. The growing industries of advertising developed forms of representa-tion that helped to integrate merchandise in the context of public spectacles.[70] One particular aspect of the crisis concerning expectations about property transfer was the growing perception in mid-Victorian England that property has important imaginary characteristics. The slowly increasing awareness, at the end of the eighteenth century, of mobile and imaginary property such as the public debt[71] was an early indication that property which is fit to circulate in the market is ever more likely to be parted from its owner. Loss of property was thus merely one particular version of a property transfer that follows econ-omic laws more and more situated beyond the domain of human error, accident, or greed. The potential collusion of economical and non-economical practices in what Pierre Bourdieu calls a general "economy of practices"[72] was also a threat to everyone bent on owning property alone.

This form of anxiety is also crucial in determining the behavior of many parties to Jarndyce and Jarndyce, who believe they are on the verge of becoming "exchange parties" to the anticipated income flowing from an asset whose status nevertheless remains obscure. The estate in ques-tion may be expected to change the hands of legitimate owners. But as long as the income that is expected to flow from it varies unpredictably, the legal determination of ownership, as well as of the estate's value in exchange, is also affected by the economic incentives of the parties to contest its ownership status. Yoram Barzel has pointed out more gen-erally that rights to an asset are often impaired to the extent that the flow of income to be derived from it can vary and/or be predicted:

When the flow of income from an asset may be affected by the exchange parties, ensuring ownership over it is problematic. When the income stream is variable and not fully predictable, it is costly to determine whether the flow is what it should have been in any particular case. Consequently it is also costly to determine whether part of the income stream has been captured by the exchange parties. The exchange parties will engage in wealth-consuming capture activities because they expect to gain from them. The delineation of ownership is problematic, then, when the income stream from the exchanged property is subject to random fluctuations and when both parties can gain from affecting that income stream.[73]

When Dickens employs the many instances of tragic death in *Bleak House*, they either end claims to property or end possession by way of bestowal or other forms of legal transfer. He generates views on the irresistible trajectories that inhere in his characters' compulsion to own. The characters do not seem to resist the ubiquitous circulation of property so much as attempt to get a share of the power to bestow it. Mill suggests that the desire to bestow is at the heart of the human drive towards self-extension: "The ownership of a thing cannot be looked upon as complete without the power of bestowing it, at death or during life, at the owner's pleasure: and all the reasons, which recommend that private property should exist, recommend pro tanto this extension of it."[74] Mill thus implicitly acknowledges that the privacy of ownership is closely associated with both the filial and public aspects of how property may be alienated. Yet he does not explore the question as to whether there inheres in the power to bestow a compulsion to do so.

While Dickens does address that question in *Bleak House*, he avoids reducing the compulsive power to bestow to a narrative representation of capitalism's death drive. One example is the novel's fairy-tale ending. John Jarndyce "alienates" Esther to Allan Woodcourt in just the way Mill summarizes, in *The Subjection of Women* of 1869, Victorian marriage relations as a form of (the husband's) private ownership: "'Allan,' said my guardian, 'take from me a willing gift, the best wife that ever man had. What more can I say for you, than that I know you deserve her! Take with her the little home she brings you'" (*BH*, LXIV, p. 915). The way a husband or guardian holds on to a wife or ward like a treasure that eludes circulations of property in excess of his expectations ironically confirms the increased unpredictability of property transfer under positive law. In the final chapter, Esther discloses how she and Allan have for seven years been cultivating their new Bleak House like a treasure (*BH*, LXVII, pp. 932ff), clearly in order to fend off the haunting legacy of the old one.

In contrast, Lady Dedlock appears to break with this culturally typical affinity between the circulation and possession of women. As soon as the truth about Esther's parentage is in danger of being publicized, Lady Dedlock feels that she can escape punishment for her affair with Captain Nemo only by radically escaping the symbolic order of deadlocked wedlock – and having to declare herself, according to its logic, an "'unworthy woman'" (*BH*, LV, p. 816). Dickens portrays her as breaking the chain of alienability, but at the price of resembling characters like Gridley, Krook, or Richard. Their deaths render questionable the redemptive fiction of death as the myth of an exchange free from alienation.

By having Lady Dedlock fail in trying to achieve earthly redemption, Dickens implies that her very efforts to turn her life away from society's exchanges of vanity reveal her yearning for redemption as tainted. In fact, redemption can be seen as a potential surplus value that may be obtained in return for attempting to escape the logic of surplus value. Lady Dedlock confesses to Esther, "'I have long *outbidden* folly with folly, pride with pride, scorn with scorn, insolence with insolence, and have *outlived* many vanities with many more. I will *outlive* this danger, and *outdie* it, if I can'" (*BH*, XXXVI, p. 567, my emphasis). Dickens illustrates the gains and losses anticipated in this resolution by having her contrast the total commensurability of exchangeable vanities ("outbid" and "outlive") with a redemptive remainder that is supposed to resist incorporation into the circulation of passions and interests ("outlive" and "outdie"). However, he is careful in letting her use the word "outlive" for both the sphere of total commensurability and that of resistance to it.

Thus effectively questioning the odds of breaking the chain of alienability, Dickens renders Lady Dedlock instead as ambiguously unable or unwilling to "repay" the "moral mortgage" of her history that "conveyed" title and class identity to her. While creating such an ambiguous effect, he may have been aware that this very ambiguity in fact existed in the contemporary language of mortgages. In fact, "equity of redemption" was a traditional economic pattern of debt in Victorian England.

Legal mortgage was the most common lender's tenure. In return for a loan, the full title was conveyed to the mortgagee. The deed specified repayment in six month's time, and after this had elapsed, the lender could call the loan in, subject to three months' notice. The borrower was entitled to repay the loan and regain his title at any time, subject to six months' notice or a fine of six months' interest in lieu. This right, the "equity of redemption," was itself a marketable tenure and its value was the difference between the market price of the property and the outstanding value of the loan. Custom limited the advance to two-thirds of the estimated value of the property; if the market value declined below the amount of the loan, the "equity of redemption" became negative and the borrower lost the incentive to repay.[75]

In variation of the standard Victorian plot of hidden or stolen estates, revealed or returned at last to their former owners, Esther's class identity is finally disclosed to her by the mother who was concealing it. While Esther's inheritance is restored, Lady Dedlock's lack of duty is not repaired. All the more is Esther, who at first also conceals knowledge about her inheritance from the reader, determined to assume that sense of duty by resurrecting the legacy of ownership. Along with the new Bleak House, she inherits Tom Jarndyce's lost will as her mother's "lost" will to assume the duty to act in response to the family curse.

By translating the legal context of "will" into a psychological one, Esther restores a sense of domestic mastery over her uncanny legacy. She thus positions her compulsion to "own" the family legacy as the product as well as the cause of possession. Her impulse to chart the unmapped curse that defined her even before she consciously "inherited" it takes shape as a ritual of possession, a recovery of sacred property that forms the sentimental centerpiece of obligations "stolen" by corrupt lawyers and other such illegitimate "conquerors." She recovers the obligations that her mother's class-defined nobility betrayed by reviving a sphere of the domestic, which she identifies, as we have seen, with a "nobility in the soul[s]" (*BH*, xxxvi, p. 562) of the laboring poor.

Esther holds on to her domesticated family curse as something that seems to have assumed a subjective value above the level of exchange value. She attempts to withhold it from the circulation of goods or exchange of gifts. Annette Weiner calls such possessions, which are intended to authenticate the authority of their owner in order to affect all other transactions, "inalienable possessions [that] are kept by their owners from one generation to the next within the closed context of family, descent group, or dynasty." Following Bateson's cybernetic formulation of schismogenesis, Weiner argues that in situations ruled by norms of reciprocity throughout Western history, there is frequently a "governor" at work in order to prevent

the constant giving and receiving in an exchange or ritual event from spinning out of control. In fact, inalienable possessions that groups or individuals hold dear to them act as that governor. Inalienable possessions do not just control the dimensions of giving, but their historicities retain for the future, memories, either fabricated or not, of the past. Not always attainable, keeping some things transcendent and out of circulation in the face of all the pressures to give them to others is a burden, a responsibility, and at best, a skillful achievement.[76]

Esther's "skillful achievement" consists of two related operations. First, she protects herself from the "dark vision" that the Bleak House of England's family curses may be the "governor" of her sentimental projects, that is to say, the "Other" ruling all her interactions with others. Second, she protects herself from the curse that defines her compulsion to "own" the family legacy by means of optimistically practicing sympathetic intercourse as a form of unconditioned reciprocity of sentiments. This very "paradox of keeping-while-giving" (Weiner) allows Esther to make effective differences in terms of contradictions. To the extent that she remains unaware of the paradox which informs her determination to make the world a better place, those contradictions may also remain unimprovable within the normative framework of tautology[77] that defines the circular logic of Chancery's self-justification. Only by remaining unaware of "the temporal and functional limits of reproduction"[78] can she effectively balance the opportunities and questions of legitimacy that she inherits.

Esther affirms and Lady Dedlock challenges the notion of the domestic as a valid form of readjusting expectations to the vicissitudes of property transfer. Different as their choices may be, both respond to the repercussions that their own disappointed expectations have on them with measures of closure – reformed domesticities, redemptive interiorities, and fantasies of anticipated conclusions to the complexity of proprietorial exchange. Their actions may fail in trying to transcend the exigencies of freely circulating property. But by presenting them as two among several alternative actions, Dickens allows us to contemplate their struggle with complicity in terms of our own: The cathartic effects generated by Esther's and Lady Dedlock's stories may, but need not, resemble the "surplus value" that the "labor" of reading a bleak story about unpredictable circulation gains in excess of its "exchange value." In other words, Dickens juxtaposes forms of (Esther's) domestic and (Lady Dedlock's) redemptive closure in order to indicate that such responses may be implicated, but need not be "deadlocked" in what they seem to oppose. To create this effect, however, Dickens has to employ the notion of property transfer as a trope that itself circulates among responses to crises of legal practices and crises of expectations.

The point about Civil Death and Substituted Judgment is that they are both based, as I have indicated throughout, on the tension between literal and metaphorical transfers of property. In Civil Death, we remember, a felon literally loses his or her right to inherit and bequeath and metaphorically inherits from his or her "precursors" the classification "corruption of blood" as the law's legacy of social death. In Substituted Judgment, an "incompetent," having "suspended" the capability to articulate or formulate a will, literally cannot bequeath. He or she thus puts the judge in a position to use the incompetent's body as the metaphor of a property to be administered and alienated by the court.

Both legal fictions can be used to manipulate established relations between death and inheritance. Such possibilities to manipulate standards of ownership by means of declaring death may not be unrelated to the curious common-law rule, mentioned by Blackstone, that "'stealing the corpse itself, which has no owner (though a matter of great indecency), is no felony.'"[79] Civil Death and Substituted Judgment allow judges and lawyers to use death as a trope so that they can reinterpret literal inheritance. Their mechanisms differ from philosophical discourse in that they serve to shift the legal authority over such reinterpretations of testators' or legislators' intentions without being publicly monitored. They differ from literary discourse in that they do not allow the use of inheritance as a trope.

Characters like Richard and Lady Dedlock come close to being considered "socially dead" before the case eventually causes their literal deaths. They "incarcerate" their lives in some sort of a metaphorical Civil Death. They also seek to restore what they feel is "proper" to them, but what was "stolen" from them as a property "alienated" by both a case and a curse. On this level, they impose closure upon their own experiences of contingency. Richard's and Lady Dedlock's imagination attempts to recover a sense of authority from the circulation of alienable property. Their imagination operates in ways that put both in line with those lawyers who apply legal fictions in questions of property transfer, as well as those philanthropists who exchange the gift of benevolence for their recipients' character formation, in order to reproduce their own authority. Similar to the professional determination of lawyers and the missionary zeal of philanthropists, Richard's paranoia and Lady Dedlock's longing for redemption establish "an *arbitrary boundary*" against what both of them experience as an intransitive quality of circulation, a boundary which Bourdieu likens to rites of institution, "by fostering a misrecognition of the arbitrary nature of the limit and encouraging a recognition of it as legitimate."[80]

The notion of property transfer thus adds a specifically legal nuance to the incarceration trope. In their literal sense, property transfer and incarceration are connected in terms of a strictly legal causality: you may get incarcerated *because* you are found to have violated rules of property transfer. Yet in both the practice of legal fictions and in literary discourse, property transfer and incarceration may be used as tropes. This connection becomes most apparent whenever tropes of property transfer and incarceration that are used in the practice of legal fictions make their entry into Dickens's literary discourse.

IS THERE SUCH A THING AS EQUITABLE UNNATURAL DEATH?

Real incarceration in Chancery's prison is Dickens's concern long before he depicts Richard and Lady Dedlock as metaphorical inmates of Chancery. Incarceration has the effect of imposing on life an anticipation of death and thus, in a strange sense, "recalls" metaphorical uses of Civil Death. Pickwick, for instance, encounters a Chancery inmate, "[who] had been there long enough to have lost friends, fortune, home, and happiness, [. . .] the iron teeth of confinement and privation had been slowly filing him down for twenty years. [. . .] 'I am a dead man; dead to society, without the pity they bestow on those whose souls have passed to judgment' [. . .]."[81] This enforcement of isolation, which in legal terms is based on "corruption of blood," amounts to the inmate's concrete isolation from family and kinship. The prison scenes in *The Pickwick Papers* certainly refer to a widespread experience of misery in contemporary prisons.[82] But Dickens also uses them to point to the damages Chancery has inflicted on local enclaves of sympathy. The elements of dysfunctional family life that characterize the Dedlocks, Pardiggles, Turveydrops, and Smallweeds illustrate this type of damage.

Consequently, in Dickens's depiction of anticipated death in the prison scenes of *The Pickwick Papers*, "corruption of blood" becomes itself a metaphor. Incarceration is no longer merely the legal response to felony, which severs blood relations by means of prison walls as well as by suspending the inmate's right to inherit and bequeath. Isolation also turns into a symptom of how Chancery damages family life. Similarly, the social dimension of *Bleak House* suggests a metaphor of the family for the two nations, a philanthropic force threatened by Chancery: "Innumerable children have been born into the cause; innumerable young people have married into it; innumerable old peole have died out of it. Scores of persons have deliriously found themselves made parties in Jarndyce and Jarndyce, without knowing the how or why; whole families have inherited legendary hatreds with the suit" (*BH*, 1, p. 52).

The isolation of Chancery inmates becomes a metaphor of the isolation of those outside Chancery prisons who cannot seem to connect or bond. The metaphor of this form of existence is once more derived from the legal semantics of Civil Death: Incarcerated for twenty years, one prisoner "had grown so like death in life that they knew not when he died."[83] Death-in-life is the metaphor of a deprivation of certain legal and moral "rights" inside and outside of prisons. It may suggest a moral right to universal sympathy. But Dickens does not seem to formulate such a right in *Bleak House*.

Instead, Dickens acknowledges the complexity of metaphorical incarceration, as Arac argues, by subjecting its articulation to different idioms. Dickens uses the sociomedical idiom of professionals and specialists such as Allan, which makes the danger of infection in slums transparent, in order to prevent the gothic idiom, for instance of Krook, from petrifying in the apocalyptic idiom of otherworldly redemption, for instance that of Miss Flite.[84] His narrative panorama of sociomedical and satanic aspects of mid-Victorian life thus establishes, according to Arac, connections between experiences inside and outside of prisons.[85] One example is the *Household-Words* article "In and Out of Jail" of 1853, in which Dickens parallels poverty and incarceration in terms of inspection.

The governor is to his jail as the physician is to his hospital. Knowledge must be coherently organized by "classification" in order for proper action to be taken. Prisons must be seen not as "so many disconnected undertakings" but as "all parts of one great whole." In order to know this totality, "we must mount with the aid of a good spirit to the highest tower in the jails"; we must let this beneficent Asmodeus unroof the houses for us and show us "how the people live, and toil, and die." For "without a just consideration for every humble figure in the great panorama" we will not properly know how to administer prisons.[86]

In his speeches on public health held around the time *Bleak House* was published, Dickens uses the notion of panoramic vision as a synekdoche, Arac claims, for the ways prisons ought to be organized by means of centralization and inspection. He concedes, however, that in *Bleak House* itself, Dickens permanently interrupts panoramic narration.[87] On the one hand, the gothic idiom connects notions of architecture and character in the Bleak House of England. On the other hand, the scientific idiom translates apocalyptic interpretations of infection and death into sociomedical progress. Yet Dickens refrains from assembling both idioms in a way that would impose on the novel's social dimension the kind of coherence which his article in *Houseword Words* presupposes as a given. In the novel, he still presents the multifaceted dangers of death, which sociohygienic achievements since the Cholera epidemics of 1830–32 and 1848–49 should have been able to reduce, as something uncanny.[88] The differences that Dickens maintains between redemptive and detectivist approaches to misery continue to prevent tensions between literal and metaphorical death from being reduced to symptoms of a moral cholera in Victorian England.

In 1850, Dickens published an article in *Household Words*, titled "The Martyrs of Chancery," which emphasized the bitter lot of those incarcerated due to "contempt of court."[89] In his study *Charles Dickens as a Legal Historian* of 1928, William Holdsworth found the injustices attacked in this article reminiscent of the ways Bentham proposed to revise the common law. But he also argued that the attacks were anachronistic, given that they were published in 1850. Holdsworth believed that Lord Lyndhurst, who followed upon Lord Eldon, the inventor of Substituted Judgment, served as the historical model for Dickens's Lord Chancellor in *Bleak House* – which would have the novel take place in 1827. He mentioned a letter by Sir Edward Sudgen, later Lord St. Leonards, written in response to the article. Sudgen considered the attacks outdated, basically because of the reforms he himself initiated.

However, Trevor Blount has convincingly shown that in the late 1840s, legal practice was still considerably lagging behind reformist intentions.[90] Thus "The Martyrs of Chancery" correctly pointed to the law's shortcomings. As late as 1850, the *Westminster Review* complained about endless procrastinations of cases and the horrendous costs resulting from them. Gridley's case, for instance, was based on the famous Challinor case of 1849, a case about a problematic transfer of property that made equity courts rich. The famous Jennings case, which began in 1798 and which was about a missing will needed to transfer enormous amounts of property, lasted eighty years before a legitimate heir was determined. Similarly, K. J. Fielding and Alec Brice demonstrated that the character of Jo the crossing-sweeper was based on the real George Ruby, specifically in connection with the equally disturbing case against Thomas Hall in 1848–49. They suspect that Dickens wrote an article published in the *Examiner*, whose author explicitly identifies with Bentham's complaints, in *The Rationale of Judicial Evidence*, about the contemporary practice of common law.[91]

The author of "The Martyrs of Chancery" comments on that practice, which in 1850 still seemed a cause for alarm:

A Chancery prisoner is, in fact, a far more hopeless mortal than a convict sentenced to transportation; [. . .] he may, and frequently does, waste a lifetime in the walls of a gaol, whither he was sent in innocence; because, perchance, he had the ill-luck to be one of the next of kin of some testator who made a will which no one could comprehend, or the heir of some intestate who made none.

Any other party interested in the estate commences a Chancery suit, which he must defend or be committed to prison for "contempt." A prison is his portion, whatever he does; for if he answers the bill filed against him, and cannot pay the costs, he is also clapped in gaol for "contempt." [. . .] Whoever is pronounced guilty of contempt in a Chancery sense is taken from his family, his profession, or his trade (perhaps his sole means of livelihood), and consigned to a gaol where he must starve, or live on a miserable pittance [. . .]. A popular fallacy spreads a notion that no one need to "go into Chancery" unless he pleases. Nothing but an utter and happy innocence of the bitter irony of "Equity" proceedings keeps such an idea current. Men have been imprisoned for many years, some for a lifetime, on account of Chancery proceedings of the very existence of which they were almost in ignorance before they "somehow or other were found in contempt."[92]

In terms of both tone and content, the article resembles Bentham's invectives against Blackstone. In his novels, Dickens frequently uses those same visions of incarceration as metaphors. Not only does Pickwick go to Fleet Prison. Oliver Twist is caught in the hands of Fagin, and Dorrit is "imprisoned" by his own habits. Therefore, Blount argues that Dickens complements real prisons like Marshalsea or Fleet by numerous metaphorical prisons or situations that resemble real incarceration, for instance life in Tom-All-Alone's or obsessions about Chancery that reach beyond mere legal questions about Jarndyce and Jarndyce.

Yet Blount has nothing to say about the specific interaction – he only assumes a dichotomy – between literal and metaphorical prisons, which I have argued takes place through the medium of legal fictions. The mechanism of Civil Death already consists of an interaction between metaphorical death and real incarceration. Thus it must be noted that instead of initiating that interaction, Dickens's literary discourse adopts and translates it from the practice of legal fictions. Due to differences in translation, legal fiction and literary fiction cannot be said to deal with exactly the same interaction between literal and metaphorical incarceration, as well as literal and metaphorical transfer of property.

The most prominent feature of this interaction between metaphorical death and real incarceration is a tension that Alexander Welsh describes as causing many Victorian anxieties about the nineteenth-century transition from theological to scientific paradigms of world-making.[93] Natural religion, Welsh argues, used to deny any notion of natural death as it was committed to the idea of an afterlife. In contrast, the law focused on unnatural death – predominantly, that is, on the possibility and probability of murder, manslaughter, or suicide. It did so on the premise that the ways in which such forms of death put an end to life threatened communities less in a theological than a criminal sense. The less natural religion could account for the existence of an afterlife, the more the law's task of finding evidence of murder, manslaughter, or suicide had to compensate for the increased gulf between death and redemption that Victorians had come to be concerned about.

Detectivist approaches to the law of evidence, Welsh continues, began to represent as well as emphasize how relevant distinctions between death and murder had become. Murder in the sense of unnatural death had of course always been understood as an external intrusion into natural life, putting an untimely end to that life based on malice aforethought. However, in the specific context of theological explanations of natural death that had turned into natural religion's embarrassment, Welsh concludes, the law at least permitted an approach *ex negativo* which substituted a legal formalization of unnatural death for the inexplicability of afterlife. Natural death could be defined as the absence of that external intrusion which forces an untimely end upon life.

This distinction between intentional and unintentional forms of ending life is also important for the conviction and punishment of murderers by means of Civil Death. For in such cases, the life of the incarcerated felon is also untimely and intentionally ended – albeit only in a metaphorical sense. While the inmate's social life ends, his or her biological life remains initially uncompromised and, if portrayed, frequently illustrates the physical and psychological "misery" of social deprivation. To end social life is thus to enter metaphorical death. In turn, this particular form of metaphorical death can enact such "unnatural" forms of life that it may itself result, as reprehended in Dickens's articles in *Household Words*, in literal death or end up being translated into forms of a death-in-life experienced outside prison walls. One obvious example in *Bleak House* is Gridley. The chapter titled "An Appeal Case" presents him as longing in vain for an otherworldly court of appeals that would redeem him before he dies (*BH*, XXIV, p. 408). He interprets this trial of life as a death-in-life that serves to justify redemption in the form of literal death.

"[. . .] it would have been far better for me never to have heard the high name of your office; but, unhappily for me, I can't undo the past, and the past drives me here!" [. . .] To the last, I'll show myself in that Court to its shame. If I knew when I was going to die, and could be carried there, and had a voice to speak with, I would die there, saying, "You have brought me here, and sent me from here, many and many a time. Now send me out, feet foremost!" (*BH*, XV, p. 269)

Creating an additional difference in translation, Dickens translates this displacement of the natural and the unnatural into the case of Lady Dedlock. She subjects her own wish to see Tulkinghorn dead, which she starts cultivating long before his actual death, to an excruciating trial of life and continues to do so even after Hortense has been disclosed as his murderer. The family curse seems to be transforming her entire life into a court drama enacted *in foro interno*.

Her enemy he [Tulkinghorn] was, and she has often, often, often wished him dead. Her enemy he is, even in his grave. This dreadful accusation comes upon her, like a new torment at his lifeless hand. [. . .] The horror that is upon her, is unutterable. If she really were the murderess, it could hardly be, for the moment, more intense. For, as her murderous perspective, before the doing of the deed, however subtle the precautions for its commission, would have been closed up by a gigantic dilatation of the hateful figure, preventing her from seeing any consequences beyond it; and as those consequences would have rushed in, in an unimagined flood, the moment the figure was laid low – which always happens when a murder is done; so, now she sees that when he used to be on the watch before her, and she used to think "if some mortal stroke would but fall on this old man and take him away from my way!" it was but wishing that all he held against her in his hand might be flung to the winds, and chance-sown in many places. So, too, with the wicked relief she has felt in his death. What was his death but the key-stone of a gloomy arch removed, and now the arch begins to fall in a thousand fragments, each crushing and mangling piecemeal! Thus, a terrible impression steals upon and overshadows her, that from this pursuer, living or dead – obdurate and imperturbable before her in his well-remembered shape, or not more obdurate and imperturbable in his coffin-bed – there is no escape but in death. Hunted, she flies. The complication of her shame, her dread, remorse, and misery, overwhelms her at its height; and even her strength of self-reliance is overturned and whirled away, like a leaf before a mighty wind. (*BH*, LV, pp. 815–16).

The third-person narrator presents Lady Dedlock as performing a displacement of natural and unnatural as well as literal and metaphorical death, which bears extraordinary consequences for her. Embodying a tomb that forebodes untimely death, Tulkinghorn reminds her, while he is still alive, of the curse that keeps surrounding her with the bleak lives of dead ancestors. His secret knowledge about her history causes her to turn her life into a probation and to bar from her Lincolnshire identity not only transgressions of moral standards but also the passive submission to guilt: "[N]oble Mausoleums [. . .] perhaps hold fewer noble secrets than walk abroad among men, shut up in the breast of Mr Tulkinghorn" (*BH*, II, p. 58).

For this reason, she lives much of her life in isolation from her environment. Her metaphorical incarceration is one that anticipates death by turning life into the grave that "her enemy" appears to be preparing for her. Tulkinghorn is a professional trained to employ the literal incarceration of Civil Death in a metaphorical sense as well. It comes as no surprise, then, that he succeeds in using the effects of such metaphorical incarceration to pressure Lady Dedlock into feeling ashamed of making her life public and stepping out of her isolation.[94]

Responding to his abuse of her family's "ghostly stories," Lady Dedlock wishes Tulkinghorn a literal death, whose "deadly meaning" (*BH*, xlviii, p. 721) she feels is already defining her own life in terms of a global metaphor. When the death she wishes for him turns into a murder she did not commit – "the key-stone of a gloomy arch" – an identity of hers begins to collapse that is more complex than that which she used to associate with the subdued intensity of hatred she directs towards Tulkinghorn and the legal profession. The life that she at this point attempts to escape from already represented a form of escape before the murder happened. Hers is an escape from the family curse, from Tulkinghorn's vicious self-interest, and into a form of death-in-life.

The next step she takes is the escape into a literal death which she begins to wish for herself as she escapes from the world of Chesney Wold. Literal death thus becomes the focus of an escape from that very metaphorical death which caused her a life in isolation. It is a soteriological form of death. To redeem metaphorical death, which she believes is her life, in literal death is to dissociate death from the incarceration trope and to recapture it by means of theological semantics. She displaces the death that figured her isolation as a disintegration of a part from the whole onto a redemptive death that transfigures the unknowable nature of an end to life into its soteriological Other. Death begins to represent (for her) a theological equity of life, suggestive of the Augustinian myth of earthly and celestial cities,[95] that contrasts redemption with the injustices of a death-in-life.

Yet Lady Dedlock does not return to the sphere of natural religion. She "chooses" unnatural death, as it were, by intentionally freezing to death on the steps of St. Martin's pauper graveyard. Throughout the novel, unnatural death is always also the symptom of a metaphorical death-in-life, both inside and outside of prisons. Lady Dedlock has a feeling, when she recognizes Nemo's handwriting, "'like the faintness of death'" (*BH*, ii, p. 62), whereas she usually is "'bored to death'"

(*BH*, II, p. 62) in Lincolnshire; and Esther receives her ominous admonition: "I must evermore consider her as dead" (*BH*, XXXVI, p. 566; see also *BH*, XLIII, p. 647). In the light of this ambiguity of literal and unnatural death, Lady Dedlock's actual death ends a process of displacements in which she emerges, sometimes as the real, sometimes the imaginary victim of Tulkinghorn, sometimes as an imaginary murderer, sometimes as a real "self-murderer." Committing suicide would in fact have made her legally guilty in terms of a felony against her self.[96] Since her suicide translates unnatural death into redemptive death, she can be said to displace the semantics of two legal fictions that figure forth meanings of her various deaths. By translating Civil Death into *felo de se*, she ultimately chooses not to leave the manipulation of legal fictions to the lawyers.

The fact that Lady Dedlock is innocent with respect to the murder of Tulkinghorn highlights an irony that is also typical of other characters. On the one hand, she comes to identify the Chancery case with the same curse that is prefigured by the Dedlock genealogy. On the other hand, the family curse causes her to undergo a trial of life which is already prefigured by the social and psychological effects the Chancery case has had on other characters even before she got involved. The local enclave of her family's genealogy protects as well as isolates her from the law's more global networkings. This irony complicates the role of the law, which she has come to hate simply because it appears to isolate people from one another.

By escaping from the world of Chesney Wold, Lady Dedlock also escapes her impending apprehension. She continues, however, to weigh potential evidence against her innocence, evidence that might render her guilty in more complex ways than in terms of murder. Her road of escape becomes a medium that allows her to determine moral guilt.

The dark road I have trodden for so many years will end where it will. I follow it alone to the end, whatever the end may be. It may be near, it may be distant; while the road lasts, nothing turns me. [. . .] To hope to do what I seek to do, I must be what I have been so long. Such is my reward and doom. If you hear of Lady Dedlock, brilliant, prosperous, and flattered; think of your wretched mother, conscience-stricken, underneath that mask. Think that the reality is in her suffering, in her useless remorse, in her murdering within her breast the only love and truth of which it is capable! (*BH*, XXXVI, pp. 567–8)

Significantly, she refuses to subject to a public mediation or trial what she acknowledges as a moral injustice she has been inflicting on others.

Instead, she internalizes moral guilt as a form of death-in-life, translates death-in-life into a private trial of life with respect to her desires, and activates conscience as a judge who is to find and interpret evidence of what she has been "murdering within her breast." This is entirely different, for instance, from the evidence discovered about the innocence of George the Trooper, for George emerges as a "good-natured man" in the sense of Fielding's Tom Jones. Lady Dedlock's private trial sharply contrasts with such confidence in the law's capacity to restore a defendant's reputation. Her "probation" anticipates Nietzschean and Freudian versions of civilization's discontents.

Lady Dedlock cannot "acquit" herself of her own past: "'To hope to do what I seek to do, I must be what I have been so long'" (*BH*, XXXVI, p. 568). At the same time, she "liberates" herself from her duties and obligations as a legal subject. In contrast, George the Trooper somewhat indulges in an abstract form of the social contract. He submits freedom and security to a civil obedience of the law and its authority and accepts imprisonment upon this premise. Lady Dedlock dissociates herself from that premise and establishes her own private jurisdiction. Thus she relinquishes the idea of the social contract, which caused Bentham's contemporary Burke to declare the basic foundation of civil society, "*that no man should be a judge in his own cause.*"[97]

She turns away from that idea, but in an ambiguous way. On the one hand, she distrusts Tulkinghorn and the legal profession in the same way that Bentham used to disqualify the social contract as a detrimental fiction. On the other hand, she appears unwilling to join contemporary reformers in substituting a transparency of norms for the professional manipulation of fictions. Rather, her private "judicial" law goes back to Locke's efforts to distinguish between the genuinely political and the paternal exercise of power.[98] The authority on which she relies is not only a paternalistic one, but also honeycombed with the imagined inevitability of a curse that "modernizes" paternalism in terms of a "law of the father."

In Lady Dedlock's case, Dickens inverts the idea that as a child one may outlive one's father, but that as a legal subject one cannot escape the social contract. Lady Dedlock considers herself subject only to a trial of life as death-in-life. She does attempt to escape the social contract to the extent that she suspects herself – "'conscience-stricken [. . . in] useless remorse'" (*BH*, XXXVI, p. 568) as she sees herself – unable to escape the "law of the father." Consequently, she subjects herself to an examination according to conscience, in which she is aware of her legal innocence and yet feels guilty. So thoroughly has she internalized the procedures of such an examination that she seems willing, perhaps more than she knows, to consider the possibility of guilt, simply because conscience has been authorized to conduct that examination.

The burden of the curse grows along with the burden of proof regarding her moral innocence, which Lady Dedlock imposes on herself but cannot translate into exoneration. What the authorities first used against her as circumstantial evidence of murder, she subsequently begins to use against her self, who no longer seems an innocent victim of circumstances. Her inversion of the social contract turns her into a subject of internal laws and authorities. These impose on her the burden of proof to provide circumstantial evidence of moral guilt.

The feeling of guilt that the social contract may cause in the innocent, who nevertheless find themselves exposed to examination or trial, is always genuine in the sense that their permanent obligation to submit to the social contract creates "guilt" as a permanent debt. Lady Dedlock, however, inherits a feeling of guilt, which she then bestows upon Esther. Her sense of guilt implies imaginary causes, for instance a reified trauma, and, once considered pathological, the possibility that she may have reduced a crisis in terms of expectations to the metaphorical self-incarceration in a prison of guilt.

Dickens repeatedly employs the metaphor of property transfer to suggest her sense of guilt as an ominous legacy of laws that specifically govern her internal psycho-judicial system. If the legal subject's obligations toward the social contract redefine indebtedness as guilt, then Dickens can be said to emphasize an uncanny quality of unquestioned assumptions about the law which has gone unnoticed by such reformers as Bentham. At the same time, Dickens continues to insist on the irony that any representation of an uncanny trial of life as death-in-life is already figured forth by the very mechanism of legal fictions such as Civil Death.

In contrast to Richard, Lady Dedlock abstains from articulating the heterogeneous contexts in which the law's exemplary economy of norms and precedents may become paradoxical. She almost refuses to bring this kind of excess into the open, thus establishing alternative internal standards for delinquency. Her impatience does not seem to increase with her self-imposed isolation, at least not to the same extent as her confusion and despair about the logic of fate do. Her struggle with the want of logic of her "fate," which places the family curse beyond the confines of Greek tragedy, shows her as both trying to justify providence and calling into question the justice of providence. To the degree that she meets that challenge, the curse moves into the next, Esther's, stage of being told.

But she also internalizes the anxiety of personal and singular experiences of guilt as a scandal indefensible by the authority of customs and norms. The more that happens, the more her intuition of a life immune to the common recurrences and repetitions of generating meaning for individual lives drives her into isolation. Her retreat is indebted, as it were, to the very legal assumptions about personality from which she chooses to escape. This particular conflict causes her metaphorical incarceration in guilt to emerge as a self-imposed Civil Death.

In contrast to Miss Flite, whose yearning for a justice rendered in terms of divine revelation represents redemption as something supernatural, Lady Dedlock does not seem to expect the revelation of a transcendent truth. Instead, the only thing expected to be revealed by her psycho-judicial system is the necessity of revelation itself. Conscience must reveal the truth about her, through the medium of an internal trial, in order for the truth to become a truth about herself. Like Miss Flite, she uses the idea of revelation to pave her road toward redemption. Unlike Miss Flite, she inverts the idea of revealed truth by making it coincide with the acts of its revelation, thus emphasizing the gulf between a truth transcendent because inaccessible and a truth particularized because revealed by individual conscience.

She "learns" from this particularized revelation that the family curse does not simply incarnate fate in single ancestors and then withdraws again to its Beyond before subsequent heirs "inherit" it. What expires in the individual sacrifices "demanded" by the law of the curse is the idea of transcendent and unrevealed truths itself. The family curse is a name for this intimate liaison between revelation and incarnation. Its persistence results from a compulsion continuously to perform the lack of revelation inherent to the notion of transcendent truths.

Lady Dedlock actually distances herself from two forms of truth – on the one hand, that truth which the law posits as equitable justice, and on the other hand, that truth which the family genealogy appears to "assign" to her in terms of (tragic) fate. She is resolved to submit her "indebtedness" to the social contract (as a legal subject) and to fate (as a subject of certain genealogical imperatives) to an internal trial. In effect, however, she renounces her very subordination to the norms and customs that define an aristocratic life of respectability, and for the sake of which she was prepared to put everything at stake.

"The complication of her shame, her dread, remorse, and misery" (*BH*, LV, p. 816) ultimately consists in the problem that after her renunciation of transcendent authorities, there is in fact no form of agency left that could forever declare her guilty. Consequently, the very conscience she invokes in order to receive equitable redemption equally begins to lose its traditional authorization to perform such appeals outside a court of equity. In the process of severing her social ties, she inadvertently collapses the distinction between public subjects and private individuals which motivated her retreat in the first place.

Her very retreat from the repressive circuits of fate weighs upon her as the redoubled guilt of having stripped conscience of its (legally uncontested) authority. Her response to that unorthodox experience of guilt consists in an act of renouncing the normative and customary basis of authority as such. She finally feels compelled to examine that authority in the isolation of an internal trial. This second-hand guilt, as it were, reveals to her the ultimate disappointment that she remains "indebted" to the very inheritances of legal and genealogical alliances that she chose to renounce. Her retreat from the social contract and from genealogical fate ironically appears to make her guilt inevitable.

Eventually, she realizes that it has become impossible to undo the initial subordination of her love for Esther to the respectable norms and customs of aristocratic family life. The guilt she projects into that act of subordination alienates her from her offspring. The redoubled guilt she projects into the act of renouncing authority as such separates her from the sphere of existing social bonds. It may in fact be due to this intuition of redoubled guilt that she finally makes the transition from metaphorical incarceration to redemptive literal death. Yet in her "case," there is no such thing as equitable unnatural death. The permanent shifts between her literal and metaphorical notions of natural and unnatural death indicate that the very mechanism of making such transitions remains "indebted" to the legal mechanism of Civil Death.

RENEWAL, RETRIBUTION, REVENGE

What Lady Dedlock "hands down" to Esther is therefore a sense of artificial legitimacy with which the contradictory effects of the case and the curse come together in the name of the person who gets to inherit Bleak House. Unmet expectations concerning that which supposedly governs property relations and family identity provide the very justification for that artificiality to continue. This justification of renewal works at the cost of splitting genealogy off from inheritance. However, Lady Dedlock fails to adopt a vantage point outside the artificial mechanisms that reshuffle her expectations. Thus she feels compelled, in a sense, to assume and repudiate her legacy simultaneously. She must accept that artificiality as a component of what it means to be a fallen aristocrat. At the same time, she must build up the expectation that it neither restricts nor determines the course of her self-examination.

The gap between Lady Dedlock's attempts at disrupting and reestablishing a continuity of social bonds is one defined by the problem that her symbolic inheritance, like her character and destiny, are not immediately available to her. Having to retrieve that inheritance, she is faced with the irony that she has not asked for it but that instead it comes to her through the reversals of law and genealogy. More importantly, the inheritance remains elusive even after she has chosen to embrace it *in foro interno*. It does not consist of a substance but the lack of it.

It is precisely in this empty space of inheritance that the national heritage of Bleak House emerges as an artificial preservation of the institution of property transfer and the respective maintenance of class distinctions. For Esther, who inherits this exposure of artificiality in the sentimental mode of renewal, to accept and embrace a heritage distinct from and lacking dependence on nature is also to enhance the motivation to protect what appears to have been discredited. Resolved to fill the void left behind by Lady Dedlock's emptying out of her inheritance, Esther adopts for the new Bleak House the same conventional basis of legitimacy with which legal fictions make the connection of names and estates in the notion of privilege look natural.

Both George, who is literally incarcerated, and Esther, who struggles with the problem of how to create meaningful continuities for her family history, manage to survive. Both counter the fantasm of being caught in their mothers' legacies. George does not even insist on defending himself, which results in a strange kind of self-acquittal that differs from Lady Dedlock's escape from the confines of a legal subject. Like Esther, as we have already seen, George translates the legal meaning of will into a psychological one.

"I did intend to read it [the account I have been drawing up], straight on end, whensoever I was called upon to say anything in my defence. I hope I may be let to do it still; but I have no longer a will of my own in this case, and whatever is said or done, I give my promise not to have any." (*BH*, LV, p. 809)

"[W]ill" here refers not only to the will of Mrs Rouncewell, his mother (*BH*, LV, p. 806), and his claims to the inheritance specified therein, but also to his faith in a legal system that actually works. Like Esther, he appears to accept that his resistance against that system is implicated in its very categories. He permanently resists – and thus implicitly accepts the validity of – the legal category "corruption of blood," used to label felons who have been subjected to Civil Death, and prefers retreat from social bonds over being designated as such in public: "'No relations shall be disgraced by me, and made unhappy for me'" (*BH*, LII, p. 764); and his mother explains that "'[. . .] when he didn't rise [to be an officer], I know he considered himself beneath us, and wouldn't be a disgrace to us'" (*BH*, LV, p. 802). He can only endure the isolation he chooses for himself by waiving claims and abandoning wills. In a sense, to translate the legal meaning of will into the sphere of conscience is to substitute one version of judgment for another.

Similarly, Esther concludes that unless the legacy of the past is conceived as a denied claim, it need not force her into metaphorical death:

[...] I saw very well that I could not have been intended to die, or I should never have lived; not to say should never have been reserved for such a happy life. I saw very well how many things had worked together, for my welfare; and that if the sins of the fathers were sometimes visited upon the children, the phrase did not mean what I had in the morning feared it meant. I knew I was as innocent of my birth as a queen was of hers [. . .]. (*BH*, XXXVI, p. 571)

But when Bucket reveals to Esther that Lady Dedlock exchanged clothes with Jenny, the brickmaker's wife, to deflect attention from her tracks, he implicitly discloses an even more complex exchange mechanism that Esther must avoid. Jenny leaves behind a dead child. Lady Dedlock symbolically bestows death upon Esther. After Captain Nemo's ominous death, the family curse turns demonic whenever Esther's personal history appears to resemble that of the working poor and especially the aristocracy. Chesney Wold, "[s]een by night, from a distant opening in the trees, the row of windows in the long drawing room, where my Lady's picture hangs over the great chimney-piece, is like a row of jewels set in a black frame" (*BH*, XII, p. 210). It is this curse of a fantasmatic complicity that Esther seeks to undo:

Dare I hint at that worse time when, strung together somewhere in great black space, there was a flaming necklace, or ring, or starry circle of some kind, of which I was one of the beads! And when my only prayer was to be taken off from the rest, and when it was such inexplicable agony and misery to be a part of the dreadful thing? *(BH*, xxxv, p. 544)

Just as George goes to prison, only to leave it as a free man without trusting the legal system's proof of his innocence, Esther suffers from small-pox, only to return to the aristocratic nexus of the necklace, whose legacy she gets to inherit.

Nemo's death is for Lady Dedlock, Krook, and Jo a legacy as fatal as Tom Jarndyce's suicide is for Richard and Gridley. The third-person narrator depicts Nemo's funeral as a legacy for generations to come and translates this particular exchange of life and death into "corruption of blood" – a metaphor that also evokes Civil Death.

[. . .] with every villainy of life in action close on death, and every poisonous element of death in action close to life – here, they lower our dear brother down a foot or two: here, sow him in corruption, to be raised in corruption: an avenging ghost at many a sick-bedside: a shameful testimony to future ages, how civilization and barbarism walked this boastful island together. *(BH*, xi, p. 202)

Death here emerges both as the simple condition for the transfer of inherited property and the symbolic mortgage that figures forth the heir's initiation into possession as reproducing the corruption caused by continuous acts of handing down burdensome capital. The narrator's thanatography concerning corrupted continuities thus differs from the typical rite of passage, which symbolically exchanges life and death, turns endings into beginnings, and announces further endings in those beginnings. Similarly, Garrett Stewart has shown in reference to the chapter titles that Dickens makes the narrative effects of a continuous antinomy of beginnings discontinuous. The legacies highlighted in *Bleak House* fail to build bridges of hope across the generations.[99] As we have seen in the case of Lady Dedlock and Esther, Dickens blurs the legal and spiritual dimensions of hope in order to perpetuate the ambiguities of death as a narrative event and metaphor.

Krook's readjustment of unmet expectations differs from Lady Dedlock's in that he comes across as seeking retribution, not renewal. With Spontaneous Combustion, he performs the very apocalyptic break with the "perplexed and troublous valley of the shadow of the law" *(BH*, xxxii, p. 498) that is announced at the opening of the novel: "[. . .] the whole burnt away in a great funeral pyre." *(BH*, I, p. 55) Dickens prefigures Krook's death by an uncanny putrescence in the air, suggesting the novel's social dimension as a global misery calling for redemption: "It is a fine steaming night to turn the slaughter-house, the unwholesome trades, the sewerage, bad water, and burial-grounds to account, and give the Registrar of Death some extra business" (*BH*, xxxii, p. 499). Just as Chancery absorbs all costs, Krook seems to buy everything and sell nothing (*BH*, v, p. 99). For his visitor Richard, the state of disintegration in which he finds Krook's accumulated bones, rags, and papers represents Chancery's consumption of lives: "One only had to fancy [. . .] that yonder bones in a corner, piled together and picked very clean, were the bones of clients, to make the picture complete." Similarly, the third-person narrator suspects connections between the unofficial Lord Chancellor and the disintegration of individual bodies as well as between the official Lord Chancellor and the disintegration of the body politic.

> The Lord Chancellor of that Court, true to his title in his last act, has died the death of all Lord Chancellors in all Courts, and of all authorities in all places under all names soever, where false pretences are made, and where injustice is done. Call the death by any name Your Highness will, attribute it to whom you will, or say it might have been prevented how you will, it is the same death eternally – inborn, inbred, engendered in the corrupted humours of the vicious body itself, and that only – Spontaneous Combustion, and none other of the deaths that can be died. (*BH*, xxxii, p. 511)

Insofar as this form of death results from the corrupt humors both of individual bodies and society as a whole, it refers to a cosmological depiction of global crisis that was of course long outdated in Dickens's time. In a nexus of crises exclusively framed by the classical pathology of humors, all symptoms of suffering are connected, even though it is not revealed how. Its qualifiers, "inborn" and "inbred," are misleading at first. They falsely encourage the reader to associate this "same death eternally" with a notion of natural death that at the same time need not necessarily be caused by corrupt humors. Thus the specific relation between Krook's individual death and the anticipated death of all Lord Chancellors replicates the more general relation between isolated symptoms of a crisis and an inscrutable complexity of expectations, which the text both insinuates and withholds from the reader.

Furthermore, Dickens leaves it rather vague as to whether in Spontaneous Combustion death occurs naturally or unnaturally. Krook's gesture of resistance may be considered "inborn" to the corrupt system and thus natural insofar as it is immanent to an omnipotent legal system. But the system itself may also be seen as unnatural due to its corruption. In this case, Krook's death might refer to a "natural" notion of afterlife, with respect to which it could be considered "inborn." The multiplicity of meanings with which Krook's body "is invested make it a site," as Françoise Jaouën and Benjamin Semple have argued more generally about the body, "that is at once threatening and exalted, a place of exile and a promised land."[100]

Such a soteriological form of death certainly represents a version of resistance designed to return to a corrupt legal system that which it is presumably incapable of processing: the spontaneous self-annihilation of legal subjects existing in a metaphorical death-in-life. However, Krook's death appears to perpetuate the curse of the case rather than bringing it to an end. Just as Nemo's death becomes a precedent for Krook's life, Krook's death becomes a precedent for Richard's life. Dying and inheriting continue mutually to provide metaphors for one another. One character's death continues to form part of another person's inheritance. Immediately after Krook's death, the Smallweeds claim his property. Immediately, the court concerns itself with "the fiction of a full-sized coffin." After Krook's combustion, there are hardly any remains left to fill the coffin (*BH*, xxx, pp. 521–3). To a certain extent, Krook's death is even cathartic for other members of the body politic. He may be said to have died the death of a scapegoat or martyr from which George and Esther have been spared.

Krook exchanges life and death like a martyr whose death symbolically renders renewal to a community in crisis. But his self-destructive resistance – provided that this is what Spontaneous Combustion means – fails to influence the development of the case in any substantial way. The fact that the case comes to an end because of documents found late but seemingly not made available to the parties corresponds to the institutional fact that equity courts like Chancery operate without a jury. The ending of Jarndyce and Jarndyce appears to remain largely unaffected by individual actions and initiatives other than those of lawyers and judges. Since the estate in question is at no point exactly determined, evidence can mutate in rather unrestricted ways and potentially turn into symptoms of crises other than that of the legal system.

One prominent example of such a mutation is Tom-All-Alone's, Tom Jarndyce's legacy, a legacy of pauperization and human alienation in slums.

This desirable property is in Chancery, of course. It would well be an insult to the discernment of any man with half an eye, to tell him so. Whether 'Tom' is the popular representative of the original plaintiff or defendant in Jarndyce and

Jarndyce; or, whether Tom lived here when the suit had laid the street waste, all alone, until other settlers came to join him; or whether the traditional title is a comprehensive name for a retreat cut off from honest company and put out of the pale of hope; perhaps nobody knows. (*BH*, XVI, pp. 273–4)

Perhaps Tom-All-Alone's is Chancery's legacy for England; perhaps it is only falsely assumed to be such a symptom of fatal transfers of property; or perhaps it is indeed such a legacy, but nobody knows. Everybody seems to talk, but nobody seems to care about Tom-All-Alone's. Equitable justice apparently comes neither from the judiciary nor the legislator.

Much mighty speech-making there has been, both in and out of Parliament, concerning Tom, and much wrathful disputation how Tom shall be got right. [. . .] In the midst of which dust and noise, there is only one thing perfectly clear, to wit, that Tom may and can, or shall and will, be reclaimed according to somebody's theory but nobody's practice. And in the hopeful meantime, Tom goes to perdition head foremost in his old determined spirit. But he has his revenge. Even the winds are his messengers, and they serve him in these hours of darkness. There is not a drop of Tom's *corrupted blood* but propagates infection and contagion somewhere. [. . .] There is not an atom of Tom's slime, not a cubic inch of any pestilential gas in which he lives, not one obscenity or degradation about him, not an ignorance, not a wickedness, not a brutality of his committing, but shall work its retribution, through every order of society, up to the proudest of the proud, and to the highest of the high. Verily, with that tainting, plundering, and spoiling, Tom has his revenge. (*BH*, XLVI, p. 683, my emphasis)

Tom's legacy is "corrupted blood" – part of the metaphorical death inflicted in the context of Civil Death. Dickens evokes the semantics of this particular legal fiction in order to illustrate how socially and medically isolated the slums are from the rest of society. What is more, Tom-All-Alone's is also "property [. . .] in Chancery" (*BH*, XVI, p. 273). The slum thus emerges as a social space controlled by the legal system to the extent that the latter incorporates the former as, in Kristeva's terms, an "other within." By presenting the slum in the gothic code of uncanny retribution, Dickens has Tom turn back on those who share a common interest in controlling misery by means of its incorporation – including many more than members of Chancery. He clearly associates the death-in-life of many characters with the way Tom's illness and pestilence are going down over England's separate classes.

Tom's vengeance has no legitimate authority before tribunals. Essentially, vengeance asks for the revision of competences or enforces the institution of new tribunals by subverting the old ones. Tom is incapable of articulating himself in an idiom appropriate for the context of jurisdiction – a "legacy" that he "hands down" to Jo – and thus lacks the legal means of bearing witness to the injustices he has had to suffer. He forms no part of the discourse of law in the sense other parties to the case do. As Jean-François Lyotard explains, the authority of vengeance is derived, not from the discourse of pleas and claims, but from the problem that in particular circumstances informal complaints have no outcome.

The law reserves the authority to establish crime, to pronounce the verdict and to determine the punishment before the tribunal which has heard the two parties expressing themselves in the same language, that of the law. The justice which the victim calls upon against the justice of the tribunal cannot be uttered in the genre of juridical or forensic discourse. But this is the genre in which the law is uttered. The authority that vengeance may give ought not then to be called a right of law. The plea is a demand for the reparation of damages, addressed to a third party (the judge) by the plaintiff (the addressor). The avenger is a justice-maker, the request (the cry) is addressed to him or her (the addressee) as to a judge. It is not transferable to a third party, even for its execution (idiolect), its legitimacy allows for no discussion, it is not measured distributively because its referent, the wrong, is not cognizable. All the same, vengeance authorizes itself on account of the plea's having no outcome. Since one is not able to obtain reparation, one cries out for vengeance.[101]

The fact that the legitimacy of vengeance is not measured distributively – for instance in terms of retribution – suggests that Dickens contrasts Tom's revenge with contemporary legal claims to compensation. The crown had always been in charge of translating the expiation of unnatural death into revenue, by means of confiscating the monetary value attributed to objects causing that death; but in 1846, unnatural death was relegated to civil tort law, and kin of the victim could claim damages entailed to them by that death.[102] This new notion of private liability for death certainly redefined the existing legal nexus of expiation and forfeiture. Nevertheless, the very legal efforts made to reach a definition of compensation in distributive terms reflect the problem that natural and unnatural death are not necessarily connected in a distributive sense.

Regarding the role of death in civil tort law, Tom's revenge therefore represents the contingent but inevitable limit of distributive justice. His revenge is meant to operate as distributive justice's "other within," a force of negation implicated in but irrecuperable by legal discourse. On the one hand, the call for retribution can be considered an act of conscience that is motivated by the legal discourse which allows conscience to operate within that discourse's limits. On the other hand, the referent of revenge is, as Lyotard puts it, not "cognizable" in the terms of the discourse whose limits – that is to say, standards of representation – the act of conscience seeks to challenge.

To bear witness to unnatural death as an injustice unaccounted for by courts of appeal is to seek para-equity. The fact that its pleas have no outcome in legal terms does not exclude the possibility of symbolic compensation. Thus it appears, oddly enough, that characters in *Bleak House* die literal deaths and live their lives as metaphorical deaths not only because of Chancery's practices but also Tom's revenge. In the latter case, Dickens lets death return as avenging death. He enacts the economy of property transfer as a psychic economy of uncanny returns to the extent that death becomes a legacy which can be inherited in different literal and metaphorical ways. For Dickens, the point about the various modalities in which this legacy can be inherited is to expose the similarity of mechanisms that perpetuate it. On the one hand, within the limits of legal discourse, claims can be made only to property, not to the entire economy of property transfer. On the other hand, Tom's revenge undercuts that economy only to perpetuate it within the psychic economy of the uncanny.

As equitable justice's "other within," para-equity is not entirely identical with utopias. Instead, it is merely suggested in the novel as a structured form of response in excess of the legal retributions available to revert poverty, misery, and illness. John Jarndyce, for instance, hints at some form of para-equity beyond those legal discourses which send letters of the alphabet back and forth between law and equity and turn Tom's will into a "dead letter" (*BH*, VIII, pp. 145–6). He contrasts the uncanny effects of corruption in equity courts, a mixture of reflection, control, retribution, and death, with a strategy of conscious forgetfulness: "'Bleak House [. . .] must learn to take care of itself'" (*BH*, LX, p. 869). While Tom interprets para-equity as revenge, John identifies it as sympathy.

Both readings are already counter-measures directed against, as well as motivated by, distributive approaches to compensating for unnatural death. This is the reason why a gothic sense of unnatural death never stops threatening John's model of sympathy: "'We are [...] equitably waltzing ourselves off to dusty death, about costs'" (*BH*, VIII, p. 145). Similarly suspicious is the fact that the coroner declares Nemo's death "accidental death" (*BH*, XI, p. 200). None of those who die during Jarndyce and Jarndyce seems to die entirely accidentally. And the death that is "symbolically exchanged" among characters who live their lives as metaphorical deaths is not anthropologically genuine either. For this kind of exchange tends to defy, instead of encourage, rebirth as renewal.[103]

Para-equity thus takes different shapes according to the different types of interests and desires that motivate characters to seek it. On the level of individual interest, characters such as Esther and George, who "survive" metaphorical death, control their own inheritances by protecting themselves against possible claims of other parties. Whenever their inheritances turn into some sort of a curse or the referent of suffered injustices, they assume control by domesticating and incorporating the inheritance of others into a code of unconditional sympathetic reciprocity. Whenever they turn a metaphorical notion of legacy into a legal claim, they see themselves as taking over an inheritance. Whenever they consider legacies as gifts, they see themselves as receiving an inheritance.

On the level of collective interest, metaphorical death is a legacy of the history of property transfer. At the core of this problem lies a sense of recognition in Victorian England, captured in *Bleak House* in the form of the uncanny, that the promises associated with the social contract, especially the apotheosis of Reason which defines its operations, are beginning to get challenged by an increasing complexity of expectations. The law either appears to lack the means of correcting corruption in the ranks of its profession or to have itself grown so complex that it can afford not even to prevent it from happening. Judges and lawyers tend to be seen as acting only to avoid putting themselves in a position of blame. In the eyes of many of Dickens's characters, they seem unwilling to coordinate different public perceptions of how new collective expectations about justice – for instance concerning its transition from peace to welfare[104] – have become more openended.

The conservative gesture, made by many of the prominent characters in *Bleak House*, to project metaphorical death on themselves or others as soon as the predictability of their bonding with others is at stake, corresponds to the conservative function Blackstone ascribes to legal fictions, which is to translate precedents from the feudal context of status to the modern context of contracts. It also corresponds to the conservative function, frequently ascribed to literature, to generate poetic justice. The production and exchange of metaphorical death in the novel reflects the characters' crisis of expectations. Both the conservative function of legal fictions to translate precedents and that of literature to generate poetic justice depend on the corrupt institutions of the social contract that they criticize.

The variety of fantasms that characters create about death thus also reflects a variety of possible responses to the complexity of unmet and readjusted expectations. Characters may want to hold the legal profession liable for unmet individual expectations. But liability is itself a legal category that they cannot challenge in order to make valid claims about the legal profession's corruption. This aporia causes them to struggle with the problem that the growing complexity of the law cannot exclusively be held responsible for the growing complexity of unmet and readjusted expectations.

A RESPONSIBLE DISSIPATION OF APORIAS

Dickens explores the pervasiveness of such aporias in Victorian culture by comparing "para-equitable" and philanthropic visions of responsibility. One prominent example is the way characters deal with transitions from metaphorical death in a life of poverty to literal death from poverty. Jo, for instance, belongs to that group of characters who literally die from the legacy of Nemo's and Tom's deaths. His life, a snail-like form of "Moving On" (*BH*, xix, pp. 319–20), ends right next to Nemo's grave. However, the slum he inhabits already defines his existence as a death-in-life: "Jo lives – that is to say, Jo has not yet died – in a ruinous place, known to the like of him by the name of Tom-All-Alone's" (*BH*, xvi, p. 272).

Jo's fever suggests an untimely end of liveliness. Dickens uses that sense of an ending as a metaphor of the cause-and-effect relation between poverty and literal death: "Dead, men and women, [. . .] dying around us every day" (*BH*, xlvii, p. 705). When Charley, Esther's servant, is confronted with Jo's life as a question concerning human mortality, she seems unable to call his "Moving On" either natural or unnatural, implying that compassion alone cannot answer that question: "'I know no more than the dead [. . .]. Perhaps the dead know better, if they could only tell us'" (*BH*, xxxi, p. 487).

Unlike Lady Dedlock, Jo seems incapable of establishing an internal psycho-judicial system that could help him to escape the invasions which the official legal system makes into his private life. Thus he submits to various interviews with the Coroner, Chadband, and Woodcourt, who designate him as the recipient of their legal, philanthropic, and medical "gifts." Jo's human authorities are paternalistic. But they are also void of the father figures against whom Lady Dedlock shaped her internal trial. Jo cannot help but submit to those authorities without even knowing the rules of compliance that they impose on him. Thus he cedes his will to the paternalistic ways in which Locke suggested paternal authority may substitute its judgment for someone else's ignorance or incapacity.

And if the father die, and fail to substitute a deputy in his trust; if he hath not provided a tutor to govern his son during his minority, during his want of understanding, the law takes care to do it. Some other must govern him, and be a will to him, till he hath attained to a state of freedom, and his understanding be fit to take the government of his will.[105]

Jo knows no other father than Nemo. Nonetheless, he accepts the Christian God as an ultimate paternal authority. It is this authority that is supposed to lead him out of the death-in-life of legal and philanthropic authorities and into an afterlife (*BH*, XLVII, p. 705). However, he knows the name of God, whom he accepts as having the power to pass judgment on him individually, as little as the meaning of truthful testimony (*BH*, XI, pp. 199–200), which the Coroner expects of him, and "the light of Terewth" (*BH*, XXV, p. 414), which Chadband promises as a general redemption.[106] The "light of Terewth" is "telescopic" for Jo in the same ironic sense as the absence of Miss Flite's apocalypse debunks the promise of individual redemption: "The light is come upon the dark benighted way. Dead" (*BH*, XLVII, p. 705).

Legal and philanthropic authorities substitute Jo's will to judgment about how he might use Tom's and Nemo's legacies for himself. For them, Jo is incompetent, at the very least in a metaphorical sense. Thus they can be said to administer his ignorance by means of applying the mechanism of Substituted Judgment. Ironically, the authorities treat him as liable for his ignorance because he is incompetent as defined in the terms of their respective discourses, which in turn puts them in a position to take on responsibility for him. Such legal and philanthropic manipulations of culpability bear witness to the institutionalized efforts to substitute someone else's judgment and administer legacies.

Laws of property and property transfer are used in this process to establish a legal semantics that operates in the philanthropic context as well. For instance, Allan Woodcourt's version of Substituted Judgment portrays Richard in terms of a promise that is simultaneously a sacred ritual: "'I will accept him as a trust, and it shall be a sacred one'" (*BH*, XLV, p. 682; see also LIX, p. 860 and LXI, p. 890). In a sense, Allan turns himself into Richard's Lord Chancellor, based on a philanthropic promise to administer his decreasing judgment. The former's unselfish action is supposed to substitute for the latter's self-less identity.

The way Dickens situates such legal metaphors of culpable identities in the philanthropic context corresponds to Welsh's observations, who follows in the wake of Max Weber's analysis of the Protestant ethic, about the Victorian nexus between an uncertainty about salvation, a concept of work as formative of character, and distributive charity.[107] The assumption that God withholds from mortals any certainty about their salvation for an afterlife is inextricably tied to the assumption that mortals must permanently work to form their character in the here-and-now. Both assumptions represent openended projects for a life based on the link between theologically inspired ethics and ethically inspired versions of capitalism. The here-and-now fundamentally defies salvation. Any sense of duty about work can never be more than a sign of salvation.

The Victorian doctrine of work served to compensate for this powerlessness. It was formulated and practiced in order to control events in the here-and-now by manipulating their potential use as evidence of salvation. As a result, the quest for salvation turned into a character-forming practice of benevolence. This practice, however, was entangled in ambiguous ways in its own precondition – a perception of misery which requires the charitable formation of character.

The Victorian attitude toward charity is the logical correlative of the doctrine of work. The attitude is chiefly distinguished by its emphasis on the character of the recipient of charity, an emphasis that inverts the long tradition of Christian charity as a practice contributing to the salvation of the charitable. The elevating influence of the gift on the giver is never denied, but the giver is asked to subordinate this (almost selfish) consideration to a concern for the effect of his gift on the recipient's character – an effect that is regarded as dubious at best. [. . .] In Calvin's theology, charity must follow from grace and cannot directly contribute to the giver's salvation; and begging and other forms of dependence were severely discouraged. The attitude toward charity that dwells on the character of the recipient can be reduced to the worry that, despite our eloquence, ordinary men will not work unless they are forced to. This worry, which sometimes amounts to a conviction, is the back-handed acknowledgement of the emptiness of the doctrine of work itself – its purely moral emphasis and the Puritan logic that makes work ultimately unrelated to the end of life.[108]

The practice of charity did not go uncontested. The workhouses of the 1830s, inspired by the New Poor Law and Malthus's theses, served to institutionalize a critical position which suspected dogmatic charity of increasing rather than reducing poverty and, as a result, sought to replace sympathetic charity with legislative activity. Other critical positions secularized the religious idea of character formation. They challenged the moral hiatus that the philanthropist Wilberforce had made from original sin and Christ's return to the practical idea of welfare. Herbert Spencer, for instance, translated charity from the context of the Protestant ethic into that of the natural selection of "strong" and "weak" characters. On the basis of this translation, he considered charity a "breach of equity."[109]

Welsh argues that Dickens held equivocal positions with respect to theories of pauperization, neither embracing nor entirely rejecting them. On the one hand, the Victorian sense of decency and shame seemed to prevent respectable subjects from receiving gifts in good conscience. On the other hand, Dickens frequently exposes the psychological economy behind such ratios of debt and credit, for instance in the case of Harold Skimpole, the poet-in-residence and parasitic houseguest at John Jarndyce's estate.

Though Dickens is of mixed minds about the economic laws that make charity inadvisable, and not nearly so concerned as some Victorians with its debilitating influence on weak characters, he thoroughly agrees that to receive charity is not respectable. However he may differ on the subject with his contemporaries, he joins them in the assumption that those who accept charity, whether in consequence of their own acts or not, are a race apart. This lesson was beaten into the Victorian mind, not by stories of able-bodied men who had been pauperized by charity, but by stories of good persons, preferably children, women, or unable men, who had refused charity in order to remain morally respectable. [. . .] It often seems as if the nineteenth century simply took literally the dictum of Christ that it is better to give than to receive – so literally that no allowance is made for a class of people who may happily receive what Christians give. [. . .] Harold Skimpole does not work, and accepts charity without feeling any guilt. His considerable power over Dickens's imagination and that of his readers is a measure of the degree to which work and avoidance of charity (i.e., receiving charity) are irrational and compulsively imposed values.[110]

According to Skimpole, charity deviates from distributive justice, insofar as that notion of justice is based on an even balance of giving and receiving. Since charity always already violates that economy, he reasons, it is sufficient for him to intend to pay a bill without actually having to carry out that intention. Skimpole's proclamation of innocence thus reflects the unexamined assumption informing the Victorian work ethic that one is not supposed to receive a pittance.

Fred Kaplan pointed out Dickens's awareness "that Benevolence oversimplified the social context and the possibilities of widespread remediation to the extent that it damaged the chances of other approaches. Under the guise of private charity, it had become a self-serving substitute for public responsibility."[111] Dickens rejected not only Puseyites and Roman Catholics, but also parts of the Evangelical movement, especially its exaggerated enthusiasm, ignorance, hypocrisy, self-serving piety, and suppression of naive sensuality.[112] He was certainly determined to practice benevolence in an authentic, unpretentious, and sensitive way that was different from Exeter Hall's institutional narcissism.

Nonetheless, his opposition must not be overrated, as Pope cautioned,[113] and for three reasons. First, Evangelicals sometimes proved to be capable of criticizing the fact that some charitable activity seemed to be designed with a view to gratifying the charitable; Lord Shaftesbury, for instance, despite the resistance he met with on the part of his Exeter Hall audience, insisted that the filthiness of slums was not the fault of the poor.[114] Secondly, Dickens's view of female philanthropists, which was reprehended by Mill, tended to be rather biased; he implied, by ridiculing the missionary role of Mrs Jellyby and Mrs Pardiggle in *Bleak House*, that women's responsibilities were primarily domestic.[115] Thirdly, he supported the so-called Theater Services, made possible by Shaftesbury's Religious Worship Act of 1855, which reflected the need to enact institutional unity in the form of mass spectacles in order to attract the working poor.[116] This is not to say, however, that *Bleak House* portrays philanthropic activities as stereotypes of what Dickens did not like about Exeter Hall. In fact, the romantic-comical role of Mrs Jellyby, the puritanical-maternal role of Mrs Pardiggle, and the cynical-crooked role of Chadband are variations of how philanthropic characters conceal their own vanity, indicative of benevolence as a complex practice, the literary representations of which cannot be reduced to moral critiques of charitable institutions.[117]

As the first among philanthropists, William Wilberforce systematically cautioned against legislating charity. Similar to some characters in *Bleak House*, he sought to keep charitable forms of equity, or philanthropic versions of para-equity, separate from the sphere of the law. He argued that religion must not be reduced to an institution merely designed to adjudicate on sins. Conversely, he claimed, sins that the law does not consider crimes must not be belittled by the generic legal term "*De minimis non curat lex*":

It is indeed a most lamentable consequence of the practice of regarding religion as a compilation of statutes, and not as an internal principle, that it soon comes to be considered as being conversant about external actions rather than about habits of mind. This sentiment sometimes has even the hardiness to insinuate and maintain itself under the guise of extraordinary concern for *practical religion*; but it soon discovers the falsehood of this pretension and betrays its real nature. [...] Indeed it is the *heart* which constitutes the man; and external actions derive their whole character and meaning from the motives and dispositions of which they are the indications. Human judicatures, it is true, are chiefly conversant about the former; but this is only because, to our limited perceptions, the latter can seldom be any otherwise clearly ascertained. The real object of inquiry to human judicatures is the internal disposition; it is to this that they adapt the nature, and proportion the degree, of their punishment.[118]

Charitable practice that is properly inspired by religion, as Wilberforce pointed out, must investigate and discover human interiority. However, he could not exclude the possibility that investigations of interiority may be used to cover up manipulations of the investigated person's will. While investigations of interiority are to be kept separate from the sphere of the law, they are based on the procedures that also inform Substituted Judgment: a translation of intentions between those who donate gifts, or issue verdicts, and those who receive gifts, or accept verdicts. Like the para-equity anticipated by some characters in *Bleak House*, Wilberforce's philanthropic vision of responsibility created a sense of aporia to the extent that it was also determined by what it was meant to oppose.

Criticizing the Christian establishment, Wilberforce complained about a lack in otherworldy orientation as well as a fixation on "law and custom."[119] His reservations about legislating charity thus built on more than a purely spiritual justification. Legislating charity protected those in need of support from having to depend on other people's willingness to help. Yet it did not liberate them from having to depend on forms of bureaucracy that tended to replace their dependence on others. The impact of personal decisions that were made within the sphere of the family, characterized by subjective risks, was then replaced by the impact of legally typified decisions made by bureaucracies, characterized by more objective risks.

What distinguished these kinds of decisions was not only the type of risks taken: while the former decision was subjective and limited by guilt, the latter was objective and self-righteous. The more important distinction between them was that the latter kind of decision eliminated the immediate interpersonal relation between donors and recipients. On the one hand, a legally enhanced form of individualism would consider it progress whenever the economic constraints defining those relations were eliminated. On the other hand, the more powerless members of society, who by and large were excluded from this ideal of establishing selfhood, would experience that kind of change as the institutionalized elimination of sympathy and charity.

At the same time, philanthropic institutions had to avoid creating the impression that the bureaucratic administration of their own benevolence eliminated interpersonal sympathy. Philanthropic institutions were not primarily interested in furthering individualism. They had to create a sense of social sheltering and the prevention of risks that both competed with state institutions and imitated the sense of sheltering traditionally provided by the family. They had to compensate for the problem that their structure resembled that of state institutions. On the receiving end, philanthropic institutions differed from state institutions only in that their justification of subsidies was motivated by an investigation of interiority for religious purposes. Just as a valid application of Substituted Judgment was defined by the incompetence of its "recipient," the philanthropic justification of subsidies was defined by the very destitution of recipients that charity is expected to eliminate.

What distinguished the ritual of philanthropic gift-giving from the mechanisms of legal fiction and legal reform was the goal of character formation, which the philanthropic donor would like to see realized in exchange for benevolence. To achieve that goal, philanthropists had to devise asymmetrical relationships that allowed donors to impose on recipients their own terms of exchange. Once both parties had internalized these terms, however, character formation (on both sides) was in danger of depending entirely on the mechanism of exchange itself. In contrast, philanthropists could not have an interest in leaving character formation as openended as all possible terms of exchange might suggest. Instead, they had to restrict emerging subjectivities to the moral mandate of a religiously defined character. They would like to see those in need of character formation turn into subjects who felt responsible for their own character formation.

The Protestant ethic, however, was continuously haunted by the very openendedness of character formation that philanthropists sought to restrict. Dickens's point about this contradiction is that sentimentally or philanthropically inspired responses to the openendedness of character formation can cause individuals to define themselves as lacking in responsibility and thus to inscribe themselves into moral and metaphysical economies of debt and credit. They begin to create vicious cycles, as pointed out by Nietzsche in *On the Genealogy of Morals*, between a demand for violence and a demand for responsibility. Those who survive Chancery's authoritative force and violence (in the sense of the equivocal German term *Gewalt*), for instance Esther and George, continue to identify, usually after a series of crises, with a cause to which they are willing to subordinate their entire lives. They readjust previously disappointed expectations accordingly and make some sort of pact with their own alienation in the new alliances for which they expect to sacrifice everything else. Those who renounce such an alliance, for instance Richard and Lady Dedlock, find themselves in a void that characteristically opens up after they have separated themselves from the sacrifices they made for their previous objects of love and devotion.

Within this constellation, as we have seen on account of the question who might be responsible for Krook's Spontaneous Combustion, Dickens plays notions of natural and unnatural death off against one another. Richard and Lady Dedlock end up separating themselves from their previous obligations in the form of literal death. Other characters continue to struggle with notions of metaphorical death and to articulate the problematic of reinstating the primacy of their desires, which they are not prepared to renounce for the sake of sympathy. In rebellion against her mother, Caddy Jellyby exclaims, "'I wish Africa was dead!' [. . .] 'I wish I was dead!' [. . .] 'I wish we were all dead'" (*BH*, IV, pp. 92, 94). In a similar fashion, Boythorn violently declares the accountability for uncomfortable public transportation a matter of individual responsibility: "'The coachman ought to be put to death!'" (*BH*, XVII, p. 298).

Bruce Robbins is correct in claiming that Dickens goes far beyond merely criticizing the professional impersonality of lawyers and certain philanthropists in *Bleak House* as the calculated effort, in a Foucauldian sense, to bypass domestic concerns by producing generically responsible individuals. He argues that Dickens's rendition of professional distance allows the reader to establish supra-ethical forms of coherence, which emphasize a systematic nexus, experienced by individuals, between the transference of aggression and the assignment of responsibility. For this reason, his reading of *Bleak House* calls for a rehabilitation of telescopic philanthropy as well as telescopic professionalism.

Africa in a sense regains its rights: it is not proximate ethics but distant politics [. . .] that should be decisive. [. . .] Given a social system which distracts attention from its own irresponsibility by distributing false accusations of responsibility among the innocent, these characters find their only freedom of thought and action in adopting the impersonality of Skimpole, of the lawyers, of professionals. [. . .] Although the professions stand for an impersonality that may provoke an individual to be "carried beyond" himself into violence, they also suggest, in the same impersonality, a means of being carried beyond the individual's rage, madness, and impotence.[120]

During the 1840s, the legal relevance of responsibility changed indeed considerably. "In the year when imprisonment for debts of less than £20 [attacked by Dickens in *The Pickwick Papers*] was abolished, 1844 (the year after the Borrioboolan expedition), the Companies Act was passed, taking the first step toward limited liability. The same concept that incarcerated a body in exchange for a business debt also of course precluded the modern corporation."[121]

In order to contemplate such relations between liability and responsibility, a certain professional distance is necessary, which Dickens simultaneously criticizes and ridicules. Robbins concludes that *Bleak House*'s narrative ambiguities account for this notion of supra-ethical responsibility. Dickens renders professionals and their institutions as both selfishly corrupt and capable of impersonal distance. Thus he manages to dissipate aporias that characters who struggle to readjust disappointed expectations experience as failed assignments of personal responsibility.

To narrate from the distance of thematized perspectivity is certainly to distance oneself, to some degree, from sympathy. But it is also to remain suspicious about the global declarations of aporia which characterize David A. Miller's account of the novel's complicity with forms of discipline.[122] By inscribing into impersonal distance a degree of strategic ambiguity, Dickens detotalizes aporias in the face of panoptical discipline. This is not to say that his social vision on the basis of sympathy and the dissipation of global aporias on the basis of supra-ethical responsibility necessarily contradict one another. Nevertheless, in order to clarify the interdependence of para-equitable and philanthropic visions of responsibility, it will be useful to emphasize the differences between his social vision and his dissipation of aporias.

In the case of sympathy being a para-equitable social vision, the exchange between donor and recipient will be considered both mutual and arbitrary with respect to that which as a result of the novel's social dimension emerges as uncanny. Insofar as the familiar is doubled in the opacity of the cursed case, it is supposed to allow for reversible exchanges between the classes, thus replacing the asymmetrical relation that defines philanthropic exchanges. However, the exchange of sympathy between the classes must remain non-institutional to avoid reifying the uncanny as a humanitarian version of frozen utopia. Moreover, in order to avoid giving up sentimentality as a strategy to activate sympathy across the classes, Dickens sometimes employs it anti-philanthropically, sometimes has it collapse in the grotesque mode.

Once Substituted Judgment makes its entry into the literary (con)text, it turns into a metaphor of this duplicity. Being part of the repertoire used by an allegedly corrupt legal profession to reproduce its own authority, Substituted Judgment also figures forth philanthropy as an alternative to legal equity: feeling sympathetic feelings *substitutes* for the partiality of passing judgments in the place of others. Thus social visions become imaginable without having to be justified by specific social norms. A literary friction between norms and their transgression, sympathy is then no longer a matrix of poetic justice. Instead, it becomes the fiction of its own anti-utopian possibility.

In the case of sympathy being an institutionalized ritual of philanthropic gift-giving, the exchange between donor and recipient will be considered asymmetrical and one-sided. Here, the exchange mechanism enacts altruism to circumvent the checks and balances of hidden self-interest. This form of exchange is as conservative as Substituted Judgment, in that the economy of the exchange, just as the legal fiction's manipulations of intention, must neither be disclosed nor made subject to debate. Insofar as the familiar is doubled in the opacity of the cursed case, philanthropy reduces its uncanny effects to the necessity to alleviate institutionally defined misery and to the assumption that the recipients of philanthropic gifts stand in need of institutionally defined character formation.

To the extent that philanthropy enacts a form of jurisdiction designed to remedy corruption in the legal system, it is para-equity. As institutionalized para-equity, however, philanthropy occasionally appears to be as rigid and corrupt as some courts of equity. In such situations, donors of philanthropic gifts such as Chadband emerge as self-appointed judges, presiding over the "case" of "incompetent" recipients on the scene of a metaphorical Substituted Judgment. In this particular function, the "judge" connects the asymmetrical ritual of exchanging philanthropic gifts with the judicial practice of legal fictions. Here sympathetic feelings no longer *substitute* for partial judgments made in the place of others. Instead, feeling sympathetic feelings *institutionalizes* the passing of judgments. Thus the necessity to help the destitute becomes imaginable in a ritualized form of sympathy, an institutionalized exchange of certain "blessings" of benevolence in return for character formation.

Philanthropic discourse on that necessity assumes that the gift of character formation forms part of an irreversible exchange. The recipient may return sympathy, but the donor is assumed beyond any need for character formation. For a donor such as Chadband, the exchange represents only a formalized quest for signs of salvation. For a recipient such as Jo, the irreversibility of that aspect of the exchange may in fact represent the *status quo*, that is, continuing barriers between classes.

The final question to be raised about para-equity concerns the status of Dickens's literary fiction in relation to legal fictions and philanthropic rituals. We have seen that the success of two Victorian institutions, law and philanthropy, is measured, according to their representatives, by how they find remedies against internal corruption. The price to be paid for such success is that institutional self-critique reproduces the same tendencies toward corruption that it claims to exorcize. Since literature is not as much bound by the pressure to affirm agendas as are legal and philanthropic institutions, it is in a better position to enact (though not transcend) the dubious success of institutional evolution as a reproduction of authority. In *Bleak House*, notions of renewal, revision, and reform, which are based on an interplay between literal and figurative death, compete with the institutional reproduction of authority. The site of Dickens's literary cross-examination of law and philanthropy may be defined as an interface between legal fictions and philanthropic rituals of character formation.

Within this interface, Dickens uses the concepts of injustice, misery, and opacity to establish different though related responses to the increasing complexity, in Victorian England, of positive law and the nature of expectations. The common law's tools for undoing injustice include equity. Philanthropy's tools for alleviating misery include para-equity. Literature's tools for dissipating aporias include narrative opacity. Legal fictions serve to determine liabilities for committed and suffered injustices. Philanthropic exchange rituals serve to determine the need for character formation. Dickens's literary fiction serves to determine responsibility in the midst of aporias.

However, liabilities for injustice are frequently manipulated, needs for character formation are frequently simulated, and prefabricated social visions are frequently mistaken for responsibility. Bentham's discourse on the corrupt practice of legal fictions, Wilberforce's discourse on the corruption of Christian philanthropy by "law and custom," and Dickens's literary discourse on an alleged corruption of expectations by Chancery's obscure practices – all three discourses are to a degree self-reflexive, that is to say, they generate duplicities in order to account for what each addresses as a problem of increasing cultural complexity. Bentham focuses on the duplicity of pragmatically justified but in practice reprehensible fictions. Wilberforce focuses on the duplicity that while legislating charity cannot create genuine moral justifications of subsidies, the philanthropization of fellow-feeling similarly subjects recipients of sympathy to its own institutional terms. Dickens focuses on the duplicity that a dissipation of aporia may generate as well as simulate responsibility.

Civil Death and Substituted Judgment enact these duplicities. We have seen how they serve to exchange deaths, intentions, and legacies among the contexts of common law, Evangelic philanthropy, and fantastic realism. We have also seen how they figure forth, in non-legal contexts, the isolation of prison inmates and the incompetence of those who find themselves subject to judicial fellow-feeling. Moreover, they are important metaphors of powerlessness in the legal, moral, and aesthetic contexts of Victorian responses to cultural complexity. In the contexts of law and philanthropy, they figure forth death to allow the control of inheritance by means of revoking civil rights and manipulating intentions – in law, concerning transfers of property in appeal cases, in philanthropy, concerning the quest for signs of salvation in asymmetrical rituals of exchange. In the context of literature, they also figure forth inheritance. Dickens uses that effect in order to liberate the significance of dying from a dichotomy of death-in-life and afterlife, which proves fatal to a number of characters.

Whenever these legal fictions operate on a literal level, they touch upon the boundaries of common-law institutions. Blackstone would see them as another remedy, Bentham as another scandal of existing legal practice. Whenever they operate on a metaphorical level, they are capable of figuring forth the very corruption they represent on the literal level. On both the literal and metaphorical level, they are employed where equitable justice is found missing. Judges use them (literally) to revisit rules for mediating and adjudicating conflicts. Philanthropists use them (metaphorically) to revisit the abuse of equity in the sphere of "law and custom," by establishing rituals of asymmetrical exchange. Dickens uses them to revisit illusions of powerlessness by dissipating global aporias.

In the context of judge-made law, they serve to revisit equity without advocating legal reform, thereby effectively protecting professional privileges. In the context of philanthropic rituals, they also revisit equity without advocating legal reform. Not only do philanthropists refrain from correcting instances of corruption in the legal system, they also perpetuate them, in a sense, by covering up the asymmetry at the bottom of the exchange of benevolence for character. In the context of *Bleak House*, they also revisit equity without advocating legal reform. Dickens's narrative dissipation of aporias and the characters' articulation of a crisis concerning their expectations do not merge into a common denominator of either legislative or moral renewal.

In contrast to law and philanthropy, *Bleak House* emphasizes needs for reform whenever individual attempts at revisiting equity stand themselves in need of correction. The novel revisits circularities in the law's self-justification by confronting them with paradoxes that the legal system cannot represent to itself – in the case of Richard, the paradox of law and crime, in the case of Lady Dedlock that of equitable unnatural death and retribution. While itself part of an institution – literary fiction – *Bleak House* need not be measured against standards of institutional validity to the extent that legal and philanthropic institutions do. Unlike law and philanthropy, Dickens can both use the notion of equity to revisit justifications of past reforms and use the notion of reform to revisit corrupt justifications of practiced equity.

CHAPTER 5

A curse gone re-cursive: the case and cause of solidarity in Conrad's The Nigger of the "Narcissus"

For what can more partake of the mysterious than an antipathy spontaneous and profound, such as is evoked in certain exceptional mortals by the mere aspect of some other mortal however harmless he may be, if not called forth by this harmlessness? [. . .] Coke and Blackstone hardly shed so much light into obscure spiritual places as the Hebrew prophets. And who were they? Mostly recluses.

Melville, "Billy Budd"

DISTRIBUTING COMPENSATORY JUSTICE AND JUSTIFYING THE DISTRIBUTION OF RISK

Like Dickens, Conrad explores the contexts in which the law's exemplary economy of norms and precedents may become paradoxical. In similar fashion, he channels this kind of excess towards the question of alternative internal standards for delinquency. Both Dickens and Conrad raise the question of excess in terms of the question as to how much the internalization of guilt in self-imposed isolation is indebted to the very legal assumptions about personality that causes conscience to operate. This question of guilt-as-indebtedness reflects an affinity, unintended by many of their characters, between the renunciation of norms or customs and the alienation from intimacy and social bonds.

Like Dickens, Conrad is concerned to question Bentham's attempt to anchor the calculus of pleasure and pain in a more or less self-regulating circuit of suffering and compensation – the utility principle. In similar ways, he variously suggests this concern throughout his early work: the postutilitarian idea of commensurating pain with its cure is already present in those philanthropic doctrines which advocate character formation as an anticipated compensation for suffering. Both Dickens and Conrad respond to certain moral and economic tensions in Victorian England between compensation and responsibility.

The different modes of supplementarity in which Dickens and Conrad respond to these tensions reflect the growing importance of insurances and tort law during the latter half of the nineteenth century. In Dickens's time, this growing importance was not yet distinct enough to form a context for the way *Bleak House* supplemented philanthropic expectations about the institutional fogginess of equitable justice. Conrad's complex treatment of solidarity, however, does take issue with the late-Victorian assumption that probabilistic approaches to compensatory justice are justified to the extent that they can be used to calculate the costs of individual damages as costs spread out over larger groups. This influential attitude towards solidarity was based, not on sentimental or philanthropic fellow-feeling, but on statistical reasoning and the rules of law which had to balance its scientific challenge with more traditional views on causation.

Insofar as this problematic became relevant for Conrad's early novels, it may be defined in two related respects: first, as an increased rationalization of the wanting logic of fate in terms of risks; and secondly, as a justification of suffering in terms of evolutionary adaptation. The opaque relations between cases and curses that caused Dickens's characters a great deal of discontent were in Conrad's time more frequently interpreted as a natural distribution of citizen-subjects' luck and mishaps. To those Victorians who opposed philanthropic notions of equity, this distribution would seem fundamentally just. In their eyes, it challenged and taught individuals to define their actions according to the risks that might bring them luck or misfortune.

In contrast, *Bleak House* still responds to contemporary assumptions that privileged prescriptive over mere normative evaluations of how nature and morality connect. While Dickens does split off fate from the norms and rules of inheritance, he eventually locates that split in Richard's and Lady Dedlock's failure to renounce modernity's dictates of law and genealogy. In the previous chapter, I argued that these dictates are embodied in the law's power to "substitute judgment" *in loco parentis* and in a family curse's power to generate aristocratic identity as the "death" of intimate bonding. What characters like Richard and Lady Dedlock "hand down" as their legacies is a sense of artificial legitimacy with which the contradictory effects of the case and the curse come together in the name of the person who gets to inherit the failed promises of Bleak House. Unmet expectations concerning that which supposedly governs property relations and family identity provide the very justification for that artificiality to continue.

Dickens enacts that justification of renewal without providing a vantage point outside the artificial mechanisms that reshuffle the expectations of his major characters. Thus the continuous creation and destruction of prescriptive evaluations as to what may constitute desired links between nature and morality causes those characters to assume and repudiate their legacies simultaneously. As a result, they end up constantly having to empty the prescriptive space, and to fill the ensuing epistemological and moral void, of inheritance as generated by the reversals of law and genealogy. They either manage or fail, first, to accept that artificiality as a component of the types of bonding that define their social identity; and second, to build up the expectation that it neither restricts nor determines the course of their self-examination *in foro interno*.

Dickens still responds to aporias arising from claims to prescriptive evaluations of how compensatory justice may be equitably distributed. Many of his characters struggle with the genealogical imperatives of an epistemological and moral void. In contrast, Conrad responds to a transitional situation in which distributive justice seems on the verge of turning into a justification of distributed risks and rationalized suffering. In this chapter, I will show that the cases and curses of such kinds of distribution reflect his characters' struggles with recursive rather than genealogical mechanisms of how articulations of suffering and claims to compensation reproduce one another. In those struggles, the reproductive cycles of suffering and equitable relief result from feedback processes between resentful complaints and legal claims. Ditching genealogical imperatives, some of Conrad's principal characters feel that they can enter those cycles at any point in time, without affecting the basic recursive mutuality of complaints and claims as such. In their understanding, feedback processes between complaints and claims may emerge from, but cannot be reduced to, the components that make up any particular reproductive cycle of injury and compensation.

Conrad's fictional response to this late-Victorian sense of a curse gone re-cursive reflects Anglo-American law's gradual transition from individualistic categories of "'moral causation' and 'free agency'" to the "'legislative' question of who should pay."[1] The skyrocketing number of railroad accidents made it obvious for everyone that dangers connected with industrialization were on the rise. As a result, judges were more frequently called upon to award damages for bodily injuries. Modifications in the domain of criminal, tort, and contract law followed, often restricting the scope of entrepreneurial liability and contributory negligence.

At stake was the problem how to separate remote from proximate causes that may or may not link one action (or its omission) to another; how to separate types of negligence that are actionable from those that are not; how to demonstrate fault on the part of an injurer or a contributor to injury; and how to separate voluntarily from involuntarily assumed risks. In the domain of tort law, for instance, legislators and judiciary confronted the felt necessity to restrict legal claims to collect damages for bodily injury with the moral ambiguities involved in distributing the burden of individual misfortune among other citizens. They essentially restricted the distribution of responsibility for individual suffering among all members of society. To the extent that they limited the scope of entrepreneurial responsibility, they also limited the scope of the binding force of solidarity for society at large. On a smaller scale, such a force also happens to be at work in insurances.

The emergence of insurances during the nineteenth century is closely connected to a type of rationality that formalizes the calculation of probable outcomes of events. Since those outcomes can derive from certain actions as well as their omission, the step from injury to compensation that defines objectifications of risk implied a devaluation of the actual intentions that constitute agency. Once insurers positivistically analyzed negligence in the context of potential events, they could objectively calculate risks outside the more unpredictable worlds of lived experience. In (simplified) contrast to proponents of free agency, insurers would interpret facts, laws, and causes in terms of the probable or improbable occurrence of events.

A rationalization of open endedness in terms of risk in fact required the insurer to suspend any judgment about the past or future causes of facts. Instead, he or she would record events without regard for their moral significance and more constant features of social life such as the desire to bond or commit a crime. Traditionally, inexplicable phenomena would be attributed to the invisible workings of divine Providence or supernatural forces that exceeded the human ability to find unchanging laws for them. In contrast, the reality of statistical facts depended on the probability with which they could be calculated to occur.

Such rationalizations of openendedness can generally do without references to nature or morality. To the extent that they did, risk defined individuals as parts of a specific kind of social totality. The mutuality and solidarity between such individuals arose from an attitude that was also at the heart of the nineteenth-century probabilistic revolution in the sciences. This attitude held that the scientific "fact" that luck and misfortune

are "naturally" distributed events also suggested that the workings of
chance can, in a nonmoral sense, be considered "equitable."

Herbert Spencer applied this sense of equity to a rationality of human
evolution when he argued that increased suffering does not necessarily
lead to a proportional increase of pain, but rather to an increased
insensitivity to pain: "[D]ivergences of sentiency [can] be expected from
the further evolution of humanity."[2] Spencer assumed that the human
ability to adjust suffered injury to the need for a "'compensatory
equilibrium'" of pleasure and pain reflected an evolutionary process
"'in which men themselves are answerable' to themselves, justice here
being simply a reflexive equilibrium, 'a definite balance, achieved by
measure.'"[3]

This notion of a "'conciliation of individual natures with social
requirements'" defined much of the nineteenth-century "functionalist
logic," which not only influenced "the practice of selective anesthesia"
and "the rational beneficence of the new-style philanthropists" but was
also "at work [. . .] in tort law."[4] Reading the nineteenth-century
tort-law treatise writer Francis Wharton in the light of Spencer, Dimock
maintains that once suffering was instrumentalized as a "usable resource,"

the rationalization of pain [became] openly economic, grounded in the tradeoff between the brute fact of suffering and the moral it could be counted on to
deliver. Nineteenth-century tort law thus stood as one of the boldest experi-
ments in commensurability, one of the boldest attempts to create a symmetrical
order out of its designated problem and solution. [. . .] Chastened by ["salutary
suffering" (Spencer)], workers would become so prudent as to make further
suffering unlikely. The cause of pain and the effect of pain were understood,
then, both to emanate from and to descend upon the same party. Mutually
entailed and inversely corresponding, they would work to neutralize and cancel
out each other. Tort law thus brought about an adaptive equilibrium in the
workforce, even as it achieved an operative equilibrium within itself, by a
method of damage control that contained the damage within the narrowest
possible compass. The problem of pain was not at all a problem here: not a
problem, because it could be counted on to take care of itself, to work toward its
own cure and its own end. [. . . For tort law,] suffering thus carried with it a
rationality of its own, a rationality that made it necessary, useful, and, in the
end, happily self-regulating. [. . .] This was the hope [. . .] of an entire age
fascinated by the phenomena of pleasure and pain and predisposed to see an
instrumental reason behind their occurrence.[5]

The way tort law instrumentalized suffering thus justified the important
role of the law as such in justifying a civic rationality of human evol-

ution. As the emergent nexus of proximate causation and limited liability implies, this rationality was also thought to be closely connected to the "evolution" of entrepreneurial activity.[6]

In *The Nigger of the "Narcissus,"* Conrad challenges this model of a self-regulating rationality of suffering. He does so by contrasting it with another way of overcoming modern aporias of humanitarian compassion: resentful solidarity. Without endorsing either alternative, Conrad cross-examines conflicting but related ways of commensurating the pain of suffered injury with the question who should pay for it. In his novella, he develops this alternative notion of solidarity as dependent on how individuals and communities manage the various forms of resentment that can turn social bonds into controlled struggles for recognition.

POSITIONED FOR PAYBACK: SOCIAL INSECURITY AND THE NEGATIVE GLITZ FACTOR

Like many twentieth-century cultural anthropologists and contemporary ethnographers trained in critical theory, Conrad seems interested in the way communities ranging from primitive groups to developed societies tend to connect the avoidance of violence and pain with claims to compensation. Like many of them, Conrad explores the question as to whether that connection may be grounded in the mechanism of symbolic founding murders or similar sacrifices of parts for the sake of the whole. Like many of them, he builds on the empirical (and perhaps obvious) fact that overarching crises often shake a community's moral foundations and push the legal means to resolve conflicts to their limits. Unlike many of them, Conrad does not attempt to answer the question as to why an instance of resentment against insurmountable barriers of social differentiation – barriers that can defy claims to individual compensation – is so often channeled toward an emissary victim.

The moral status of such designated victims is highly ambiguous. The victim who takes the blame is often also considered a celebrated figure of sorts. One effect of this negative glitz factor is that the victim's ambiguous moral status also allows for the conditions that define social differentiation at any given point to be rearranged in times of crisis. To be sure, such rearrangements may happen in the name of including the excluded in new solidarities against common enemies. Occasionally, though, all the uncompensated will be granted is participation in spectacles that allow them to name emissary victims. Claims to compensation for lost struggles for recognition then obviously shift from an individual experience of social insecurity toward a momentary sense of collective gratification.

Emergence of solidarity in such moments is as ambiguous as the moral status of the victims themselves. On the one hand, this type of solidarity works to perpetuate resentment. It provides a justification for rearranging, first, the conditions for present or future articulation of resentment and, second, the reasons why resentment as such should be employed to break up or modify existing structures of social differentiation. On the other hand, resentful solidarity entails the hope that structures of participation in social bonding may be distributed sentimentally. It thus suggests that these structures can somehow permanently be detached from the technical rigor of instrumental reason. For the emissary victim's suffering always also invites empathy from spectators who occupy marginal positions relative to centers of communal significance. To the extent that that type of empathy promises to transcend instrumental reason, it also lends itself to justifying new and different ways to commensurate pleasure and pain.

As a consequence of this duplicity, cultures of resentment can be said to generate solidarity, in the late-Victorian context, as a supplement to instrumental reason. In fact, resentful solidarity supplements the very notion of instrumental reason with which the logic of torts limits a community's obligation to bear the responsibility for individually sustained injury. As I argued before, the logic of torts that emerged during the nineteenth century balanced the rationale of insurances with contemporary rationalizations of suffering. It served to connect moral epistemologies of causation with legal classifications of responsibility. In performing that task, the logic of torts relied on certain economic assumptions, some of which protected entrepreneurial activity. In contrast, the logic of resentful solidarity implies that legal limits to responsibility may always be put to the test in nonlegal ways.

Those who subscribe to the latter view will therefore seek to challenge existing legal standards for determining responsibility. They will feel justified in contending that the economic premises of limited liability which govern the logic of torts can prevent resentment from finding its just articulation. In fact, appeals to justice emerge in scenarios of resentful solidarity as part of a political contestation that is no longer limited to legal procedures. That does not necessarily mean, however, that those appeals are intended either to transcend or to exclude the law. In fact, their iterability may be structured like that of ritual promises. Rather, appeals to resentful solidarity fuel, as Conrad suggests, a mutual reinforcement of empowerment and resentment. The point is of course that this mutual reinforcement politicizes economic premises of tort law in ways that would have been entirely unacceptable to the legal formalists of the day.

Conrad's conflation of legal and "para-legal" notions of solidarity, which I will explore in detail, allows us to reexamine his take on resentment. Fredric Jameson describes Conrad's vision and literary use of resentment as an "ideologeme," a narrative practice employed to provide "imaginary resolution[s]" to social and economic contradictions.[7] Rereading Nietzsche's narrative of *ressentiment* in *On the Genealogy of Morals*, Jameson correctly notes that the "diagnostic double standard" that inheres in the structure of articulated resentment is "autoreferential."[8] By "autoreferential" he means that resentment reiterates itself unconsciously, or "transform[s]" itself "dialectically",[9] in the very narrative strategy of intellectuals and artists who appear to insist on renouncing its revolutionary appeal.

Jameson then goes on to apply that same notion of reiteration or transformation to a number of Conrad's texts, including *The Nigger of the "Narcissus."* The novel strikes him as an exercise, first, in "recoding [. . .] the human pole of the labor process in terms of the whole ideological myth of *ressentiment*" that Nietzsche unearthed; second, in "contain[ing]" resentment in the "existentializing metaphysics" of the malevolent and humanity-defying sea; and third, in "rework[ing]" that containment "in melodramatic terms, in a subsystem of good and evil which now once again has villains and heroes."[10] Jameson concludes that Conrad's "ideologeme" of resentment reflects a "production of [narrative] form"[11] that represses resentment's autoreferential structure. Thus he is in a position to read *The Nigger of the "Narcissus"* against the grain, that is to say, contrary to Conrad's own famous statement in the "Preface" to the novella, as focused upon "all the things which Conrad preferred not to see [. . .]."[12]

While Jameson is right in describing resentment as an ideologeme, Conrad does not miss its autoreferentiality – at least not in *The Nigger of the "Narcissus."* In fact, Conrad uses his protagonist's ambivalent character both to insinuate and blur melodramatic distinctions between "villains and heroes." In doing so, he separates modernity's cultural productivity, or "autoreferentiality," of resentment from its identification with moralistic prudery and the hypocritical denunciations of those whose real accomplishments others envy. He thus explores the scale between a sense of nostalgia that is often associated with the effective reciprocity among members of a group – a reciprocity which social differentiation has broken down – and the various reinforcements of solidarity, both legal and nonlegal, that are supposed to help deal with that breakdown in reciprocity.

Conrad does not endorse "imaginary resolution[s]" to social and economic contradictions. Nor does he merely sublimate the ideological impact of their failures, as Jameson argues, in the "production of [narrative] form." Instead, Conrad "makes [his readers] see" the ambivalent things that can happen to the social tensions between egalitarian rivalry and hierarchical resentment when characters shift them to fictitious universes where they get to escape the isolation of their worldly failures and to share an unsatisfied desire for power with their fellows. In order to provide an alternative or para-"mythical" narrative about resentment, he invokes the contemporary logic of torts. On the one hand, Conrad presents a group of individuals defined by the fictitious negative totality of their shared failure to participate in processes of empowerment promised by the "grand narrative" of emancipation. On the other hand, he suggests that they are simultaneously subjected to a legally justified distribution of risks and a rationalization of suffering. Thus he is in a position to explore how this specific mutuality of political and legal narratives about solidarity and resentment can affect what Victorians experienced as an overwhelming impact of modernity on social differentiation.

Conrad is certainly far from embracing the full (and ambivalent) implications that twentieth-century legal realism had by letting nonlegal concerns interfere with formalism's proclaimed autonomy of the law. He does, however, seek to challenge the scope of contemporary legal questions concerning the relevance of causation for matters of responsibility. In the legal domain, that relevance reflected the influence scientific notions of causation had on the widespread sense of morality that vindicated individual rights in the form of claims to compensation. For a court to determine whether someone caused someone else's injury, and thus to hold that person liable without being charged with an arbitrary redistribution of damages, it was necessary to establish objective "chains of causation."

This rationale also included "intervening" or "supervening" causes sufficient to break those chains. In such cases, the burden of compensation would shift toward another potential injurer. Discussing the remote cause of instigation, James Fitzjames Stephen used the case of Iago and Othello to explain the legal approach to supervening causes. In

Stephen's opinion, Iago could be convicted as an accessory to Desdemona's murder only because he told Othello: "Do it not with poison, strangle her in her bed" (IV, i, 210), but not because he had told him of "facts" that in turn created a motive to murder her: "It would be an abuse of language to say that [Iago] had killed [Desdemona], though no doubt he has been the remote cause of [her] death."[13] Only if Othello's act had been not fully voluntary, according to Stephen, would Iago's instigation have amounted to causing the "principal offender" to "commit" the crime.

But John Stuart Mill's *System of Logic* of 1843 had already stirred up a debate over the metaphysical assumption, which to some extent informed the concept of causation in Anglo-American law, that voluntary human agency has a moral primacy over and responsibility for most events that occur in nature. At stake was the transition from an alleged objective character of causation to a nonmoralistic, probabilistic view on liability and negligence. One strategy to achieve this was to emphasize consequences instead of causes. Thus, while Iago did not strictly speaking cause Othello to act as he did, the principal offender's act could be described as a consequence of the instigation and liabilities be assigned accordingly. Moreover, the consideration was gaining ground that someone may be held liable, without any imputation of guilt on his or her part, for consequences that could be foreseen as likely to occur. To the extent that organized labor was appropriating the statistical foundation of this idea, the new liaisons between liability, negligence, and probability began to impede previous efforts to limit entrepreneurial liability, particularly where workers' compensation was at stake. Thus legal formalists were forced into the position of having to uphold an objective character of causation against growing criticism.

In contrast, skeptics such as Nicholas Green argued that the use of science to introduce an objective sense of morality into legal concepts of causation covered up what should actually be rendered visible: the politics of the law. Elaborating on Mill's argument that the cause of a given event is the sum of all of its antecedents, Green deconstructed, as it were, the official binary opposition between proximate and remote causes. As Horvitz explains, Green's deconstruction paved the way toward more elaborate theories of responsibility, for instance that of Oliver Wendell Holmes, who argued that the tests of liability should be considered external to and independent of a person's motives or intentions. In the final analysis, Green's and Holmes's arguments implied that questions concerning the difference between strict (objective) liability and negligence could no longer be settled by means of purely deductive reasoning. To assign liability "[without] objective causation" was to rely simply on "the fairness of the distribution of risk":[14]

In the 1870s few were yet prepared to agree that the infusion of moralism into law made it political. [. . .] By the end of the nineteenth century, however, orthodox legal thinkers would begin to downplay the "moral" element in causation while emphasizing the scientific basis of objective causation in law. But as they thereby implicitly conceded their own growing skepticism about the objectivity of moral categories, they laid themselves open for the final assault on causation by the legal realist heirs of Nicholas Green, who would not only show the illicit moralism of legal causation but also the collapse of causation in the natural sciences as well.[15]

As it turned out, the problem involved in commensurating suffering with compensation and separating strict liability from negligence was that such projects could end up generating endless "chains of causation." In a world of random events, connections between causes and events ceased to be necessary in order to determine liability. One effect was that against the backdrop of statistical correlations of facts and causes, the role of agency in tort law finally lost its traditional metaphysical foundations.

Another effect, one not too hard to imagine, may have been that both jurists and laypeople felt more encouraged to manipulate agency, for instance in order to fabricate causes for symbolic compensation. Making similar use of this possibility, Conrad's protagonist manipulates the ethnocentric environment in which he finds himself to generate forms of resentful solidarity. The black man's "method" is probabilistic in that he tries to make symbolic compensation for racism and ethnocentrism occur as events in tangled "chains of causation" – events "likely" to be "caused" by imperialist practices on British vessels. Like professional opponents of the "doctrine of objective causation," he does deconstruct the official sense of causality that regulates behavior in this particular environment. But instead of assuming that everybody's risks are fairly distributed, he makes an attempt at taking over his superiors' authority to assign liabilities.

The protagonist's manipulations of solidarity would not work the way they do if they could not draw implicit support from the inherited value, expressed in nineteenth-century theories of the modern state, that communal welfare is an entity greater than the sum of all the individually pursued interests which the idea of welfare is supposed to promote. For this is in fact the position that both Hegelians and Benthamites arrived at, even though they approached it from diametrically opposed philosophical poles. The protagonist can also make implicit use of a related development, namely that the combination of an increasingly complex need to protect society's welfare and an increasing sensitivity in matters of social justice caused state legislation to develop stricter norms for liability. Anyone acting in areas affected by legislation that protected public welfare would more and more often have to accept the burden of finding out the grounds for incurred liability at his or her own peril.

To some degree, the protagonist joins tort law's new project of deconstructing the increasingly arbitrary causal relationship, in matters of liability, between agency and intentionality. However, he reconnects those components as he provokes others to inculpate themselves for holding him as a symbolic prisoner of their ethnocentrism. His attempt to manipulate culpability works (only) to the extent that some of them are already willing to be reminded of their own experiences of victimization. As one consequence, the distribution of people whom others may consider liable for offending the community's welfare begins to appear more and more arbitrary. They sometimes act like spectators to, or even defendants in, a symbolic trial that involves dramatic reversals of retribution and compensation. To the extent that that happens, the protagonist appears successful in connecting the idea of liability for public offenses with the idea of recovering symbolic damages for marginalization.

Conrad dramatizes this undertaking as a complex exercise in performative agency. He does so in order to show in what ways such formations of resentment can be effective, even as they conspire with more official contemporary notions of solidarity derived from the idea of a fair distribution of risks. With respect to the more general postcolonial problem as to whether responsibilities for racism and ethnocentrism can or should be "limited," Conrad explores the extent to which an assignment of liabilities for these exclusionary practices reproduces the very conditions for marginalization that it is intended to overcome.

Addressing the same problem in postcolonial times, neopragmatist philosopher Richard Rorty endorsed a postmetaphysical form of human solidarity – one which takes the curse off ethnocentrism without reducing our responses to the historical contingencies that brought ethnocentrism into existence to an identification with humanity as such. To escape that dilemma, Rorty insisted on a certain sense of self-doubt, in democratic states, about one's sensitivity to the pain and humiliation of others.[16] His argument that the "liberal ironist," whom he advocates, is capable of distinguishing private questions about pain from public questions about the point of life may invite different responses. On the one hand, one might feel uneasy about the problem that the relation between obligations and contingency may itself be contingent. On the other hand, one might take Rorty's sophisticated nonfoundationalist optimism as symptomatic of a bourgeois intellectualism in its nostalgic decline. In the light of this problematic, it does not seem overstated to say that the politics of irony considerably contributes to many tensions in contemporary debates, as reflected in our now internally divided curricula, on the politics of representation in postethnocentric societies.

What distinguishes Conrad from the liberal tradition associated with Rorty's argument is his refusal to stop worrying about a problem that, in Rorty's view, cannot be sufficiently solved, that is, his refusal to live with the "contradiction [. . .] between an ironic awareness of the contingency of all norms, beliefs, and values and the necessity nonetheless to affirm a commitment to community, compassion, and self-invention."[17] This "irreducible antagonism [that] divides compassion and irony, faith and suspicion, commitment and contingency"[18] emerges in Conrad's *The Nigger of the "Narcissus"* as a schism between racial and national identity. On the one hand, Conrad would certainly *not* have advocated the politics of that schism in the postcolonial terms of "subaltern" identities – identities to be formulated in deconstructive relationships with the various racisms and nationalisms that they are meant to subvert and often used to describe colonial and postcolonial subjects.[19] On the other hand, he does find himself excessively concerned, in *The Nigger of the "Narcissus,"* with the problem that when the schism between racial and national identity is pronounced – such as in the case of protagonist Jim Wait – race tends to lose its power to hold the trust, or interest, of those outside its ranks and is perpetuated as part of that schism.

Like Rorty, Conrad does not endorse the "Nietzschean attitude"[20] of maintaining a distinction between the aesthetic and the moral in order to privilege the former over the latter. Unlike Rorty, he refuses to settle for an undecidability understood as integral to the aesthetic-moral complex. As one critic has claimed for *The Secret Agent,* the anarchic indecision at the bottom of Conrad's irony "creates its own obligations" to understand and (re)create worlds – despite the ironic "imperative" "*not* to permit the emigration of moral truths from the text to the world."[21] Similarly, *The Nigger of the "Narcissus"* may productively be read as a political ironist's, but not specifically a liberal ironist's cross-examination of solidarity and resentment.

Furthermore, the novel may productively be read as an exploration of the question as to whether the various mechanisms Conrad demonstrates as operating between solidarity and resentment properly frame the problem of solidarity when considered in racial and national terms. By discussing how legal fictions and rituals make their entry into Conrad's text, and thus drawing on the languages of law and cultural anthropology, I will show how different notions of equitable justice work to perpetuate the schism between racial and national identity as a mutual reinforcement of solidarity and resentment. I begin by describing the protagonist's project in the form of this question: How would one have to go about suggesting evidence of imperialist ethnocentrism that in view of an unspecified common good identifies some of its practitioners as liable wrongdoers?

A CASE OF MURDER OR A CURSE OF EXPIATION?

The often-expressed maxim "The absence of evidence is no evidence of absence" not only appeals to common sense but would also be hard to refute. Nonetheless, the courtroom stategy of narrative visualization, or using words appropriate to make something evident, has a double-edged quality that perhaps this maxim does not entirely cover. Verdicts may be derived from what is made visible as well as what is not made visible (or made invisible), from traceable evidence as well as the likelihood of unseen conspiracies. This double-edged quality of visualization has, since Aristotle, been reflected in (but not restricted to) the growing number of cross-examinations of legal and dramatic or fictional diegesis.[22] Equally, expectations toward equitable justice are generally associated with a notion of evidence employed to visualize something that is absent, based on its similitude with alleged causes for withheld justice. Whenever causes for withheld justice come on narrative display, however, visualization can easily be used to substitute an absence of evidence by causes for the chains of events whose connection may be otherwise inaccessible.

Consequently, narrative visualization does not so much provide sufficient similitude with the events, actions, and motives under scrutiny as it allows to stage events, actions, and motives in the light of the expectation to bring something about, for instance "racial justice." Solidarity may thus arise from a collective investment in bringing about racial justice as a form of distributive or compensatory justice. However, what happens if visualization rests on *simulacra* that defy similitude, indicate the very artificiality with which they render form to a fantasmatic figuration, and thus dissimulate equity? The problem of solidarity then arises in the form of the question as to who controls that dissimulation of equity. And the attempts to answer that question often confront the necessity to include what was previously excluded from the benefits of justice with another necessity – namely, the necessity to control the admissibility of evidence for any exclusion from justice. In order to explain how Conrad addresses that question, I will first introduce James Fitzjames Stephen's legal model of evidence, which was prevalent in Conrad's times, and then move on to argue how it may be used to read *The Nigger of the "Narcissus"* as its dissimulation.

When Stephen published *The Indian Evidence Act* in 1872, British law traveled to India. The novelty of this act lies in its attempt, in the tradition of Bentham's legal positivism in *The Rationale of Judicial Evidence* of 1827 and against the tradition of classical common-law theory, to define the relevancy of facts. Like Bentham in his later years, Stephen made a plea for statutes and principles, although he also criticized Bentham for his alleged lack of practical mastery of the law.[23] *The Indian Evidence Act* is still the law in India. And the 130 pages of Stephen's introduction are still part of the several thousand pages of commentary that have since grown around the act.

Stephen's efforts to simplify British law for the Indian context triggered his attempt at supplying the lacking definition for relevant facts in British common law as it existed at the time. In doing so, Stephen insisted, as he referred to Mill's *System of Logic*, on determinable correspondences between "facts in issue" and facts that cause, result from, introduce, explain, or even obscure facts in issue, thus tending either to prove or disprove them. Stephen therefore operated within the aforementioned paradigm of "objective causation." In many instances, his *Digest of the Law of Evidence* reflects the comprehensive positivist effort to classify the complexities of "intervening" and "supervening" causes."

Similarly, the argument Stephen made in his introduction to *The Indian Evidence Act* is based on principles of inductive reasoning and as such drew some criticism. More importantly, he used five murder cases to illustrate the general principles of evidence as he saw it, namely to show what "makes the existence of one fact a good ground for inferring the existence of another."[24] Stephen maintained that since "[murder cases] involve capital punishment and excite peculiar attention, the evidence is generally investigated with special care."[25] However, he fell short of explaining why murder cases "show so distinctly the connection between fact and fact."

This inconsistency in Stephen's and other contemporary discourses on evidence has caught the attention of literary critic Alexander Welsh. It leads him to conclude that common "associations [of unnatural death] with desecration and pollution" and "a sense of violation of human life" gave rise to an entire jurisprudence of causation in the nineteenth century. This new type of jurisprudence refined existing degrees of liability for homicide – murder, manslaughter, accident, and self-defense – in order "to determine when a death may be attributed to the conduct of a particular person."[26]

Stephen inscribed his own discourse on circumstantial evidence into the tradition of Burke and Bentham. In this tradition, murder cases often served to support arguments for higher degrees of probability beyond reasonable doubt. But why murder cases? Welsh explains the sense of importance which unnatural death used to have in violating communal expectations by referring to a covert nexus between law and natural religion. Law applied to the dead body theories of circumstantial evidence in order to indicate murder or suicide. Similarly, natural religion commonly interpreted the dead body as evidence of the immortality of the soul.

In short, both discourses applied "strong representations" to achieve their different goals, namely that a prisoner is guilty or that Christianity is true.[27] On the one hand, law exploited the dynamic relation between law and fact in order to diminish uncertainties in matters of fact. On the other hand, natural religion had to recover lost ground. Its rhetoric of inference could cover up only insufficiently the undeclared *a priori* assumptions it claimed to discover in the evidence selected to prove the soul's immortality. Criminal law ultimately shifted the attention paid to the dead body away from the theological question about the death we all have to die. Instead, it adopted the notion that unnatural death can bear witness to how natural life may have been terminated due to malice aforethought.

As that attention shifted, however, law still responded to the same general crisis of "unnaturally" violated life that natural religion used to take care of. Stephen's discourse on relevant facts with regard to evidence thus externalized natural religion's sense of probation in a private "trial of life." Circumstantial evidence now suggested that a murderer could be detected and convicted at all times. No longer did it "prove" the truth of an afterlife. Instead, it now served to reduce the theological dimension of unnatural death to cases of homicide and to make liable those who caused the untimely death of others: "If murder thus compensates for death, and a trial of the few for the probation of the many, it can further be noted that well into the nineteenth century the sentiments of natural religion were directly supportive of the use of evidence at law."[28]

James Wait, the "nigger" on the "Narcissus" and protagonist of Conrad's novella, does not die as a result of murder but as a result of tuberculosis. However, the way he himself and the crew anticipate his impending death in the context of alleged "malingering"[29] constantly suggests something more than death due to illness. Apart from our common experience that in fiction nobody seems to die accidentally, Wait's death is time and again associated with his incarceration by the captain and his victimization on the part of some crew members. As readers who know that he is going to die, we are provoked by Conrad to join the I- and we-narrators in a search for concealed causes for what in legal terms might be called wrongful death. It is a narrative search for evidence, not of murder, but what contributes to Wait's natural or unnatural death and why the way he and the crew anticipate it creates an impression of desecration and pollution.

This "sense of a violation of human life" (Welsh) certainly accounts for the crew's anxieties about Wait not dying for so long. Those anxieties eventually contribute to a crisis about authority on the ship. They suggest a ritual of expiation that is supposed to compensate for the various shortcomings or setbacks caused by Wait's impending death. Many times, these aspects of ritual supersede the evidentiary aspects of a simple case of fraud on his part. The narrator suggests the possibility that Wait may be turning his anticipated natural death into the anticipated trial of an unnatural death caused by someone other than himself: [To Podmore:] "'Go away! Murder! Help!'" (*NN*, p. 86).

It seems rather unlikely that Wait really expects to be killed the moment he exclaims "Murder!" But he does evoke the sense of desecration and pollution that according to Welsh was at the time still associated with unnatural death. More importantly, he also inverts the role Stephen thought circumstances ought to play in the relations between causes and consequences of unnatural death. One might assume that Podmore is, contrary to the narrator's account, planning to let Wait die from mere exposure to his strange acts of preaching. But even if that were the case, Stephen would still argue that that death must, in order that the accused may be convicted, be a consequence, on ordinary causal principles, of what Podmore did to Wait. (Yet he did not physically harm him.) It would not even be enough that Podmore's psychotic attempts to convert Wait to Christianity were a necessary condition of the death. Criminal law would require any advocate of Wait's "cause" to show that the death was a consequence of those attempts.

The matter gets more intricate, however, if these causal relations include Wait's illness as part of the coexisting circumstances of his death. For as long ago as Hale, it was thought that "if a man be struck by some such disease which possibly by course of nature would end his life in half a year and another gives him a wound or hurt which hastens his end by irritating and provoking the disease to operate more violently or speedily, this hastening of his death sooner than it would have been is homicide or murder."[30] Stephen's Victorian version holds that "a person is deemed to have committed homicide, although his act is not the immediate or not the sole cause of death, if by any act he hastens the death of a person suffering under any disease or injury which apart from such act would have caused death."[31] Wait does of course not actually die at this point. But the lack of that formal requirement, as it were, complicates rather than dismisses or disclaims the problematic tensions between causes and consequences that were already part of the contemporary legal debate.

By exclaiming "Murder!", Wait emerges as someone trying to invoke, if not assume, a judge's authority to admit certain "coexisting circumstances" as evidence of homicide or murder. Building on the legal premise that an existing illness or susceptibility of the victim does not break the chain of causation regarding homicide or murder, Wait creates the impression that his death is prematurely near and that Podmore's "acts," like those of other crew members allegedly preying on his illness, thus "hasten his [Wait's] end." In the light of this strange rationale, it seems almost fitting that Wait apparently neither takes much care of his illness nor asks for or even accepts treatment. Criminal law considered the irresponsible conduct of a patient no defense to charges of homicide. As Stephen put it, "If [accused] inflicts a bodily injury on another, which would not have caused death if the injured person had submitted to proper surgical or medical treatment, or had observed proper precautions as to his mode of living," the injurer is deemed to have committed homicide if death follows.[32] If Podmore had actually wounded Wait (again, he did not) in an attempt to murder him, and if Wait had later died as a consequence of that wound, no matter whether it was mortal or not, Wait's negligence in attending to wounds that might have accelerated his decline in health would not have exonerated the wounder from criminal liability.

The point is of course that Wait *does* die later, though not from wounds any crew members inflicted on him, but from the illness he refused to have them attend to. On the one hand, while their attendance could not have prevented his death, it might have eased his suffering. On the other hand, a premature disclosure of the illness might have made future employment more difficult, in case he initially expected to survive his trip on the "Narcissus." Instead of settling with either alternative, however, he apparently decides to raise the question as to whether the death he is expecting is a consequence merely of this illness. To the extent that crew members begin to speculate on other possible causes, perhaps some sort of unfair and degrading treatment on other ships that Conrad's novella tells nothing about, Wait is already in a position to manipulate culpability.

In such a scenario of death, Mill's aforementioned notion that the cause of an event is the sum of all its antecedents takes on an ominous dimension. For this view would place on all previous superiors of Wait's the risk of his death, which might not have occurred but for the gross negligence they could (or could not) be proven to have displayed by exploiting his good health. Despite the fact that risk liability has generally little place in criminal law, Wait would succeed, if indeed he wanted to create such a scenario, in separating negligent actions from possibly good intentions and in submitting certain causal principles adopted in tort law to his private fantasies of enforcing a penal policy. His odd success would be measured according to how convincing it is to the crew that his seemingly unreasonable refusal to have his illness attended to does not break the chains of speculative causation which he establishes by suggesting himself as the scapegoat for racist and ethnocentric practices on British vessels.

Moreover, he seems to be successful to the extent that he does not express this idea, provided he actually intends to, as a claim to compensation. For as soon as he did, he would have to take issue with the significant legal problem that while all injuries inflicted on a workman produce changes in his body which do indeed continue despite a refusal to undergo treatment, some "consequences" may well carry limitations that prevent the illness or disability from being attributed to the original scene where the injuries in question occurred. By not explaining the reasons why he refuses his illness to be attended to, he also avoids the impression that his refusal comes across as a binding choice of conscience, one that he would not be allowed to abandon in case superiors or crew suspected him, as in fact they do, of merely "shamming sick" (*NN*, p. 88) in order to escape his duties. Instead, he seems to use his silence to suggest that what is wrongful about the death he is waiting for cannot be redeemed by the authority of national law.

The narrator suggests that one part of the crew feels sympathetic to that anticipation of a wrongfully redemptive death as well, especially those who see their own lives endangered by the austere, or stubborn, way the captain handles the ship during a powerful storm (*NN*, pp. 54ff). In contrast, the superiors, for instance Baker, who with his "delicate tact" "refuses to take [the crew's anxieties] seriously" (*NN*, p. 33), seem inclined toward debunking the sacrificial pathos with which sailors like Donkin use the ambivalence of Wait's illness to destabilize customary and, in their view, binding rules of cooperation. Other crew members, the narrator indicates, find comfort in appealing to supernatural causes. They label Wait a perpetrator violating what they assume to be the unwritten, natural, and eternal "laws" of the sea: "Land. The land that draws away life from sick sailors. [. . .] Here was the land [. . .] – there was that corpse. Cause and effect" (*NN*, pp. 109, 116).

Whatever Wait's "case" may be or is made to be, the various parties, who form small competing pseudo-communities according to what they make Wait stand for, are equally affected by what each has projected onto Wait, whether they have genuinely self-protective or plain strategic reasons for doing so. For some, Wait becomes the prisoner of his image of the "gaol" in which he sees himself confined (*NN*, p. 83). Philanthropically inclined crew members are sometimes so overwhelmed by Wait's unscrupulous abuse of their benevolence that they turn themselves into "cheerful accomplices in a clever plot." They read his impending but not yet occuring death as a symptom that "[t]he universe conspired with James Wait" (*NN*, p. 106). Even the captain, who eventually confines Wait to the sick-bay, is somewhat overwhelmed by the crew's resentment against his act. For he was trying to prevent just that when he decided to confine Wait, by way of an alleged act of "compassion over the incertitudes of life and death" (*NN*, p. 94), and let him "go out in his own way" (*NN*, p. 93). The curse of Wait's case repeatedly suggests more than evidence for concealed causes of his death. At the very least, Conrad distorts the way Stephen would be looking for "evidentiary relevances."

Wait's case is not a murder case that would simply set off predictable investigative procedures. For a case is already being made by himself and other characters long before he dies. Instead, the characters make certain decisions concerning how to act upon the interpretive decisions they have made about Wait's status, combining means to be chosen and ends to be attained in what Alfred Schütz called "motivational relevances."[33] Conrad thus enables the reader to observe, and perhaps even participate in, the production of "strong representations" – religious, legal, or literary representations that "insist on submitting witnesses to the test of corroborating circumstances" and that "mirror without mystery the Pauline evidence of things not seen."[34] With Stephen, British law travels to India in a simplified form[35] and mysteriously aligns the question of unnatural death with the idea of concealed facts putting peculiar pressure on judicial inference. With Conrad, Stephen's exported law seems to be traveling from Bombay back to London and no less mysteriously aligns unnatural death with the idea of an interaction between ritual and law.

THE MULTIPLE BORDERS OF RESENTMENT, OR: ALTRUISM ON TRIAL

Traveling on the high seas, the "Narcissus" is occupying a "zone" where national sovereignty over matters of injury, responsibility, and compensation is often questionable or in dispute.[36] Similarly, the "Narcissus" is itself an isolated legal space, a confined space which mirrors various standards of jurisdiction and even legislation when it comes to resolving conflicts nonviolently. It mirrors standards of legislation in so far as Conrad emblematically suggests the "Narcissus" as the ship of state put to a test outside the national borders, "a fragment detached from the earth [. . .] like a small planet" (*NN*, p. 21). It mirrors standards of jurisdiction in so far as it confronts the authority of the captain, figuring as the crew's Lord Chancellor, with the crew's concerns about contemporary efforts to reform unsatisfactory working conditions on British vessels.

Samuel Plimsoll's humanitarian reforms in 1875 and 1876 were directed against the abuse and exploitation of seamen. Plimsoll's reforms were effective in saving sailors' lives and in preventing them from being confined or jailed for refusing to serve on unseaworthy vessels.[37] In the novel, however, Plimsoll's sentimental appeals, as voiced by various crew members and the we-narrator (*NN*, pp. 78–9), come across, in the eyes of the I-narrator, as mutinous resentment. And as conflicts arise in a grey area between these two spaces of jurisdiction – the maintenance of order on the part of the owners or their representatives and the call for reform on the part of some sailors – attempts at conflict "management" resort not only to legal devices but also to rituals of expiation.

The crew's resentment challenges the defense mechanisms that the captain's jurisdiction customarily upholds against conflicts. The touchstone of conflict, both projected onto and enhanced by Wait – whose "moribund carcass" is the "fit emblem of their aspirations" (*NN*, p. 90) – registers different representations of the crew's various unfulfilled aspirations. This is what anthropological critics such as Eric Gans have in mind when they relate representations to a deferral of violence. In this view, a heightened risk of violence must be expected if each member of a group at the periphery can get in on the consumption of an object at the center. The central object is then turned into an ostensive sign that indicates an aborted gesture of appropriation. The object's deferral by the sign takes place in a community defined by the reciprocal conditions of the sign's emission. In such a prototype of an exchange system, the object then becomes sacralized and/or sacrificed.

No individual member of the community can ever appropriate the ritual reproduction of that scene of representation on his or her own. But some get a greater share than others in the sacrificial feast that holds the potential violence of egalitarian rivalry in check. Nonetheless, a discrepancy remains between the competition for socially recognized significance and the inaccessibility of the center for those at the periphery. This continuous discrepancy keeps alive what Gans calls a culture of drowned resentment.[38] Modifying assumptions about the founding murder as a self-reduplicating victimage mechanism[39], Gans here refers to the concept of *ressentiment* as Conrad's contemporary Nietzsche employs it in *On the Genealogy of Morals* and *The Antichrist*. But by going beyond Nietzsche's reference to Judeo-Christian morality, he views it as a tension between center and periphery that is constitutive of cultures in general.[40]

Nevertheless, when the we-narrator, at the opening of section V, calls Wait's suffering "demoralising" (*NN*, p. 103) for the crew, Nietzsche's assessment of pity, in *The Antichrist*, as a translator of powerlessness into egoism comes to mind.[41] Much as Wait may be viewed by his sympathizers among the crew members as the equivalent of a tragic hero, they have no desire to stand in his place. In their eyes, he seems to have taken the blame for the sins of his persecutors, who declare him simply to have taken advantage of the crew's wavering submission to pity. In taking the blame for his persecutors' resentment, he confirms the others in their submission to the necessity of social difference. Wait's power, as opposed to the captain's, is never wholly legitimate. Despite "the provoking invincibleness of that death he felt by his side" (*NN*, p. 54), he is always a potential victim of the crew's dissatisfaction. While they go at great pains to identify with the victim's sufferings, they actually examine him from the safety of the periphery, which consoles for the lack of centrality: "[. . .] we wished to save ourselves from the pain of remorse, but did not want to be made the contemptible dupes of our sentiment" (*NN*, p. 30).

This dubious impact of sentimentality also reveals to them that the structure of resentment perpetuates social differentiation according to the parameters of center and periphery. They get to see themselves as only once more seeking to repeat the ritual mechanism of sacralizing the victim of persecution from the vantage point of surviving spectators. Wait's death emerges as the "death of an old belief [that] shook the foundations of our society. A common bond was gone; the strong effective and respectable bond of a sentimental lie" (*NN*, p. 115). Whenever they are willing to acknowledge the very perpetuation of resentment they have been seeking to overcome, Wait turns from a sacred object into an uncanny mirror of their paradoxical desire, reflecting their "weird servitude" (*NN*, p. 31): "[. . .] we hated him because of the suspicion; we detested him because of the doubt. We could not scorn him safely – neither could we pity him without risk to our dignity. So we hated him, and passed him carefully from hand to hand" (*NN*, p. 54). Which raises the question as to how the legal measures taken against Wait relate to these uncanny features of ritual.

In order to answer this question, we must take a closer look at the various challenges to solidarity on the "Narcissus." Bruce Henricksen argued, by elaborating on Ian Watt's remarks in *Conrad in the Nineteenth Century*, that the multiplicity of voices in Conrad's *The Nigger of the "Narcissus"* consists of contradictory discourses about solidarity – idealizing, paternalistic, moralizing, legalistic, and philanthropic – on the part of both characters and narrators.[42] The novella confronts the nostalgia for an organic community of sailors, based on conservative co-operation, with a subversive sense of sympathy with those who suffer or seem to suffer, based on a communal resentment against inflexible hierarchies of power and property.

Henricksen shows how Conrad sustains that confrontation by means of a strategic inconsistency between the two narrators ("we" and "I"). The "we"-narrator, he explains, glorifies the crew's obedience in opposition to Donkin's greed as well as Wait's self-pity. In contrast, the "I"-narrator subjects that sense of obedience to panoptical inspection, thus violating formal consistency in the interest of surveillance. The same narrator who was supposed "to make you see" ("Preface," *NN*, p. xlix) finds himself ironically subverted at the end of the novel, when he clouds the dialogical origins of his own narrative – the crew's heteroglossia of the "divers tones" in their "thick mutters" and "ringing voices" (*NN*, p. 10), most obvious in characters such as Wamibo and the Scandinavians – with monological nationalistic aspirations.[43]

Human altruism seems somehow on trial.[44] The different voices create "centrifugal and centripetal forces within the social unit that is forming across linguistic, national, and racial boundaries" and "inevitable differences in a period of colonialism and expansionism."[45] The voices articulate various kinds of evidence for genuine and simulated altruism. Those who seem most sympathetic to the ones who suffer (for instance Belfast) are often portrayed as neglecting a sense of duty necessary for the common good of the ship. In contrast, those who seem most unsentimental in their attempts at sustaining solidarity (for instance Singleton) are often portrayed as neglecting a sense of sympathy necessary to safeguard the crew from what seems an exploitative ignorance on the part of their superiors.

Taken as a whole, these voices make nostalgia for solidarity ambivalent. The ship is no longer the monolithic microcosm of a culture "traveling" through the liminal situation of ownership conflicts. The microviewpoints of Conrad's competing voices constitute a battle over narrative power within the liminal ritual of communal transition, suggestive of the idea that anthropologists like Renato Rosaldo[46] replace concepts of *limen* [threshold] (Victor Turner)[47] by concepts of *border* in order to delineate communities as interactions of multiple voices. No longer is it evident what kind of community, supposedly as a whole, goes through an unstable process of transition. The "threshold" event marking the peak of a communal crisis may not be experienced at all as one single communal event. Instead, it is far more likely to be experienced as different events constituted as such in different narratives. In other words, liminality emerges as a scene of competing representations. On that scene, performances of the communal crisis by means of ritual mechanisms border on each other and, in doing so, affect borderlines between performances.

As the "Narcissus" faces a crisis in terms of solidarity, contrasting with as well as reinforced by a "crisis in nature" – the powerful storm on

its voyage from Bombay to London – contradictory legal and philanthropic acts of "crisis management" result from those multiple approaches to solidarity. The most prominent of those acts may be the
incarceration of Wait. As I indicated before, the sick Caribbean sailor
has tuberculosis from the moment he enters the ship and dies from it
toward the end the novel. His incarceration, as ordered by Captain
Allistoun, in turn evokes contradictory responses. The few nostalgics on
board, such as old Singleton, urge Wait to "'get on with [his] dying'"
(*NN*, p. 30). They somewhat transform the posture of Wait's waiting into
a Kierkegaardian *sickness-unto-death*. Those who work to ease his suffering, like young Belfast, "as sentimentally careful of his nigger as a model
slave-owner" (*NN*, p. 104), develop a certain anxiety about having to see
him die (*NN*, p. 95). They somewhat transform Wait from a tribal totem
into their psychopathological double.

David Manicom demonstrated how Wait, in waiting to die, creates
fictions about his illness. Not only do these fictions allow him to perform
death as a way of masking his will to life. They also make him narcissisti-
cally embrace and get caught up in them. Furthermore, Manicom
correctly notes, as he refers to Frege's distinction between sense and
reference, that Wait's deceit does not merely make his illness ambiguous. This ambiguity co-depends on the various narrative perspectives
projected on the illness. Hence the ambiguity actually reflects what
Frege calls a "coextensiveness" of equally valid statements about a
withheld fact. To the extent that the divergent perspectives mutually
comment on one another's spheres of fiction-making, Manicom calls the
resultant self-reflexivity of fiction-making with regard to the illness
"narcissistic narrative."[48] He thus successfully transcends a dichotomy
commonly attributed to narcissism: Wait's version of it amounts neither
to the self-referential psychodynamics of individuation nor to a personality disorder frequently displayed in maladaptive self-cathexis.[49]

Wait is not the only fiction-maker in Conrad's novella who ends up
caught in the confinement of his own fictions. The legal ramifications of
Wait's incarceration – as I mentioned, he is eventually found "shamming sick" (*NN*, p. 88), allegedly in order to escape his duties – make him
both a case of fraud with regard to nostalgic solidarity and a case of
sympathy with regard to his occasionally ignored real sickness. Both the
superiors and the crew turn Wait into a symptom of the crisis regarding
solidarity each thinks pervades the 'Narcissus.' Both kinds of narration
construct Wait's narcissism as a curse somehow harking back at the
various cases of fraud and sympathy made of him.

Both parties, the narrators are suggesting or at least implying, seem to use Wait as a scapegoat for the shortcomings of their respective aspirations. To the nostalgics as well as the superiors, he is a threat to boundary maintenance between the ranks and classes. To most of the crew members – except for Donkin, who strategically employs the case of Wait's "'blooming himposyshun'" (*NN*, p. 81) for his own contradictory agenda of "'black fraud'" (*NN*, p. 30) – Wait's suffering eventually turns into a redemption from their own real or imaginary sufferings. The various anxieties about his death, coupled with the peculiarly benign winds after his death, in fact implicate even the narrators in the sailors' attempts at turning Wait's curse into a case of supernaturalism. The fact that the supernatural element extends Wait's sacralization beyond his death, as another means of deferring violence, further suggests that solidarity on the "Narcissus" is closely related to the anthropological notion of resentment that Gans claims, as I mentioned earlier, is generally constitutive of cultures.

However, the ominous black man Wait does not simply turn into an emissary victim of the others' self-deceptions, much as these self-deceptions are based on satanic archetypes of racism.[50] After all, his death is not the result of a founding murder, for he dies from his illness. The text raises questions, though, about how accidental or unnatural his death is in other than medical terms. The text raises questions, that is, about the various explicit and implicit appropriations of his death as either inevitable in nature or wrongful by implication.

ANTICIPATING WRONGFUL DEATH

The sense of expiation that cases of unnatural death aroused in the communities affected by them had established, in British common law, a legal articulation of the problem that formally lasted until 1846. By that time, the legal institution of deodands – an alloy of biblical and pre-Christian traditions, which made religious expiation compatible with increases in the Crown's revenue – was replaced, in a statutory change[51], by individual compensation. If an inanimate object had directly or indirectly caused death, that object, until 1846, was confiscated by the Crown as a deodand. The monetary value attributed to it could be claimed and forfeited by the authorities in charge (the Crown, the court). In contrast, kin of the deceased had no right of action to recover the damages entailed by the death.

These restrictions were similar to the practice of forfeiture and prohibition of burial that applied, until 1823 (1870), to cases of suicide.[52] In both homicide and wrongful death (where no direct human agency needed to be involved), either the convict's fortune or the instrument of murder – which could belong to either the person causing the death or to the victim – was confiscated. The principle of deodands allowed for confiscation under the premise that even

where the injury to the victim would not only have been amenable to compounding, but also where this remedy was obligatory, death was not compoundable. [. . .] The unnatural death of a human being was, at the very least, a quasi-crime; the effect of it transcended mundane considerations, and entailed expiation in one form or another. This expiation is naturally directed towards God, the transcendent sovereign of human society, who is thought to demand and expect it, but in practical terms, is demanded and received by the king, his earthly magistrate. Finally, and most importantly, moral culpability is not a necessary condition for imputation of guilt, except in terms of the magnitude of the penalty. Guilt can be contracted very much like a disease; one may be afflicted with it not only unwittingly, but even against one's most earnest efforts and precautions.[53]

Things changed with the abolition of deodands in 1846 when wrongful death was relegated to civil tort law. Kin of the victim of such a death could now recover damages entailed to them by that death. Correspondingly, expectations about individual compensation – and, along with it, toward the compoundability of death – rose without altogether obliterating the nexus between religiously founded expectations toward life and legal definitions of death. The principle of deodands translated expiation into the forfeiture of an *offending thing*. And while that principle was subsequently "transfigured" into a "judicial fiction" rather than given up entirely,[54] questions of private liability for death now could become more important.

This development ran parallel with certain reforms in the 1840s that loosened the legal rigor of responsibility in general. When imprisonment for business debts of less than £20 ended in 1844, the Companies Act was passed. It opened up the sphere of limited liability, which was further formalized in the Partnership and Limited Liabilities Acts (1855) and the Joint Stock Companies Act (1856). It was still felt to be immoral for an ordinary commercial business to be carried on under conditions which might allow the partners to escape paying its debts. But now joint stock companies, prototypes of the modern corporation, began to generate "a new form of business association in which the members might not know each other personally, need not necessarily work together, and could not 'be called upon to contribute to the debts and liabilities of the company.'"[55] Businesspeople such as those owning the 'Narcissus' began to look for returns on their raised capital anywhere in the world economy, thus potentially fueling the economic irresponsibilities commonly attributed to capitalist imperialism.[56] Liability and responsibility began to deviate from one another in terms of corporative and personal accountability. Hence Nietzsche's persistent efforts to debunk a nonhistorical understanding of responsibility and the economy of pity.

Nonetheless, it is important to keep in mind that confiscations and forfeitures previously based on the principle of deodands continued in the fiction of "*reipublicaedand*"[57], which still allowed the state to collect revenue from harm suffered by individuals. Moreover, tort law still classified harm in terms of its impact either on the community or the individual. Depending on which road was taken in a given case, harm – for instance that associated with wrongful death – would either be a matter of objective liability or depend on the injurer's fault.

All actions resulting in harms are thus enacted within a single spectrum, at the one end of which the harm is seen as in its entirety befalling the community as a whole, and the other end representing harms affecting exclusively – or almost exclusively – the individual suffering the injury consequent upon the harm. Exactly where this spectrum will be segmented is entirely a function of socio-economic forces intertwined with the legacy of each cultural and historical tradition. Two doctrines, however, operating in directly opposite directions, tend to determine the degree of liability in any given instance of wrongdoing. Within the spectrum, the closer a wrong lay to the end where the harm was considered exclusively – or nearly so – a communal one, the more likely was the standard of objective liability to be invoked against the wrongdoer. The closer the wrong fell towards the end of the spectrum where a harm was viewed as little more than a private injury, the greater was the insistence that liability be dependent on fault.[58]

We can now see more clearly the legal backdrop against which Wait's behavior appears, not only to the crew but also to the superiors, irresponsible with respect to what each considers to be the common good. For a victim of imperialism and racism, however, it would seem that any claim for retribution "that casual St. Kitts nigger" (*NN*, p. 27) may want to make will have no authority before tribunals within the British court system. Retribution usually revises or subverts the competences of existing tribunals, which claim the right to investigate crimes, to authorize verdicts, and to determine punishments. To be sure, Wait chooses not to articulate resentment in the official legal idiom. He thus foregoes the legal means to bear witness to the injustices he and his race suffered on British vessels. But he decides also not to call for a retribution, whose authority would be based only on the legal inconsequence of an informal complaint.

Legal inconsequence, however, does not preclude symbolic compensation. Wait appears to be entirely aware of the uncanny effect the few prophetic innuendos he makes about his impending death has on crew members – suggestive of Herman Melville's remark[59] quoted in the epigraph to this chapter. He may strategically act out the psychic economy of a returning repression on their part, based on an economy of satisfaction for racist and imperialist injustices against him that is legally unaccounted for. He may be crafting the death that he has to suffer as a retributive death, intended to haunt representatives and institutions of imperialism in his own local environment. By separating liabilities for imperialism and responsibilities for the common good, he is in a position to create and use the ambiguity of his illness against others just as much as he may suffer from the fear of dying.

One of the ways in which Wait uses his illness clearly is, as previously indicated, the performance of an anticipated wrongful death. He enacts the pathetic stipulation of a racist curse, ubiquitously masked by guilt-ridden sympathy, and on the verge of turning into a case of retribution: [To Belfast:] "'You wouldn't call me nigger if I wasn't half dead, you Irish beggar! [. . .] You wouldn't be white if you were ever so well . . . I will fight you [. . .] in fine weather [. . .]'" (*NN*, pp. 58–9). To perform an anticipated death is to reinsert into the "modern" notion of "dirty death," as Alan Friedman points out, Victorian elements of "aesthetic death."[60] Eventually, Wait reinstates in the corporative context of the ship a sense of expiation necessitated by the desecration and pollution of an unnatural-because-wrongful death. This sense of expiation is derived, in conspicuous ways, from the legal principle of deodands. Wait's symbolic retribution "exploits" the crew's "capital" – cooperation in conjunction with sympathy. He turns an impending death into a retributive "forfeiture" of their sympathies and is thus able to target and manipulate the very foundation of their compassion.

Stephen's alignment of unnatural death with the relevancy of facts returns to England as a cross-over between jeopardized judicial inference and ritualistic expiation. Similarly, Wait's performance of an anticipated wrongful death "returns" to the corporative context as the manipulation, by quasi-legal strategies, of a sense of expiation derived from a context that preceded the days of limited liability. The crew, the superiors, and the owners emerge in such a plot as collectively liable. The ones who are most responsive to that plot – sympathetic crew members like Belfast – engage in Wait's reversal of imperialist victimization. They consequently see themselves as victims. Sometimes they feel like victims of the exploitative practices attacked by Plimsoll, sometimes like victims of their own complicity with racist and ethnocentric imperialism. At the same time, they can remain in the safety of the periphery.

This fiction of their self-victimization, however, still depends on Wait's status of a sacrificial object at the center. In other words, it still depends on the confinement of the central figure. For the confinement is itself a necessary precondition for their peripheral status to be defined as sympathetic to the one "confined in the center." The fiction of their self-victimization helps them to interpret the curse of racist and ethnocentric imperialism as a sublime ritual of expiation. Wait leads them to realize that, as Ross Chambers points out in a more general context, "to scapegoat a mediator is to absolve oneself of the 'crime' of mediation and to naturalize a powerful discursive community, but to do so through what is itself an act of mediation (the act of producing a difference between oneself and the mediating other)."[61]

Such is the way in which Conrad has Wait manipulate the need for solidarity on the part of some crew members. He can thus suggest that that need is implicated in a repetition, quite typical of Western cultures, of the very sacrificial situation from which they want to spare Wait. From that perspective, their sentimental condemnation of his sacrifice becomes transparent "as a pure economy of barter between man and the divine powers." In fact, this sentimental tradeoff is none other than the spiritualized version of a "sacrificial 'economism' [that] runs through Plato, Christianity, Hegel, and Bataille."[62]

Like the forces of corporate power, Wait's performance of an economy of pity grows as a tension within the old order of center and periphery. Wait's resentment of the market economy, whose imperialism victimized him, and the resentment he instills in others both thrive on their hostility to a market exchange. Paradoxically, this type of exchange allowed for more egalitarian mechanisms of a cultural recentering of power in the first place. Wait performs the decentralized resentment of the market world, which cannot be grasped as a totality simply by being hostile to it, on the limited scene of resentment on the ship. He thus renders himself capable of evoking a new ritual center that competes with the captain's.

The way he "emits" himself as a sign in the center of a communal scene suggests that he ridicules a deferral of violence in terms of *collective* sympathy. Instead, in what emerges as a somewhat romantic gesture, he seems almost independent of the social whole and its collective sympathy. On a strategic level, however, he appears to exploit this romantic effect of aloofness as a means to exploit the bourgeois order, where supply and demand replace ritual interaction as the basis for exchange and distribution. In fact, he appears to exploit it for purposes of manipulating the crew's economy of pity, which in turn depends on "objects of suffering."

Collectivity in such a bourgeois context will always seem inauthentic to individual sympathy. Much as it grants individual sympathy a certain degree of freedom from collectively binding forms of charity, it will also emerge as the individual's target of critique. Wait seeks to repeat in individuals trying to attend to him his own romantic performance of an expulsion from the social order that displaces the old ritual center of attention for the superiors. For the unverbalized communication he establishes with his chosen audience, it is crucial that sympathy depend on intersubjective intuition rather than a sacrally mediated communal sharing. Thus it becomes easier for him to exploit the myth of a precommunal scene of desire for the potentially conflictual relation among the peripheral spectators of an aesthetic scene he himself has created.

As a result of this strategy, he seeks to repeat in his audience an intuition of centrality experienced as independent of the community. In doing so, he turns to his advantage the paradox that such recentered selves conceive of themselves as invulnerable to expulsion by the community. Simultaneously, the personal nature of the very intuition of recentered centrality remains in fact constituted by this expulsion. Not only does Wait aestheticize himself as the ambiguous referent of that paradoxical structure. He also personalizes the "public" scene of his audience's participation in the exile of the new central figure. Thus he feigns his own self in the multiple individual representations of him among the crew as a misarticulated subaltern victim of imperialism and racism. He emerges as the victim of a "new imperialism" that, as Chris Bongie puts it, has begun to "recode" subalterns and ex-slaves as "objects of paternalism."[63]

Wait discovers the center not only for himself but also for others. Furthermore, he reveals the crew's ritual of expiating an anticipated unnatural-because-wrongful death as a scene of representations which can generate multiple recenterings. Conrad here shifts the question of how peripheries are related to centers to how "parts [are] related to wholes."[64] As Wait takes possession of the center, he begins to use the impact of this conquest on the community as if the center were a *marketable property*. In a sense, he reverses the situation of Melville's Tahitian "superior *savage*," who in "Billy Budd" receives, but does not appropriate Christianity's "gift" of character formation: "It was like a gift placed in the palm of an outreached hand upon which the fingers do not close."[65] Wait thus appropriates the common-law principle of ownership in terms of mastery and domination, which Orlando Patterson traces back to a logic by which Roman law justified the social death of slaves through the idea of absolute possession.[66]

The impact of taking possession of the center becomes Wait's power to "bestow" significance within the community. This nexus of proprietorial power and the privilege to "bestow" significance may also be discerned in other Victorian writers such as George Eliot – for instance in the way Daniel Deronda's racial identity is "restored" to him based on a sense of duty-bound ownership:

[T]he centrality, for possession, of the "power to bestow" often asserts itself in the utter identification of proprietal prerogative with his power; an owner's power over his or her property becomes, simply, an owner's power to alienate it [. . .]. An idea of proprietorial power reposited primarily, even exclusively, in the "power to bestow" may dwell in the happiest alliance with the market economy, but it does so by severely restricting the boundless ambitions for mastery that form a deep part of the ideological heritage of possession.[67]

Instead of restricting his ambitions for mastery, Wait claims the center and "alienates" his new "property." He does so by provoking individual crew members to perform acts of individual sympathy. In fact, some of them, particularly Belfast, feel as if they were individually in a position to take possession of a center, while collectively remaining in the safety of the periphery. At the same time, however, Wait frustrates expectations among crew members that a duty-bound owner of the center may indefinitely exercise proprietorial power over the common good of the ship ("the whole").

As far as communal expectations toward a common good are concerned, crew and superiors begin to experience such a dissociation of duty for the sake of "the whole" from the possession of the center. This development in turn triggers a number of different attempts at recentering relations of parts to wholes. On the one hand, Belfast imitates Wait's detachment from the crew. He feels encouraged to do so because Wait's presumed intuitive knowledge of victimization convinces him of his own intuition that in a "culture" of conflicts all collective norms operate *a posteriori* to intersubjective sympathy. On the other hand, Singleton detaches himself from the worldly resentment generated by Wait's performance. He insists upon an impersonal intuition of solidarity, seeking to transcend a scene of representations where individuals carry out their conflicts merely as a competition of personal desires.

In similar fashion, Donkin rejects Wait's heroism of withdrawal from the communal scene. But he also detaches himself from Singleton's rejection of worldly desire. Instead of suppressing desire as the bourgeois motor of exploitation that Wait appears to accuse his audience of and that Singleton must despise in favor of ascetic impersonality, Donkin releases desire in himself and the crew as a revolutionary phenomenon – mutiny. He reformulates the intersubjective sympathy "distributed" by Wait for retributive ends as just another imposition of restraint, on the part of ship-owners and superiors, on the supposedly healthy desires of an exploited crew. Belfast, Singleton, and Donkin thus create different fictions in order to reshuffle those configurations of center and periphery which compete with each other, as "parts related to wholes," in the production, distribution, and exploitation of solidarity on the "Narcissus."

CODA: THE VERDICT OF CONFINEMENT

This situation of mutual fiction-making becomes more complex as the captain confines Wait to his cabin. Wait's incarceration eventually opens up another legal space – an intersection of legal fictions and rituals of solidarity. Both are different means for Conrad's characters to deal with experiences of the same crisis. Legal fictions, for example parenthood in the case of adoption, have in common with literary fictions the fact that any disbelief with regard to their falsehood, despite the knowledge of it, is generally suspended – with respect to legal fictions for the sake of substantial and procedural expediency, and with respect to literary fictions for the sake of self-reflexivity. Two specific legal fictions, pervasively employed in nineteenth-century England and by Conrad's time seemingly obsolete, are Civil Death and Substituted Judgment. These legal fictions resemble Conrad's scenes of crisis "management." Accordingly, I consider them in relation to the nexus of unnatural death and cursed inheritance which may be ascribed to Wait's incarceration.

To the extent that legal fictions are self-reflexive for the sake of expediency, they form part of the entire set of legal structures which transforms itself according to its own laws.[68] Given the juridical tension between principle and precedent characteristic of British common law, such transformations used to take place more or less apart from the formalizing power of codification[69] and are still based on the self-"display" of actors and institutions in the application of norms.[70] Those transformations do not solely contain within themselves the principles of their own dynamic. They also depend on the "field" of relations between themselves and other institutions with certain autopoietic features – such as secular rituals or literature – potentially competing to influence jurisdiction: "[. . .] while the juridical field derives the *language* in which its conflicts are expressed from the field of conceivable perspectives, the juridical field *itself* contains the principle of its own transformation in the struggles between the objective interests associated with these different perspectives."[71]

In Civil Death, we remember, incarcerated felons were deprived of their civil rights as well as their right to inherit and bequeath. They metaphorically died to the community.[72] This legal fiction originated in the medieval clerical distinction between worldly natural life and monastic contemplative life. *Civiliter mortuus* was later reinterpreted as an expiatory confinement designed to let an old identity die in order to trigger a new and better one. Basically, anyone convicted of treason or felony would lose civil rights and could no longer inherit. Moreover, his or her fortune was subject to forfeiture on the part of the Crown. While the legal criteria of forfeiture and corruption of blood gradually lost their impact in England and were practically not adopted in the United States, Civil Death often resulted in a transfer of the felon's fortune to heirs *as if* he or she were already dead.

Once applied, this form of fictitious death would cause life-long prison terms and end the right to sue, to ask for credit, to marry, and to vote. But the relationship between legal and social death, as well as the exclusion from inheritance and bequest, marks the core of this fiction. Thus it is significant that the same statutory change which abolished the implications of forfeitures in cases of deodands and suicides [*felo de se*] in 1870 (33 & 34 Vict. ch. 23) also ended the forfeiture and corruption of blood resultant from Civil Death. Now the fortune would be handed over to an "administrator" instead of the convict losing it forever. Nonetheless, it remained an open question whether a civilly dead person was entitled to inherit and bequeath.

In Substituted Judgment, a judge's decision substituted for the missing will of an incompetent as soon as the label "incompetent" had marked the incompetent as isolated from the faculty to articulate herself or himself according to the requirements established by the court.[73] From 1816, the Lord Chancellor in Chancery could extend his authority to administer the fortunes of lunatics and idiots – later generalized in the category "incompetent" – into the judicial realm of equity. Restricted by certain "evidentiary constraints," he was allowed to impersonate the "donative intent" of an incompetent *as if* that incompetent possessed right reason.

Obviously, the authority with which a judge may move from administered to substituted rights is at stake in such an act of impersonation. Substituted Judgment enables a judge to control the fortune of a lunatic, idiot, or incompetent, including their bodies in the case of today's organ transplants, where the law of informed consent applies. Equity courts were in a position to grant money by circumventing principles of property transfer, while they often did not have to account for the reasons why an incompetent was considered less alive and his or her fortune more in need of protection.

Substituted Judgment suggests that the judge has access to the unarticulated intention of an incompetent. It further suggests that the incompetent has had a genuine intention capable of being substituted by the judge – an intention which the incompetent would have, if he or she were now capable of having intentions. It inverts the principle of action by proxy, which translates a given will into a set of actions as long as its constituent is still alive. Not unlike Civil Death, Substituted Judgment brackets certain rights, particularly the right to transfer property, and specifically by way of substituting intentions.

The metaphorical death in literal confinement (Civil Death) corresponds to the substituted right to control fortunes to be inherited or bequeathed (Substituted Judgment). The substitution is the effect of a metaphor that translates action by proxy into displaced intention. It "literally" affects premises of property transfer. In short, both legal fictions can be used to withhold rights and displace intentions that connect metaphorical death with literal inheritance and bequest. Thus they resemble the events leading to and resulting from Wait's incarceration, with the important difference from their occurrence in literary fiction that in their genuine legal context judges employ death as a trope while taking inheritance and bequest very literally.

Ironically, Wait dies literally and the "case" of his illness creates the effect of a curse, as a rather metaphorical inheritance, on the ship's community. The ambiguity of faked or real illness and of unnatural or natural death mirrors the ambiguity, on the part of the crew and the captain, of faked or real sympathy, faked or real solidarity, and faked or real responsibility. During the storm, Wait's sick-bay in the deck-house (*NN*, pp. 33–4) turns into the prison cell of a "grave" (*NN*, p. 78), where "[a]ll the doors [. . .] become trap-doors" (*NN*, p. 48) and where he ends up "screaming and knocking [. . .] with the hurry of a man *prematurely* shut up in a coffin" (*NN*, p. 49, my emphasis).

This situation clearly anticipates Wait's later vision of his life "hover[ing] affectionately around the imposture of his ready death" (*NN*, p. 77). At night, his cabin has "the brilliance of a silver shrine where a black idol [. . .] received our homage" and where Donkin, "officiat[ing]" like a priest before a sacred object (*NN*, p. 77), eventually seeks to inherit the contents of Wait's sea-chest. Wait later projects, in a moment of hallucination, this space of confinement or death-in-life into his own chest: "He expanded his hollow chest. [. . .] There was no more air – and he had not finished drawing his long breath. But he was in a gaol! They were locking him up" (*NN*, p. 83). It then turns out that Podmore indeed turned the key and locked Wait up, only to later project a Christian version of hell on him, a confinement from which he fails to liberate him. It is this sequence of events that Conrad concludes by having the captain incarcerate Wait for "shamming sick" (*NN*, p. 88).

The captain isolates Wait as a subject of legal punishment. Crew members isolate him as the object of greed (Donkin), missionary zeal (Podmore), or pity (Belfast). Both captain and crew seek to gain control over the ambiguity concerning Wait's unscrupulous self-pity. If that sense of self-pity is justified, the crew can turn it into a cause for sentimentality and philanthropy. If it is unjustified, the superiors can turn it into a cause for sanctions. Wait's analogy of chest and prison, extending into the cursed inheritance of his desirable sea-chest, exemplifies his suspicion that both captain and crew confine the ambiguity of his inaction within real or imaginary prisons (sick-bay, hell) that are associated with metaphorical death.

Metaphorical death, then, emerges itself as the metaphor for an isolation from the group, a declaration, as it were, of "social death." Metaphorical death is an isolation from the group, although there is some additional ambiguity as to whether that isolation is also caused by the group. Generally speaking, the reasons for metaphorical death can of course vary or, as in Wait's case, remain somewhat obscure. Civil

Death here implies that enforced confinement is a response to or manipulation of the formation of solidarity. Not only does Wait's social death suggest resentment as a given predicament of this particular naval "culture." The fiction also rearranges that death, in an indirect way, for various strategic purposes: the success of greed (Donkin), missionary zeal (Podmore), or pity (Belfast).

Captain Allistoun performs a Substituted Judgment over Wait when contrary to Wait's confessed recovery from illness he gives out the order "'that this man is not to be allowed on deck to the end of the passage'" (*NN*, p. 88). I agree with Cedric Watts' interpretation that the captain here tells "a compassionate lie by declaring that Wait is to be confined to his cabin as a punishment for malingering." This is indeed "a compassionate falsehood," one whose "political error" Allistoun later recognizes as reproducing resentment (*NN*, p. 139): "'When I saw him standing there, three parts dead and so scared – black amongst that gaping lot – no grit to face what's coming to us all [. . .]. Sorry for him – like you would be for a sick brute. If ever creature was in a mortal funk to die!. . . . I thought I would let him go out in his own way. Kind of impulse. It never came into my head, those fools. . . .H'm! Stand to it now – of course'" (*NN*, p. 93).

Watts is certainly right here, and not only because "compassionate falsehood" is also an essential component of Substituted Judgment. However, there are different kinds of falsehood to be distinguished in Wait and Allistoun, and so Watts' argument needs to be qualified further. On the one hand, Wait feigns his health and thus runs the risk of causing resentment against himself, particularly on the part of those crew members who pity him for his illness. On the other hand, Allistoun feigns Wait's confessed health as a feigned illness. More importantly, he feigns this judgment of his as a Substituted Judgment passed in the middle of, but without succumbing to, the crew's controversy over Wait's health or illness. He typifies the activity of appeals court judges, who make their judgments in the absence of a jury.

This feigned judgment suggests at least two different motives. First, Wait is to be spared humiliation before the crew, which may be the reason why Wait himself decides to feign his health in that moment. Secondly, Wait is to be granted the illusion (in case he has such an illusion) that he may stay alive – an illusion granted, but embedded in such fierce rhetoric that the crew is likely to take Allistoun's Substituted Judgment to be a real judgment. To be sure, Watts deserves credit for claiming that the captain may be blending feigned punishment with real compassion. But one would have to add that there is nothing unequivocal about Allistoun's seeking to alleviate Wait's anxieties about dying. The captain may just as well seek, by enacting compassion as punishment, to prevent the crew from taking over his privileges of jurisdiction on the ship and from punishing or sacrificing Wait by themselves.

In the latter case, even Allistoun's surprise at the crew's refueled resentment – "'It never came into my head, those fools. . . . .'" (*NN*, p. 93) – may be feigned. He may have, in the final analysis, created the fiction of a necessary punishment either in order to exonerate others from the burden of feigning for the sake of philanthropy or in order to maintain for himself the privilege to employ the fictions necessary for him to remain in charge of resolving conflicts. Again, in the latter case, he would be taking away from the crew the very power to declare Wait a mere scapegoat for their anxieties. In either case, Allistoun can claim the authority to determine which kinds of "evidence" and "chains of causation" – resentful formations of solidarity on the ship, Wait's unspoken history of victimization etc. – enter his "verdict."

Civil Death confines Wait's "outrageous" otherness – "belonging wholly neither to death or life, and perfectly invulnerable in his apparent ignorance of both" (*NN* 110) – in the space of the familiar in order to domesticate it. Substituted Judgment domesticates what the ambivalence of illness – 'compassionately' sublimated by the captain in terms of "the incertitudes of life and death" (*NN*, p. 94) – has rendered strange or uncanny. Against the backdrop of Conrad's fiction, these legal fictions reveal striking similarities with rituals employed to secure symbolic jurisdiction. While the crew isolates Wait socially in order to sacralize him, the captain, in compassionately punishing Wait, substitutes for Wait's will in order to counteract the crew's symbolic employment of Civil Death against Wait. He can thus be said to compete with Wait for the power to "inscribe" a sense of "finitude," based on "separation",[74] into the social relations between crew members.

These particular employments of legal fictions as rituals for securing symbolic jurisdiction are nostalgic with respect to the myth of an organically self-transforming community. They are vehicles of self-interest, however, with respect to conflicts of social diversity in which rituals of securing jurisdiction compete with one another. Therefore, whenever Conrad has a narrator evoke either conservative cooperation or subversive sympathy as the be-all-and-end-all of diversity, the very evocation of community may always already be marked by the very self-interest on the basis of which a ritual helps to feign a particular sphere of jurisdiction that is to be secured. The transformations of a microcosmic society during the voyage of the "Narcissus" translate the crisis-resolving mechanism of a liminal ritual into more differentiated borderlines between solidarity and resentment. It comes as no surprise, then, that as soon as the voyage is over, the law of the land takes over again. With the narcissistic pathos of nationalism, the narrator looks back on the ship's community as evidence abroad of the "ship mother of fleets and nations" and "great flagship of the race" (*NN*, p. 121), as "a fragment" of England's nation, now no longer "detached from the earth."

Jim Wait's unpronounced history as a potential victim of racist practices on British vessels appears to crew members on the "Narcissus" as distressingly particular – hence, not universally appealing. What makes Wait a compelling figure for some white crew members, however, is that they associate him with a potential healer of the wounds inflicted by an asymmetrical social and political differentiation among crew and superiors. Quick to exploit the ambiguity of his health status, he mirrors their uneasiness as another ambiguity – one of imperialist exploitation and remorse. He feeds on the crew's need to transcend social (and sometimes political) hierarchies, as if their suspicious but sympathetic attempts to turn him into a celebrity could also transcend the racial divide. Soon, however, Wait turns their uneasiness into a symptomatic form of "evidence" for an anticipated murder on their part. He thus also mirrors the captain's later verdict against him by inflicting on the crew a sense of trial-as-probation. By means of it, he manages to reformulate their solidarity in terms of remorse.

This "trial" of an anticipated "murder," including its outcome, raises the stakes of Wait's and the crew's different cross-over ambitions. Before the captain's verdict, the hype surrounding Wait's alleged but unconfirmed political ambitions depends on a radical denial of the racial bad faith that persists in pockets of the microcosmic British society on the "Narcissus." Post-verdict, Wait's plausibility as a healer hinges on a negative charisma – his ability to translate the crew's need for a transcendence of the political divide between themselves and the superiors into a fictitious erasure of race. For many whites on the ship, nothing short of Wait's repudiation of any group solidarity with blacks – an illusion of colorlessness extended into an investment in whiteness – will satisfy them. Therefore, whenever his racial identity highlights a schism between racial and national identity, race itself seems to lose universal political appeal. Rather, it persists as something para-national. Thus, the transcendence, or erasure, of Wait's racial identity becomes the condition for its "survival" alongside national identity, at least until the law of the land takes over again. This is the paradox that Wait's bizarre success both reinforces and obscures.

CHAPTER 6

Conclusion

It occurs to them all that there is more to any of them than any of them suspects.
But sometimes we need coaxing to act on our own accord. [. . .] Tell me how free
I am.   Richard Powers, *Prisoner's Dilemma*

On the literary sites of sentimentality, philanthropy, and solidarity,
Sterne, Dickens, and Conrad play off on the diversity of functions that
legal fictions can perform. All three share the assumption that the
modern disjunction of equity and legal fiction – a disjunction that
Shakespeare staged early on by interweaving the legal and tragic aspects
of Ophelia's suicide – changed conventional expectations toward equitable justice. This change also includes literature's role in endorsing or
questioning such expectations. Whatever the disadvantages of that
disjunction for the project of Enlightenment, the authors build on the
assumption that that change also opened up fictional spaces for modern
literature to articulate marginal voices. For that reason, all three relocate the mechanism of legal fictions in literary contexts.

One result of that relocation is that they end up challenging a certain
confidence, spread by many Enlightenment thinkers, that critical reason
is a viable instrument with which to pursue equity. To the extent that
the law had become more positive and thus more rapidly alterable,
critical reason appeared to end up having to solve problems that it had
itself created, for instance Hobbes's attempt, after the civil war, to
depoliticize conscience. To be sure, the notion of critique can in principle always be an effective remedy for potential injustices committed by
positive law. But the rapid changes in definitions of injustices which
positive law initiated also began to affect definitions of remedies. Those
changes gradually deprived critical reason of a sovereign status. Thus all
three authors obviously feed on the same sense of irony: While legal
fictions were being disconnected from equity by those who criticized
them as suspicious instruments of power abuse, they also indicated, in

243

the context of literature, a growing destabilization of critical reason's equitable force.

With the increasing dominance of positive law, expectations toward the function of critical appeal diversified. This explosion of expectations eventually also multiplied equity's institutional authority into more temporary remedies for past injustices. Legislation was still expected to remedy past judicial injustices, and the judicial interpretation of rules was still expected to remedy past legislative shortsightedness. But other rhetorical institutions of appeals, such as sentimentality, philanthropy, and solidarity, began to claim authority for an equitable distribution of remedies as well. One result was that these nonlegal ways of distributing remedies began to affect the mechanisms which fueled the reproduction of legal authority – mechanisms reflected frequently in the power to erect, maintain, and relocate cultural boundaries in terms of gender, class, and ethnicity.

To open up historical perspectives on that development, I have used each literary author to highlight different stages of how particular views on the belatedness of appeals have affected the reproduction of their authority. The legal institution of equity certainly declined along with the destabilization of critical reason's sovereign status. But the supplementary force of equity may be said to have survived in the rhetorical institution of modern literature. As a rhetorical convention operative on the cognitive level of truth-finding, it can still be adjusted to the languages of law and fact. Alternatively, as a strategy operative on the pragmatic level of negotiating between legal and nonlegal contexts, it can still be redirected toward externalizations of conscience in sentimentality, philanthropy, and solidarity.

Most importantly, however, the momentum of equity can still persist in literature, not as an appeal to the higher or later authority of the natural or the real, but as an appeal to the possibility that complicities (including literature's own) with modernity's commensurability of signification may be usefully challenged. If so, it is not impossible even for canonical texts of modern literature to affect, instead of merely replicate, the inherited structures and authority of appeals. What makes modern literature an appropriate site for equity's persistence is its specific ability to reconfigure the traditional tropes of supplementary relationships, such as the general–particular, the generic–singular, and the dominant–marginal.

As they implement legal fictions into literary contexts, Sterne, Dickens, and Conrad explore the ambiguous possibilities contained in the power as well as the desire to transform disadvantages. The limits of literature in influencing any reproduction of authority are of course that it is itself an institution whose rhetorical authority is not foundational. But its advantage lies in emphasizing an affective dimension of metaphor that can unleash certain aspects of legal fictions which the law tends to curb. The disloyalty with which the authors translate legal into nonlegal fictions sometimes triggers new and unparalleled articulations of marginality, both supplementing and exceeding the nexus of law, equity, and conscience.

Notes

1 INTRODUCTION

1 See Rey Chow, *Writing Diaspora: Tactics of Intervention in Contemporary Cultural Studies*, Bloomington: University of Indiana Press, 1993.

2 See Mark Poster, *The Mode of Information: Post-Structuralism and Social Contents*, Cambridge: Polity Press, 1990; *The Second Media Age*, Cambridge: Polity Press, 1995.

3 See Chana Kronfield, *On the Margins of Modernism: Decentering Literary Dynamics*, Berkeley: University of California Press, 1996.

4 *Contingencies of Value: Alternative Perspectives for Literary Theory*, Cambridge, MA: Harvard University Press, 1988.

5 See Wendy Steiner, *The Scandal of Pleasure: Art in An Age of Fundamentalism*, Chicago: University of Chicago Press, 1995, p. 211.

6 For a current example, see my "Miniatures and Monstrosities of Recursive Valorization: On Barthelme and Gaddis," *Arizona Quarterly* 54, 1 (1998), 97–124.

7 Butler, *Bodies That Matter: On the Discursive Limits of "Sex"*, New York: Routledge, 1993; Guillory, *Cultural Capital: The Problem of Literary Canon Formation*, Chicago: University of Chicago Press, 1993; Bhabha, *The Location of Culture*, London: Routledge, 1994.

8 See Jacques Derrida, *Of Grammatology*, trans. Gayatri Chakravorty Spivak, Baltimore: Johns Hopkins University Press, 1976, pp. 144–5.

9 See *The Gold Standard and the Logic of Naturalism*, Berkeley: University of California Press, 1987, p. 27.

10 *Thick and Thin: Moral Argument at Home and Abroad*, Notre Dame: University of Notre Dame Press, 1994, pp. 26ff.

11 *Situating the Self: Gender, Community, and Postmodernism in Contemporary Ethics*, Cambridge: Polity Press, 1992, pp. 228–9.

12 Bhabha, *The Location of Culture*, p. 251.

13 See *Rhetoric* 1373b1-1374b22 and *Nicomachean Ethics* 1137a32-1138a3. See also Wesley Trimpi, *Muses of One Mind: The Literary Analysis of Experience and Its Continuity*, Princeton: Princeton University Press, 1983, pp. 241–361.

14 *Ethics* 1130a6–1131a6.

15 See Kathy Eden, *Poetic and Legal Fiction in the Aristotelian Tradition*, Princeton:

Princeton University Press, 1986, pp. 25–61.

16 See Wolfgang Iser, *The Fictive and the Imaginary: Charting Literary Anthropology*, Baltimore: Johns Hopkins University Press, 1993, Epilogue.
17 Richard Posner, *Law and Literature*, 2nd rev. edn., Cambridge, MA: Harvard University Press, 1998, pp. 143–4.
18 "*Hamlet*, Hales vs. Petit, and the Hysteresis of Action," *English Literary History* 60 (1993), 17–55: 38. See also Katherine Eisaman Maus, "Proof and Consequences: Inwardness and Its Exposure in the English Renaissance," *Representations* 34 (1991), 29–52.
19 See Brook Thomas, *The New Historicism and Other Old-Fashioned Topics*, Princeton: Princeton University Press, 1991, p. 199.
20 See Thomas, *American Literary Realism and the Failed Promise of Contract*, Berkeley: University of California Press, 1996, pp. 26–7, 29, 35–6.
21 Wai Chee Dimock, *Residues of Justice. Literature, Law, Philosophy*, Berkeley: University of California Press, 1996, pp. 8–10; see also pp. 23–7.
22 See for instance Drucilla Cornell, "From the Lighthouse: The Promise of Redemption and the Possibility of Legal Interpretation," *Cardozo Law Review* 11 (1990), 1687–714: 1709ff.
23 See Margreta de Grazia, "Sanctioning Voice: Quotation Marks, the Abolition of Torture, and the Fifth Amendment," *Cardozo Arts and Entertainment Law Journal* 10 (1992), 545–66.
24 See Jane Gaines, *Contested Culture: The Image, the Voice, and the Law*, Chapel Hill: University of North Carolina Press, 1991, p. 23.
25 Jean-Luc Nancy, *The Inoperative Community*, trans. Peter Connor et al., Minneapolis: University of Minnesota Press, 1991, p. xxxviii.
26 See Cathy Caruth, "Introduction," *American Imago* 48, 1 (1991), 1–9.
27 See Anita Allen, "The Jurisprudence of Jane Eyre," *Harvard Women's Law Journal* 15 (1992), 173–209: 179.
28 See David Kairys (ed.), *The Politics of Law. A Progressive Critique*, New York: Pantheon, 1982, and Roberto Mangabeira Unger, *False Necessity: Anti-Necessitarian Social Theory in the Service of Radical Democracy*, Cambridge: Cambridge University Press, 1987.
29 See *There's No Such Thing as Free Speech . . . and It's a Good Thing Too*, Oxford: Oxford University Press, 1994, p. 208.
30 See Costas Douzinas and Ronnie Warrington, *Justice Miscarried: Ethics and Aesthetics in Law*, Hemel Hempsted: Harvester, 1994, ch. 1.
31 See *Law and Literature*, Introduction.
32 See Herrnstein Smith, *Contingencies of Value*, and Fish, *Doing What Comes Naturally: Change, Rhetoric, and the Practice of Theory in Literary and Legal Studies*, Durham, NC: Duke University Pres, 1989.
33 See James Boyd White, *Justice as Translation: An Essay in Cultural and Legal Criticism*, Chicago: University of Chicago Press, 1990.
34 See Richard Weisberg, *Poethics, and Other Strategies of Law and Literature*, New York: Columbia University Press, 1992, and Robin West, *Narrative, Authority, and Law*, Ann Arbor: University of Michigan Press, 1993.

35 See *Totality and Infinity*, trans. Alphonso Lingis, Pittsburgh: Duquesne University Press, 1969.
36 See François Ewald, "Norms, Discipline, and the Law," trans. Marjorie Beale, *Representations* 30 (1990), 138–61: 155.
37 For a similar distinction between "justice" and "care" see West, *Caring for Justice*, New York: New York University Press, 1997, pp. 9, 23.
38 See Frederic Maitland, *The Constitutional History of England*, Cambridge: Cambridge University Press, 1965, pp. 462–84, and P. S. Atiyah, *The Rise and Fall of Freedom of Contract*, Oxford: Clarendon Press, 1979, pp. 359–97.
39 See also Louis Knafla, "Conscience in the English Common Law Tradition," *University of Toronto Law Journal* 26 (1976), 1–16, and Thomas Green, *Verdict According to Conscience: Perspectives on the English Criminal Trial Jury, 1200–1800*, Chicago: University of Chicago Press, 1985.
40 See Thomas, *The New Historicism*, pp. 122, 214–15.

2 TRAPPINGS OF A TRANSNATIONAL GAZE: LEGAL AND SENTIMENTAL CONFINEMENT IN STERNE'S NOVELS

1 Daniel Defoe, *Robinson Crusoe*, ed. Michael Shinagel, New York: Norton, 1975, p. 217.
2 Ibid., p. 220.
3 *The Figure of Theater: Shaftesbury, Defoe, Adam Smith, and George Eliot*, New York: Columbia University Press, 1986, pp. 85–6.
4 Ibid., p. 98.
5 Ibid., pp. 99–100.
6 See Kathy Eden, *Poetic and Legal Fiction in the Aristotelian Tradition*, Princeton: Princeton University Press, 1986.
7 See David Lieberman, *The Province of Legislation Determined: Legal Theory in Eighteenth-Century England*, Cambridge: Cambridge University Press, 1989, pp. 219ff, 257ff.
8 See Louise Harmon, "Falling Off the Vine: Legal Fictions and the Doctrine of Substituted Judgment," *Yale Law Journal* 100, 1 (1990), 1–71: 9–15.
9 See R. A. Samek, "Fictions and the Law," *Toronto Law Journal* 31 (1981), 290–317: 314ff, and Aviam Soifer, "Reviewing Legal Fictions," *Georgia Law Review* 20 (1986), 871–915: 874–82.
10 See also Owen Barfield, "Poetic Diction and Legal Fiction," in *Essays Presented to Charles Williams*, ed. C. S. Lewis, 5th edn., Oxford: Clarendon Press, 1978, pp. 106–27.
11 See Kim Lane Scheppele, "Facing Facts in Legal Interpretation," *Representations* 30 (1990), 43–77.
12 33 and 34 Vict. ch. 23.
13 Douglas Hay, "Property, Authority, and the Criminal Law," in *Albion's Fatal Tree*, ed. Hay et al., New York: Pantheon, 1975, pp. 17–63: p. 20.
14 Ibid., p. 18.

15 Ibid., p. 19.
16 *Crime and the Courts in England 1660-1800*, Princeton: Princeton University Press, 1986, pp. 141ff, 451ff, 495ff, 513ff. See also Leon Radzinowicz, *A History of English Law and Its Administration from 1750*, 3 vols., London: Stevens, 1948, I, p. 31.
17 See John G. A. Pocock, *Virtue, Commerce, and History. Essays on Political Thought and History, Chiefly in the Eighteenth Century*, Cambridge: Cambridge University Press, 1985, pp. 68–9, 112.
18 See Patrick Brantlinger, *Fictions of State: Culture and Credit in Britain, 1694–1994*, Ithaca: Cornell University Press, 1996, p. 144.
19 See Martin Kayman, "Lawful Writing: Common Law, Statute, and the Properties of Literature," *New Literary History* 27, 4 (1996), 761–84: 777.
20 See James Grunebaum, *Private Ownership*, London: Routledge and Kegan Paul, 1987, pp. 52ff, 86ff.
21 *The Rape of Clarissa*, Minneapolis: University of Minnesota Press, 1982, p. 15.
22 "Sentimentality as Performance: Shaftesbury, Sterne, and the Theatrics of Virtue," in *The New Eighteenth Century*, ed. Felicity Nussbaum and Laura Brown, New York: Methuen, 1987, pp. 210–30: p. 218.
23 *Virtue, Commerce, and History*, p. 45.
24 Stephen Holmes, *Passions and Constraint: On the Theory of Liberal Democracy*, Chicago: University of Chicago Press, 1995, p. 5.
25 Pocock, *Virtue, Commerce, and History*, p. 50.
26 *The Province of Legislation Determined*, pp. 12–13.
27 See for instance Judith Frank, "'A Man Who Laughs is Never Dangerous': Character and Class in Sterne's *A Sentimental Journey*," *English Literary History* 56, 1 (1989), 97–124.
28 *Adam Smith's Politics*, Cambridge: Cambridge University Press, 1978, p. 165.
29 *Cultural Capital: The Problem of Literary Canon Formation*, Chicago: University of Chicago Press, 1993, pp. 316–17.
30 *The Differentiation of Society*, New York: Columbia University Press, 1982, p. 5.
31 Ibid., p. 267.
32 *A Sentimental Journey through France and Italy*, ed. Graham Petrie, intro. A. Alvarez, Harmondsworth: Penguin, 1984, p. 27 [abbr. *SJ*].
33 *Tristram Shandy*, ed. Ian Campbell Ross, Oxford: Oxford University Press, 1983, bk. VII, ch. xxxiii–xxxiv, pp. 421–4 [abbr. *TS*].
34 "Sensibility as Argument," in *Sensibility in Transformation. Creative Resistance to Sentiment from the Augustans to the Romantics*, ed. Syndy McMillen Conger, London: Associated University Presses, 1990, pp. 63–82: p. 71. See also Chris Jones, *Radical Sensibility: Literature and Ideas in the 1790s*, London: Routledge, 1993, p. 7.
35 *Imagining the Penitentiary: Fiction and the Architecture of Mind in Eighteenth-Century England*, Chicago: University of Chicago Press, 1987, pp. 26–7.
36 See also Patricia Meyer Spacks, *Desire and Truth: Functions of Plot in Eighteenth-Century Novels*, Chicago: University of Chicago Press, 1990, p. 121.

37 *Eighteenth-Century Sensibility and the Novel: The Senses in Social Context,* Cambridge: Cambridge University Press, 1993, Preface.
38 Ibid., Introduction.
39 See "'A Man Who Laughs is Never Dangerous'."
40 *The Beautiful, Novel, and Strange: Aesthetics and Heterodoxy,* Baltimore: Johns Hopkins University Press, 1996, p. 156.
41 Ibid., pp. 157–8.
42 *Political Constructions: Defoe, Richardson, and Sterne in Relation to Hobbes, Hume, and Burke,* Ithaca: Cornell University Press, 1988, p. 255.
43 *The Theory of Moral Sentiments,* ed. Dugald Stewart, New York: Kelley, 1966, p. 274 [abbr. *TMS*].
44 Brook Thomas, *American Literary Realism and the Failed Promise of Contract,* Berkeley: University of California Press, 1996, p. 34.
45 *Promises, Morals, and Law,* Oxford: Clarendon Press, 1981, pp. 2–4.
46 See Susan Staves, "Toby Shandy: Sentiment and the Soldier," in *Approaches to Teaching Sterne's Tristam Shandy,* ed. Melvyn New, New York: MLA Press, 1989, pp. 80–6: pp. 82–3.
47 *A Treatise of Human Nature,* ed. L. A. Selby-Bigge, 2nd rev. edn. P. H. Nidditch, Oxford: Clarendon Press, 1978, pp. 516–25 [abbr. *T*].
48 John Locke, *The Second Treatise of Government,* ed. J. W. Gough, 3rd edn., Oxford: Blackwell, 1966, p. 33.
49 See Mary Murray, *The Law of the Father? Patriarchy in the Transition from Feudalism to Capitalism,* London: Routledge, 1995, p. 96.
50 "Engendering Accounts in Sterne's *A Sentimental Journey,*" in *Johnson and His Age,* ed. James Engell, Cambridge, Mass.: Harvard University Press, 1984, pp. 531-58: pp. 538, 546. See also Mark Madoff, "'They Caught Fire at Each Other': Laurence Sterne's Journal of the Pulse of Sensibility," in *Sensibility in Transformation,* pp. 43–62: p. 56.
51 Annette Baier, *Postures of the Mind. Essays on Mind and Morals,* Minneapolis: University of Minnesota Press, 1985, p. 175.
52 See *Trust and Power,* ed. Tom Burns, trans. Howard Davis et al., Chichester: John Wiley & Sons, 1979, pp. 35–6.
53 "Living Alone Together," *New Literary History* 27, 1 (1996), 1–14: 14.
54 *Reflections on the Revolution in France,* ed. Connor Cruise O'Brien, Harmondsworth: Penguin, 1969, p. 150.
55 John Mullan, *Sentiment and Sociability: The Language of Feeling in the Eighteenth Century,* Oxford: Clarendon Press, 1988, p. 159.
56 "Of the Rise and Progress of the Arts and Sciences," in *Essays Moral, Political, Literary,* ed. Eugene Miller, Indianapolis: Liberty Classics, 1985, pp. 111–37: p. 126.
57 Ibid., pp. 130–1.
58 Ibid., p. 133.
59 *Between Men: English Literature and Male Homosocial Desire,* New York: Columbia University Press, 1985, p. 69.
60 "'A Man Who Laughs Is Never Dangerous'," 120.

61 *Laurence Sterne: Tristram Shandy*, Cambridge: Cambridge University Press, 1988, pp. 46–7, 50–1.
62 "Of Refinement in the Arts," in *Essays Moral, Political, Literary*, pp. 268–80: p. 271.
63 Kay, *Political Constructions*, p. 261.
64 See Marshall, *The Figure of Theater*, pp. 167–92.
65 See Arthur Hill Cash, "The Sermon in *Tristram Shandy*," *English Literary History* 31 (1964), 395–417.
66 Frank, "'A Man Who Laughs is Never Dangerous,'" 105.
67 Ibid., 121n.12.
68 Albert Hirschman, *The Passions and the Interests*, Princeton: Princeton University Press, 1977, p. 111.
69 *Letters of Laurence Sterne*, ed. Lewis Perry Curtis, Oxford: Clarendon Press, 1967, pp. 398–9n.3.
70 *Cross Channel*, New York: Vintage, 1996, p. 207.
71 See Harmon, "Falling Off the Vine."
72 See Judith Butler, "'Conscience Doth Make Subjects of Us All'," *Yale French Studies* 88 (1995), 6–26: 13.
73 *On the Genealogy of Morals*, trans. Walter Kaufman, New York: Vintage, 1969, p. 87.

3 REINSTITUTIONALIZING THE COMMON LAW: BENTHAM ON THE SECURITY AND FLEXIBILITY OF LEGAL RULES

1 *Bentham's Prison: A Study of the Panopticon Penitentiary*, Oxford: Clarendon Press, 1993.
2 Ross Harrison, *Bentham*, London: Routledge and Kegan Paul, 1983, p. 122.
3 John Bender, *Imagining the Penitentiary: Fiction and the Architecture of Mind in Eighteenth-Century England*, Chicago: University of Chicago Press, 1987, p. 220.
4 See Harrison, *Bentham*, pp. 233ff, 273ff.
5 *The Philosophy of Money*, trans. Tom Bottomore and David Frisby, Boston: Routledge, 1978, p. 83.
6 *A Theory of Justice*, Oxford: Clarendon Press, 1972, pp. 226–32.
7 See L. J. Hume, *Bentham and Bureaucracy*, Cambridge: Cambridge University Press, 1981; Douglas Long, *Bentham on Liberty: Jeremy Bentham's Idea of Liberty in Relation to His Utilitarianism*, Toronto: University of Toronto Press, 1977; and David Lyons, "Utility and Rights," in *Ethics, Economics, and the Law*, ed. J. Roland Pennock and John Chapman, New York: New York University Press, 1982, pp. 107'38.
8 See Harrison, *Bentham*; Frederick Rosen, *Jeremy Bentham and Representative Democracy*, Oxford: Clarendon Press, 1983; Gerald Postema, *Bentham and the Common Law Tradition*, Oxford: Clarendon Press, 1986; and Paul Kelly, *Utilitarianism and Distributive Justice: Jeremy Bentham and the Civil Law*, Oxford:

Clarendon Press, 1990.
9 *Utilitarianism and Distributive Justice*, p. 9.
10 See Alfred W. B. Simpson, "The Common Law and Legal Theory," in *Oxford Essays in Jurisprudence*, ed. Simpson, 2nd series, Oxford: Clarendon Press, 1973, pp. 77–99.
11 *The Constitution of Liberty*, Chicago: University of Chicago Press, 1960, p. 163.
12 Quoted in J. G. A. Pocock, *The Ancient Constitution and the Feudal Law. A Study of English Historical Thought in the Seventeenth Century*, Cambridge: Cambridge University Press, 1957, pp. 33–41.
13 4 vols., 3rd edn., (repr.) Chicago: Callaghan and Co., vol. I, p. 17 [abbr. *CLE*].
14 *A History of the Common Law of England*, ed. Charles Gray, 3rd edn., Chicago: University of Chicago Press, 1971, p. 40.
15 See Simpson, "The Common Law and Legal Theory," p. 79.
16 See Clifford Geertz, "Common Sense as a Cultural System," in *Local Knowledge: Further Essays in Interpretive Anthropology*, New York: Basic Books, 1983, pp. 73–93.
17 Hayek, *The Constitution of Liberty*, p. 462.
18 *A History of the Common Law*, p. 45.
19 Quoted in Louis Knafla, *Law and Politics in Jacobean England: The Tracts of Lord Chancellor Ellsmere*, Cambridge: Cambridge University Press, 1977, p. 219.
20 See Simpson, "The Common Law and Legal Theory," p. 94.
21 See Hale, *A History of the Common Law*, pp. xxiii–xxv.
22 *Reflections on the Revolution in France*, ed. Connor Cruise O'Brien, Harmondsworth: Penguin, 1969, pp. 194–5.
23 Ibid., p. 117.
24 See Hale, *A History of the Common Law*, pp. 39–46.
25 See Christopher Hill, *Intellectual Origins of the English Revolution*, Oxford: Oxford University Press, 1975, pp. 257–8.
26 See Hill, *Some Intellectual Consequences of the English Revolution*, Madison: University of Wisconsin Press, 1980, pp. 29–30.
27 Coke, quoted in Hayek, *The Constitution of Liberty*, p. 65.
28 Hale, "Reflections by the Lrd. Chiefe Justice on Mr. Hobbes His Dialogue of the Lawe," in William Holdsworth, *A History of English Law*, 16 vols., 7th rev. edn., ed. A. L. Goodhart and H. G. Hanbury, London: Methuen, 1956, vol. 1, pp. 499-513: pp. 502–3.
29 See Postema, *Bentham and the Common Law Tradition*, p. 37.
30 Ibid., pp. 40–60.
31 Blackfriars edn., Latin text and English translation, 60 vols., New York: McGraw-Hill, 1964–75, vols. 28 (1966) 1a2ae.90–97, and 37 (1975) 2a2ae57-62, trans. T. Gilby.
32 *Leviathan*, ed. Crawford B. McPherson, Baltimore: Johns Hopkins University Press, 1968, XXVI, pp. 316–17.
33 See David Gauthier, "Thomas Hobbes: Moral Theorist," *Journal of Philosophy* 76 (1979), 547–59.

34 Hobbes, "Author's Preface," *De Cive*, ed. Howard Warrender, Oxford: Clarendon Press, 1983, pp. 29–38.
35 Reinhart Koselleck, *Critique and Crisis: Enlightenment and the Pathogenesis of Modern Society*, Oxford: Berg, 1988, pp. 28–9.
36 *The Elements of Law*, vol. 4 of *The English Works of Thomas Hobbes*, ed. William Molesworth, 11 vols., (repr.) Aalen: Scientia, 1962, 1 ch.4 sec.6.
37 *Leviathan*, XVII, p. 227.
38 See Herbert L. A. Hart, "Commands and Authoritative Legal Reasons," in *Essays on Bentham: Jurisprudence and Political Theory*, Oxford: Clarendon Press, 1982, pp. 243–68: p. 253.
39 *Leviathan*, XXVI, p. 312.
40 Ibid., p. 314.
41 Ibid., p. 314.
42 "Reflections by the Lrd. Chiefe Justice on Mr. Hobbes," pp. 503–5.
43 Postema, *Bentham and the Common Law Tradition*, pp. 36–7.
44 *Leviathan*, XXVI, p. 328.
45 *A Dialogue between a Philosopher and a Student of the Common Laws*, ed. Joseph Cropsey, Chicago: University of Chicago Press, 1971, p. 101. Hobbes wrote this dialogue in response to Bacon's *The Elements of the Common Lawes of England*.
46 See *Introduction to the Principles of Morals and Legislation*, in *The Works of Jeremy Bentham*, ed. John Bowring, 11 vols, Edinburgh: William Tait, 1838–43, vol. I, pp. 1–154 [abbr. *Bowring*].
47 See John Dinwiddy, *Bentham*, Oxford: Oxford University Press, 1989, pp. 54–72.
48 Stephen Holmes, *Passions and Constraint: On the Theory of Liberal Democracy*, Chicago: University of Chicago Press, 1995, p. 245.
49 See Long, *Bentham on Liberty*, pp. 207–20.
50 *Of Laws in General*, ed. Herbert L. A. Hart, London: Athlone, 1970, XIX, p. 2.
51 See Crawford B. McPherson, *The Life and Times of Liberal Democracy*, Oxford: Oxford University Press, 1977, ch. 2.
52 *Property and Political Theory*, Oxford: Blackwell, 1984, p. 98.
53 *A Theory of Property*, Cambridge: Cambridge University Press, 1990, pp. 194–5.
54 Ryan, *Property*, Milton Keynes: Open University Press, 1987, p. 59.
55 *A Comment on the Commentaries and A Fragment on Government*, ed. J. H. Burns and Herbert L. A. Hart, London: London University Press, 1977 [abbr. *CoC* and *FoG*].
56 David Lieberman, *The Province of Legislation Determined: Legal Theory in Eighteenth-Century England*, Cambridge: Cambridge University Press, 1989, p. 170.
57 See Postema, *Bentham and the Common Law Tradition*, pp. 413–21.
58 Ibid., p. 415.
59 Ibid., pp. 407–8.
60 See Harrison, *Bentham*, pp. 106–34.

61 See Louise Harmon, "Falling Off the Vine: Legal Fictions and the Doctrine of Substituted Judgment," *Yale Law Journal* 100, 1 (1990), 1–71.
62 Harrison, *Bentham*, pp. 12–13.
63 See James Steintrager, *Bentham*, London: Allen and Unwin, 1977, pp. 20–43: pp. 28ff.
64 See L. J. Hume, *Bentham and Bureaucracy*, pp. 171–5, 216–19.
65 See Rosen, *Jeremy Bentham and Representative Democracy*, pp. 179-81, and Harrison, *Bentham*, pp. 144–5.
66 Koselleck, *Critique and Crisis*, p. 39.
67 Jonathan Lamb, "Fictions of the Law," in *The Rhetoric of Suffering: Reading the Book of Job in the Eighteenth Century*, Oxford: Clarendon Press, 1995, pp. 128–50: p. 135.
68 See Lieberman, *The Province of Legislation Determined*, pp. 199ff.
69 See Ronald Graveson, "The Restless Spirit of the Law," in *Jeremy Bentham and the Law*, ed. George Keeton and George Schwarzenberger, London: Stevens, 1948, pp. 101–21.
70 See Dinwiddy, *Bentham*, pp. 55, 57.
71 See Bender, *Imagining the Penitentiary*, pp. 167ff.
72 See *Bentham's Theory of Fictions*, ed. Charles Ogden, Paterson, NJ: Littlefield, Adams, and Co., 1959, pp. xvii–xix, cxiii–cxxi, cxxviii–cxxxiv, 118–25, 141–50 [abbr. *ToF*]. See also Steintrager, *Bentham*, pp. 22–6, Dinwiddy, *Bentham*, pp. 54–8, and Harrison, *Bentham*, p. 30.
73 "The Self-Reproduction of Law and Its Limits," in *Essays on Self-Reference*, New York: Columbia University Press, 1990, pp. 227–45: p. 231.
74 See Dinwiddy, *Bentham*, p. 57.
75 See Kim Lane Scheppele, "Facing Facts in Legal Interpretation," *Representations* 30 (1990), 43–77.
76 "Principles of Legislation," in *The Theory of Legislation*, ed. Etienne Dumont, trans. R. Hildreth, Bombay and New York: Tripathi, 1975, pp. 1–52: pp. 42–3, 54. See also pp. 108–11, 112–14, and Hart, "Bentham and Beccaria," in *Essays on Bentham*, pp. 40–52: pp. 43–4.
77 *Of Laws in General*, xv, 12n.1. See Hume, *Treatise* pp. 293–4, 303, 316ff, 353, 363, 365, 489, 581ff, 592, and Duncan Forbes, *Hume's Philosophical Politics*, Cambridge: Cambridge University Press, 1975, pp. 105–6.
78 Lieberman, *The Province of Legislation Determined*, pp. 233–4.
79 See Steintrager, *Bentham*, pp. 23ff.
80 *The Fictive and the Imaginary: Charting Literary Anthropology*, Baltimore: Johns Hopkins University Press, 1993, pp. 110-30: pp. 116–17.
81 Ibid., p. 117.
82 Quoted in Ogden, *ToF*, p. xxv.
83 Iser, *The Fictive and the Imaginary*, p. 119.
84 Ibid., p. 113.
85 Quoted in Ogden, *ToF*, p. xliii.
86 Iser, *The Fictive and the Imaginary*, pp. 113–14.
87 See Wesley Trimpi, *Muses of One Mind: The Literary Experience and Its Continuity*,

Princeton: Princeton University Press, 1983, pp. 241–361.

88 Postema, "Fact, Fictions, and Law: Bentham on the Foundations of Evidence," *Archiv für Rechts- und Sozialphilosophie*, Beiheft 16 (*Facts in Law*), ed. W. Twining, Wiesbaden, 1983, pp. 37–64: p. 46.

89 Ibid., p. 58.

90 See Postema, *Bentham and the Common Law Tradition*, pp. 456–7.

91 Ryan, *Property and Political Theory*, p. 99.

92 *A Sociological Theory of Law*, ed. Martin Albrow, trans. Elizabeth King and Martin Albrow, London: Routledge and Kegan Paul, 1985, p. 161.

4 APORIAS OF RETRIBUTION AND QUESTIONS OF RESPONSIBILITY: THE LEGACY OF INCARCERATION IN DICKENS'S *BLEAK HOUSE*

1 *Bleak House*, ed. Norman Page, Harmondsworth: Penguin, 1971 [abbr. *BH*].

2 *Representative Government*, London: Everyman, 1954, p. 235.

3 *The Industrial Reformation of English Fiction: Social Discourse and Narrative Form 1832–1867*, Chicago: University of Chicago Press, 1985, p. 231.

4 Ibid., p. 235.

5 Ibid., p. 237.

6 *Bentham and the Common Law Tradition*, Oxford: Clarendon Press, 1986, p. 463.

7 "Tautologies and Paradox in the Self-Description of Modern Society," in *Essays on Self-Reference*, New York: Columbia University Press, 1990, pp. 123–43: p. 136.

8 For an overview of these positions, see Simon During, "Post-Foucauldian Criticism: Government, Death, Mimesis," in *Genealogy and Literature*, ed. Lee Quinby, Minneapolis: University of Minnesota Press, 1995, pp. 71–95, and Warren Montag, "'The Soul Is the Prison of the Body': Althusser and Foucault, 1970–1975," *Yale French Studies* 88 (1995), 53–78.

9 *Seminars* XI (*The Four Fundamental Concepts of Psycho-Analysis*, ed. Jacques-Alain Miller, trans. Alan Sheridan, New York: Norton, 1981) and XIV (*La logique du fantasme*). For a brief summary, see Slavoj Žižek, *For They Know Not What They Do: Enjoyment as a Political Factor*, London: Verso, 1991, pp. 146–9, and Marcelle Marini, *Jacques Lacan: The French Context*, trans. Anne Tomiche, New Brunswick: Rutgers University Press, 1992, Dossier 65 (on *The Logic of Fantasy*, Reports 1967–68, Anonymous Edition 1981), pp. 204–8.

10 *The Works of Jeremy Bentham*, ed. John Bowring, 11 vols., Edinburgh: William Tait, 1838–43, IX, p. 77.

11 *The Sentiment of Reality: Truth and Feeling in the European Novel*, London: Allen and Unwin, 1983, p. 157.

12 Humphrey House, *The Dickens World*, London: Oxford University Press, 1941; Raymond Williams, "Dickens and Social Ideas," in *Dickens 1970. Centenary Essays*, ed. Michael Slater, New York: Stein and Day, 1970; and Robert Newsom, "Pickwick in the Utilitarian Sense," *Dickens Studies Annual*

23 (1994), 49–71.

13 See P. S. Atiyah, *The Rise and Fall of Freedom of Contract*, Oxford: Clarendon Press, 1979, pp. 359–97.

14 See Jonathan Arac, *Commissioned Spirits: The Shaping of Social Motion in Dickens, Carlyle, Melville, and Hawthorne*, New Brunswick: Rutgers University Press, 1979, ch. 5.

15 See John Butt, "*Bleak House* in the Context of 1851," *Nineteenth-Century Fiction* 10 (1955), 1–21.

16 See Murray Krieger, *The Tragic Vision. Variations on a Theme in Literary Interpretation*, Chicago: University of Chicago Press, 1966, pp. 138–40n.

17 Quoted in John Butt and Kathleen Tillotson, *Dickens at Work*, London: Methuen, 1957, p. 185.

18 See Susan Shatto, *The Companion to Bleak House*, London: Unwin Hyman, 1988, p. 29, and James Boasberg, "Chancery as Megalosaurus: Lawyers, Courts, and Society in *Bleak House*," *University of Hartford Studies in Literature* 21 (1989), 38–60: 41.

19 See William Holdsworth, *Charles Dickens as a Legal Historian* [1928], New York: Haskell House, 1972, pp. 79–115.

20 See Marjorie Stone, "Dickens, Bentham, and the Fictions of the Law," *Victorian Studies* 29 (1985), 125–54.

21 See Alexander Welsh, *The City of Dickens*, Oxford: Clarendon Press, 1971, p. 212.

22 See Kim Lane Scheppele, "Facing Facts in Legal Interpretation," *Representations* 30 (1990), 43–77.

23 Quoted in Howard Fulweiler, *"Here a Captive Heart Bursted": Studies in the Sentimental Journey of Modern Literature*, New York: Fordham University Press, 1993, pp. 83–4.

24 *Discipline and Punish: The Birth of the Prison*, London: Allen Lane, 1977.

25 "Discipline in Different Voices: Bureaucracy, Police, Family, and *Bleak House*," *Representations* 1, 1 (1983), 59–89: 78.

26 See also Terry Eagleton, *Criticism and Ideology. A Study in Marxist Literary Theory*, London: Humanities Press, 1976, pp. 129–30, and *The Ideology of the Aesthetic*, Oxford: Blackwell, 1990, pp. 49ff.

27 "Telescopic Philanthropy: Professionalism and Responsibility in *Bleak House*," in *Nation and Narration*, ed. Homi Bhabha, London: Routledge, 1990, pp. 213–30.

28 Michel de Certeau, *The Practice of Everyday Life*, trans. Stephen Rendall, Berkeley: University of California Press, 1984, p. 140.

29 Ibid., p. 88.

30 Ibid., pp. xix–xx.

31 *The Ideology of the Aesthetic*, p. 53.

32 Norman Feltes, *Modes of Production of Victorian Novels*, Chicago: University of Chicago Press, 1986, pp. 7–10.

33 De Certeau, *The Practice of Everday Life*, p. 132.

34 See also Luhmann, *A Sociological Theory of Law*, ed. Martin Albrow, trans.

Elizabeth King and Martin Albrow, London: Routledge and Kegan Paul, 1985, p. 26, and *The Differentiation of Society*, New York: Columbia University Press, 1982, p. 151.

35 Julia Kristeva, *The Kristeva Reader*, ed. Toril Moi, trans. Léon Rudiez and Séan Hand, New York: Columbia University Press, 1986, pp. 96–7.

36 *Bodies That Matter: On the Discursive Limits of "Sex"*, New York: Routledge, 1993, p. 53.

37 See Newsom, *Dickens on the Romantic Side of Familiar Things: 'Bleak House' and the Novel Tradition*, University of California, Santa Cruz: The Dickens Project, 1988, pp. 47ff.

38 See Ned Lukacher, *Primal Scenes: Literature, Philosophy, Psychoanalysis*, Ithaca: Cornell University Press, 1986, ch. 8.

39 See *Charles Baudelaire: A Lyric Poet in the Era of High Capitalism*, London: Verso, 1983, pp. 49–50, 69–70.

40 *Dickens, Violence, and the Modern State: Dreams of the Scaffold*, New York: St. Martin's Press, 1995, pp. 71–97.

41 See Vladimir Nabokov, *Lectures on Literature*, ed. Fredson Bowers, New York: Harcourt Brace Jovanovich, 1980, pp. 62–124: pp. 74–8, 89–90, 108.

42 Ibid., pp. 68–9.

43 See Arac, *Commissioned Spirits*, pp. 9ff, 123ff.

44 See Butt and Tillotson, *Dickens at Work*, pp. 182–7.

45 See J. Hillis Miller, "The Interpretive Dance in *Bleak House*," in *Charles Dickens's Bleak House*, ed. Harold Bloom, New York: Chelsea House, 1987, pp. 13–36: pp. 16–19.

46 See David Owen, *English Philanthropy, 1660-1960*, Cambridge, MA: Harvard University Press, 1964.

47 Bell, *The Sentiment of Reality*, p. 158.

48 *Lectures on Literature*, p. 83.

49 See also Christopher Herbert, "The Occult in *Bleak House*," in *Charles Dickens's Bleak House*, pp. 121–38.

50 Luhmann, *A Sociological Theory of Law*, p. ix.

51 *A Comment on the Commentaries and A Fragment on Government*, ed. J. H. Burns and H. L. A. Hart, London: London University Press, 1977, pp. 509–10.

52 See *The Practice of Everyday Life*, p. 132.

53 See *Critique of Judgment*, trans. James Creed Meredith, Oxford: Clarendon Press, 1991, p. 92.

54 *Commentaries on the Laws of England*, 4 vols., 3rd edn., repr. Chicago: Callaghan and Co., I, p. 61, my emphasis [abbr. *CLE*].

55 "The Force of Law: The 'Mystical Foundation of Authority'," *Cardozo Law Review* 11 (1990), 920–1045: 997.

56 *Anti-Oedipus*, trans. Robert Hurly et al., London: Athlone, 1983, p. 176.

57 *Black Sun: Depression and Melancholia*, trans. Léon Rudiez, New York: Columbia University Press, 1989, p. 42. See also p. 47.

58 See Nabokov, *Lectures on Literature*, p. 77.

59 See David Lieberman, *The Province of Legislation Determined: Legal Theory in*

Eighteenth-Century England, Cambridge: Cambridge University Press, 1989, pp. 133–41.

60 Ibid., p. 135.

61 Ibid. pp. 133–4.

62 Ibid., p. 135.

63 Ibid., p. 136.

64 *A Treatise of Human Nature*, ed. L. A. Selby-Bigge, 2nd rev. edn., P. H. Nidditch, Oxford: Clarendon Press, 1978, pp. 485–91, 526.

65 Ibid., pp. 115–16, 293–4, 316–21, 363, 365, 583, 592.

66 See John Gray, "John Stuart Mill on the Theory of Property," in *Theories of Property: Aristotle to the Present*, ed. Anthony Parel and Thomas Flanagan, Waterloo, Ontario: Wilfried Laurier Press, 1979, pp. 257–80: pp. 264–68.

67 See *Principles of Political Economy* [1848], ed. Donald Winch, New York: Penguin, 1979, p. 376.

68 See C. R. B. Dunlop, "Debtors and Creditors in Dickens's Fiction," *Dickens Studies Annual* 19 (1990), 25–47: 39ff.

69 See Barbara Gottfried, "Fathers and Suitors: Narratives of Desire in *Bleak House*," *Dickens Studies Annual* 19 (1990), 169–203: 179–80.

70 See Thomas Richards, *The Commodity Culture of Victorian England. Advertising and Spectacle, 1851–1914*, Stanford: Stanford University Press, 1990, pp. 3, 21–2.

71 See John G. A. Pocock, *Virtue, Commerce, and History. Essays on Political Thought and History, Chiefly in the Eighteenth Century*, Cambridge: Cambridge University Press, 1985, pp. 68–9, 112.

72 *Outline of a Theory of Practice*, trans. Richard Nice, Cambridge: Cambridge University Press, 1977, p. 183.

73 *Economic Analysis of Property Rights*, Cambridge: Cambridge University Press, 1989, p. 5.

74 *Principles of Political Economy*, p. 376.

75 Avner Offer, *Property and Politics 1870–1914: Landownership, Law, Ideology and Urban Development in England*, Cambridge: Cambridge University Press, 1981, p. 137.

76 *Inalienable Possessions: The Paradox of Keeping-While-Giving*, Berkeley: University of California Press, 1992, pp. 6–7.

77 See Luhmann, "Tautologies and Paradox in the Self-Description of Modern Society," p. 125.

78 Remi Clignet, *Death, Deeds, and Descendants: Inheritance in Modern America*, New York: de Gruyter, 1992, p. 58.

79 Quoted in Russell Scott, *The Body as Property*, New York: Viking, 1981, p. 7.

80 *Language and Symbolic Power*, ed. John Thompson, trans. Gino Raymond and Matthew Adamson, Cambridge, MA: Harvard University Press, 1991, p. 118.

81 *The Pickwick Papers*, intro. Alec Waugh, London: Collins, 1963, ch. XLII, pp. 594–5.

82 See Canon T. B. Scrutton, "The State of Prisons as Seen by John Howard

and Charles Dickens," *Dickensian* 62 (1966), 112–17.

83 *The Pickwick Papers*, ch. XLIV, p. 626.
84 See *Commissioned Spirits*, pp. 7–12.
85 Ibid., p. 19.
86 Quoted in Ibid., p. 19.
87 See Ibid., pp. 119–20.
88 Ibid., pp. 123–38.
89 See also *BH*, I, p. 51.
90 See "The Documentary Symbolism of Chancery in *Bleak House*," *Dickensian* 64 (1968), 106–11, 167–71.
91 See "Charles Dickens on 'The Exclusion of Evidence'," *Dickensian* 64 (1968), 131–40, *Dickensian* 65 (1969), 35–41.
92 *Household Words*, ed. Anne Lohrli, Toronto: University of Toronto Press, II, pp. 250–1 (7 Dec. 1850) [authorship unconfirmed].
93 See *Strong Representations: Narrative and Circumstantial Evidence in England*, Baltimore: Johns Hopkins University Press, 1992, pp. 163–78.
94 On Tulkinghorn's "character," see Richard Weisberg, *Poethics, and Other Strategies of Law and Literature*, New York: Columbia University Press, 1992, pp. 67–73.
95 See Welsh, *The City of Dickens*, pp. 59ff.
96 See Olive Anderson, *Suicide in Victorian and Edwardian England*, Oxford: Oxford University Press, 1987, pp. 282–94.
97 *Reflections on the Revolution in France*, ed. Cruise Connor O'Brien, Harmondsworth: Penguin, 1969, p. 150.
98 See *The Second Treatise of Government*, ed. J. W. Gough, 3rd edn., Oxford: Blackwell, 1966, pp. 3–4.
99 "Epigraphic Chapter Titles and the New Mortality in *Bleak House*," in *Charles Dickens's Bleak House*, pp. 81–109: pp. 102–3.
100 "Editors' Preface: The Body into Text," *Yale French Studies* 86 (1994), 1–4: 3.
101 *The Differend: Phrases in Dispute*, trans. Georges van den Abbeele, Minneapolis: University of Minnesota Press, 1988, pp. 30–1.
102 See Jakob Finkelstein, "The Goring Ox: Some Historical Perspectives on Deodands, Forfeitures, Wrongful Death, and the Western Notion of Souvereignty," *Temple Law Quarterly* 46 (1973), 169–290: 197–205.
103 See Jean Baudrillard, *Symbolic Exchange and Death*, trans. Iain Hamilton Grant, Thousand Oaks, CA: Sage, 1993, ch. 5.
104 See Luhmann, *Political Theory and the Welfare State*, trans. John Bednarz Jr., New York: de Gruyter, 1990, p. 42.
105 *The Second Treatise of Government*, p. 30.
106 See Fielding and Brice, "Charles Dickens on 'The Exclusion of Evidence'," Norris Pope, *Dickens and Charity*, New York: Columbia University Press, 1978, p. 130, and Stewart, "Epigraphic Chapter Titles," p. 90.
107 See *The City of Dickens*, pp. 75ff.
108 Ibid., pp. 86–7.
109 *Social Statics*, London: J. Chapman, 1851, pp. 380–1.

110 *The City of Dickens*, pp. 92, 97, 99.
111 *Sacred Tears: Sentimentality in Victorian Literature*, Princeton: Princeton University Press, 1987, p. 56.
112 See House, *The Dickens World*, pp. 128-30, and Butt and Tillotson, *Dickens at Work*, pp. 84, 180, 185–6.
113 See *Dickens and Charity*, pp. 11, 31.
114 Ibid., p. 8.
115 Ibid., pp. 139–40.
116 Ibid., p. 143.
117 See A. Abbott Ikeler, "The Philanthropic Sham: Dickens' Corrective Method in *Bleak House*," *College Language Association* 24, 4 (1981), 497–512.
118 *A Practical View of the Prevailing Religious System of Professed Christians in the Higher and Middle Classes in This Country Contrasted with Real Christianity* [1797], ed. Hugh Martin, London: SCM Press Ltd., 1958, pp. 69–72.
119 Ibid., pp. 108–9.
120 "Telescopic Philanthropy: Professionalism and Responsibility in *Bleak House*," pp. 223–5.
121 Ibid., p. 218.
122 See "Discipline in Different Voices."

5 A CURSE GONE RE-CURSIVE: THE CASE AND CAUSE OF SOLIDARITY IN CONRAD'S *THE NIGGER OF THE "NARCISSUS"*

1 Morton Horvitz, "The Doctrine of Objective Causation," in *The Politics of Law. A Progressive Critique*, ed. David Kairys, New York: Pantheon, 1982, pp. 201–13: p. 211.
2 *The Principles of Ethics*, 2 vols., repr. New York: Appleton, 1892, 1, p. 175.
3 Wai Chee Dimock, *Residues of Justice. Literature, Law, Philosophy*, Berkeley: University of California Press, 1996, p. 166.
4 Ibid.
5 Ibid., pp. 162–3.
6 See P. S. Atiyah, *The Rise and Fall of Freedom of Contract*, Oxford: Clarendon Press, 1979, pp. 504–5, 754ff.
7 *The Political Unconscious: Narrative as a Socially Symbolic Act*, Ithaca: Cornell University Press, 1981, p. 118.
8 Ibid., p. 202.
9 Ibid., p. 205.
10 Ibid., pp. 215–16.
11 Ibid., p. 271.
12 Ibid., p. 269.
13 *A History of the Criminal Law of England*, 3 vols., London: Macmillan, 1877, III, p. 8.
14 "The Doctrine of Objective Causation," p. 211.
15 Ibid., p. 206.

16 *Contingency, Irony, and Solidarity*, Cambridge: Cambridge University Press, 1989, p. 198.

17 Paul Armstrong, "The Politics of Irony in Reading Conrad," *Conradiana* 26, 2 (1994), 85–101: 85.

18 Ibid., 86.

19 See Homi Bhabha, *The Location of Culture*, London: Routledge, 1994, pp. 237, 244ff.

20 Rorty, *Contingency, Irony, and Solidarity*, p. 142.

21 Geoffrey Galt Harpham, "Abroad Only by a Fiction: Creation, Irony, and Necessity in Conrad's *The Secret Agent*," *Representations* 37 (1992), 79–103: 100–1. See also his *One of Us: The Mastery of Joseph Conrad*, Chicago: University of Chicago Press, 1996, Introduction.

22 See Kathy Eden, *Poetic and Legal Fiction in the Aristotelian Tradition*, Princeton: Princeton University Press, 1986.

23 See *Digest of the Law of Evidence*, ed. George Chase, New York: George Chase, 1898, pp. xxiv–v.

24 *The Indian Evidence Act* (I. of 1872), with an Introduction on the Principles of Judicial Evidence, London: Macmillan, 1872, p. 56.

25 Ibid.

26 *Strong Representations: Narrative and Circumstantial Evidence in England*, Baltimore: Johns Hopkins University Press, 1992, pp. 163–4.

27 Ibid., p. 165.

28 Ibid., p. 174.

29 *The Nigger of the 'Narcissus'*, ed. Cedric Watts, Harmondsworth: Penguin, 1989, p. 53 [abbr. *NN*].

30 Matthew Hale, *Pleas of the Crown* [1678], intro. P. R. Glazebrook, London: Professional Books, 1972, I, p. 428.

31 *A Digest of the Criminal Law of England*, 3rd edn., London: Macmillan, 1883, art. 262 [d].

32 Ibid., art. 262 [b].

33 *Reflections on the Problem of Relevance*, ed. Richard Zaner, New Haven: Yale University Press, 1970, p. 46.

34 Welsh, *Strong Representations*, p. 8.

35 See Taslim Elias, *British Colonial Law. A Comparative Study of the Interaction between English and Local Laws in British Dependencies*, London: Stevens, 1962, p. 249.

36 See Jakob Finkelstein, "The Goring Ox: Some Historical Perspectives on Deodands, Forfeitures, Wrongful Death, and the Western Notion of Souvereignty," *Temple Law Quarterly* 46 (1973), 169–290: 231.

37 See Watts, *NN*, p. 138.

38 See *The End of Culture. Toward a Generative Anthropology*, Berkeley: University of California Press, 1985, pp. 301–2, and *Originary Thinking: Elements of Generative Anthropology*, Stanford: Stanford University Press, 1993, pp. 52, 119.

39 See René Girard, *Things Hidden since the Foundation of the World*, trans. Stephen Bann and Michael Metteer, London: Athlone, 1987.

40 *The End of Culture*, pp. 171–5.
41 See Watts, *NN*, p. 140.
42 "The Construction of the Narrator in *The Nigger of the "Narcissus"*, *PMLA* 103 (1988), 783-95: 786ff.
43 Ibid., 785.
44 Jetty de Vries, *Conrad Criticism 1965–1985: The Nigger of the "Narcissus"*, The Netherlands: Phoenix Press, 1989, p. 56.
45 Henricksen, "The Construction of the Narrator," 786.
46 See *Culture and Truth. The Remaking of Social Analysis*, Boston: Beacon Press, 1989, pp. 96–7, 216–7.
47 See *From Ritual to Theatre: The Human Seriousness of Play*, New York: Performing Arts Journal Publications, 1982.
48 "True Lies/False Truths: Narrative Perspective and the Control of Ambiguity in *The Nigger of the "Narcissus"*, *Conradiana* 18, 2 (1986), 105–18: 107, 113, 117.
49 See Marshall Alcorn Jr., "Conrad and the Narcissistic Metaphysics of Morality," *Conradiana* 16, 2 (1984), 103–23: 104–5.
50 See *NN*, p. 27.
51 9 & 10 Vict. ch. 62 (1846) and 33 & 34 Vict. ch. 23 (1870).
52 See Olive Anderson, *Suicide in Victorian and Edwardian England*, Oxford: Oxford University Press, 1987, pp. 282–94, and Barbara Gates, *Victorian Suicide: Mad Crimes and Sad Histories*, Princeton: Princeton University Press, 1988, pp. 3–8, 152.
53 Finkelstein, "The Goring Ox," 197.
54 Ibid., 251–2.
55 Norman Feltes, "Community and the Limits of Liability in Two Mid-Victorian Novels," *Victorian Studies* 17, 4 (1974), 355–69: 359.
56 See Eric Hobsbawm, *Industry and Empire: An Economic History of Britain since 1750*, Harmondsworth: Penguin, 1968, p. 118.
57 Finkelstein, "The Goring Ox," 251.
58 Ibid., 260.
59 "Billy Budd," in *Billy Budd and Other Tales*, New York: Signet Classics, 1961, pp. 35–7.
60 See *Fictional Death and the Modernist Enterprise*, Cambridge: Cambridge University Press, 1995.
61 "No Montagues without Capulets: Some Thoughts on 'Cultural Identity'," in *Explorations in Difference: Law, Culture, and Politics*, ed. Jonathan Hart and Richard Bauman, Toronto: Toronto University Press, 1996, pp. 25–66: p. 47.
62 Jean-Luc Nancy, "The Unsacrificeable," trans. Richard Livingston, *Yale French Studies* 79 (1991), 20–38: 26.
63 "Exit Nostalgia: Conrad and the New Imperialism," in *Macropolitics of Nineteenth-Century Literature: Nationalism, Exoticism, Imperialism*, Philadelphia: University of Pennsylvania Press, 1991, pp. 268–85: p. 282.
64 Brook Thomas, "Parts Related to Wholes and the Nature of Subaltern

Opposition," *Modern Language Quarterly* 55,1 (1994), 79–106.

65 "Billy Budd," p. 78.

66 See *Slavery and Social Death*, Cambridge, MA: Harvard University Press, 1982, pp. 30–1.

67 Jeff Nunokawa, *The Afterlife of Property: Domestic Security and the Victorian Novel*, Princeton: Princeton University Press, 1994, p. 84.

68 See Torstein Eckhoff, "Feedback in Legal Reasoning and Rule Systems," *Scandinavian Studies in Law* 22 (1978), 39–51: 46ff, and John Rogers and Robert Molzon, "Some Lessons about the Law from Self-Referential Problems in Mathematics," *Michigan Law Review* 90, 5 (1992), 992-1022: 1014–16.

69 See David Lieberman, *The Province of Legislation Determined: Legal Theory in Eighteenth-Century England*, Cambridge: Cambridge University Press, 1989, pp. 122ff, 257ff.

70 See Arthur Jacobson, "Autopoietic Law: The New Science of Niklas Luhmann," *Michigan Law Review* 87, 6 (1989), 1647–89: 1683–5.

71 Pierre Bourdieu, "The Force of Law: Toward a Sociology of the Juridical Field," trans. Richard Terdiman, *Hastings Law Journal* 38 (1987), 805–53: 816–17.

72 See Kim Lane Scheppele, "Facing Facts in Legal Interpretation," *Representations* 30 (1990), 43–77.

73 See Louise Harmon, "Falling Off the Vine: Legal Fictions and the Doctrine of Substituted Judgment," *Yale Law Journal* 100, 1 (1990), 1–71.

74 Nancy, "The Jurisdiction of the Hegelian Monarch," trans. Mary Ann and Peter Caws, in *The Birth to Presence*, trans. Brian Holmes et al., Stanford: Stanford University Press, 1993, pp. 110–42: p. 140.

Index

JUL 0 3 2024

WITHDRAWN

JUL 0 3 2024

DAVID O. McKAY LIBRARY
BYU-IDAHO